LET NOT YOUR
HEART
BE
TROUBLED

*A Pastor's Counsel
& Comfort to Those
Who Suffer*

MICHAEL L. GOWENS

Sovereign Grace Publications
Shallotte, North Carolina

LET NOT YOUR HEART BE TROUBLED:
A Pastor's Counsel & Comfort to Those Who Suffer
Published by Sovereign Grace Publications
Post Office Box 1150
Shallotte, North Carolina 28459
Email sovgracepublications@gmail.com
www.sovgrace.net

ISBN 978-1-929635-24-5

Scripture quotations, unless otherwise noted, are from the King James Version.

Printed in the United States of America

To Lori,
With thanksgiving to God for your love to me,
your heart of faith in Him,
your steady support of my ministry,
and your encouragement to complete this project.
Indeed, God blessed the broken road…it surprises me every day.

CONTENTS

Introduction
Let Not Your Heart Be Troubled

Just hours before he went to the cross, the Lord Jesus preached his final sermon to his disciples. I am impressed by the tender way he began the message: *"Let not your heart be troubled: ye believe in God, believe also in me. In my Father's house are many mansions: if it were not so, I would have told you. I go to prepare a place for you. And if I go and prepare a place for you, I will come again, and receive you unto myself; that where I am, there ye may be also"* (Jno. 14:1-3).

If there was ever a moment when our Lord would have been justified to think only of himself, this was it. Instead, Jesus is concerned to comfort and encourage his disciples. Here in the shadow of the cross, the Savior is preoccupied with their peace and well-being, not his own pending pain and suffering. How tender is this scene!

It is significant that he did not say, "Let not your *life* be troubled." Such an imperative would be supremely unrealistic. They would never be able to obey that exhortation, for trouble is inevitable in life, just as sparks inevitably fly upward (Job 5:7). No one living in a world that is under the curse of sin will escape tribulation in life (Jno. 16:33; Job 14:1). Instead, he urges, "Don't let the trouble in your life get inside your heart." When trouble in life makes its way inside of a person's heart, then that individual has real trouble indeed.

"Let not your heart be troubled..." Is it possible for the believer to live in a world of trouble with quiet peace in his heart? Paul and Silas would answer "yes." Bound with fetters and chains in a Philippian jail, these two triumphant souls knew how to rejoice at midnight: *"And at midnight, Paul and Silas prayed and sang praises to God, and the prisoners heard them"* (Acts 16:25). Their fellow prisoners had heard plenty of men curse and blaspheme God and complain of injustice, but they had never heard songs of praise or prayers of fervor and humility, especially at midnight.

What was their secret? Although Paul and Silas were physically bound, they were spiritually free. Their bodies were imprisoned, but not their souls. Madame Guyon, a 17ᵗʰ century Christian mystic, also found herself incarcerated for her faith after publishing a book on prayer. The book entitled *A Short and Easy Method of Prayer* contained sentiments considered heretical by the Roman Catholic Church. But though Guyon's body was bound, her heart was not. She wrote these lines at some point during her eight-year incarceration (1695-1703):

> A little bird I am,
> Shut from the fields of air,
> And in my cage I sit and sing
> To Him who placed me there;
> Well pleased a prisoner to be,
> Because, my God, it pleaseth Thee.
>
> Nought have I else to do,
> I sing the whole day long;
> And He whom most I love to please
> Doth listen to my song;
> He caught and bound my wandering wing;
> But still He bends to hear me sing.
>
> Thou hast an ear to hear
> A heart to love and bless;
> And though my notes were e'er so rude,
> Thou wouldst not hear the less;
> Because Thou knowest as they fall,
> That love, sweet love, inspires them all.
>
> My cage confines me round;
> Abroad I cannot fly;
> But though my wing is closely bound,
> My heart's at liberty;
> For prison walls cannot control
> The flight, the freedom of the soul.
>
> O it is good to soar
> These bolts and bars above!
> To Him whose purpose I adore,

> Whose providence I love;
> And in Thy mighty will to find
> The joy, the freedom of the mind.

Many further examples could be cited from the annals of Christian history documenting believers who knew the reality of a calm and quiet heart in the midst of tremendous storms of trouble and affliction. Fanny Crosby, the blind hymnwriter, whose heart of gratitude and love for God overflowed in over 8,000 Christian hymns and gospel songs, in spite of her physical limitations; Joseph Spafford, who wrote the classic "It Is Well With My Soul" at the approximate place in the Atlantic where three of his daughters had perished at sea; Polycarp, the post-Johannine pastor of the church at Smyrna, who insisted he be allowed to stand at the stake unbound while the fires were kindled around him; or Latimer, who turned to Ridley as they awaited martyrdom at the stake in 1555 and said, "Be of good comfort, Master Ridley, and play the man"—each case demonstrates that it is possible to have peace within and calmness of soul, even though the external circumstances of life are replete with trouble.

How is it possible to maintain an untroubled heart in the face of such troublesome circumstances in life? Jesus answers that this inward poise of spirit is possible by faith in God and in the Lord Jesus Christ: *"...ye believe in God, believe also in me..."*

Paul strikes the same note in Romans 15:13: *"Now the God of hope fill you with all joy and peace in believing, that ye may abound in hope through the power of the Holy Ghost."* Note that inward joy and peace comes by means of believing. When a burdened soul responds to God's word in terms of fixing its focus once more on the character, the blessings, and the promises of God, joy and peace fills the heart. "Let not your heart be troubled, but believe in me." That's the message of the Lord Jesus.

The ability to maintain a steady focus on the Lord, however, is not something indigenous to human nature. Instead, the very opposite is the case. Man by nature is ingrown and self-absorbed. "Man's chief problem," said Calvin, "is that he is turned-in upon himself and his greatest need is to be turned outside of himself toward God and others." This natural self-preoccupation makes it impossible for a person prior to regeneration to turn to God. The natural man has neither the desire nor the capacity to seek the Lord (2 Ths. 3:2; Rom. 3:10-11).

But what about the regenerate child of God, i.e. those identified by the declarative clause *"ye believe in God"*? The fact that John 14:1 includes both a declarative [stating a fact] and an imperative [giving a command] clause is significant. Notice that the Lord Jesus addresses people who have already been given the gift of faith—*"ye believe in God"*—and calls upon them to further *"believe also in me."* This imperative clause suggests that the act of turning outside of self and toward the Lord Jesus Christ in believing trust is a spiritual discipline, a habit that must be cultivated and developed, not an automatic response.

The key to an untroubled heart in the face of a troubled world, in other words, involves the habit of maintaining a believing focus on the Lord instead of on self and the troublesome circumstances we face. When God's child keeps his eyes on the Lord Jesus Christ (cf. Heb. 12:2), he can, like Peter walking on the water, do the impossible. But when he loses focus on Christ and becomes preoccupied with the boisterous winds and waves of trouble around him, he inevitably sinks beneath the torrents of despair.

Each chapter in the following pages develops this basic dynamic, i.e. **faith in God is the secret to inner calmness and spiritual poise**. Regardless of the particular nature of your personal struggle, both the goal before you and the means whereby you may attain that goal are rooted in this disciplined habit of turning outside of self and reaching upward in faith toward God and the Lord Jesus Christ.

The answer to your heartaches, in other words, will be discovered when you learn that the Lord is himself your everlasting "portion" (Lam. 3:24; Ps. 73:26) and "exceeding great reward" (Gen. 15:3). It is only when the believer finds peace and happiness in the knowledge that Christ is his "all in all" that the sufferings of this present time will pale into insignificance. Affliction becomes light when the Christian maintains focus on the Savior and the things that He has prepared for them that love Him (cf. 2 Cor. 4:17-18).

"Thou wilt keep him in perfect peace whose mind is stayed upon thee, because he trusteth in thee" (Is. 26:3). This is the Old Testament parallel to Jesus' exhortation, *"Let not your heart be troubled; ye believe in God, believe also in me."* That's the bottom line message that I intend to convey in these pages. It's a simple theme to which most Christians would readily offer theoretical consent, but, I suspect, find quite difficult to implement when crisis comes.

Many of us, I suppose, are like the woman who reached out to touch the hem of Jesus' garment. We have been successful in terms of touching the border of this discipline but we have found it challenging to sustain the grasp. So, as simple as the message may sound on the surface, the actual cultivation of this sustained spiritual discipline is challenging at the least.

I suspect that few of us will ever make much progress in learning to trust God consistently until we have had ample struggles that occasioned the need to move beyond this native habit of self-sufficiency and independence. Suffering is God's school, and trials His curricula, for growing strong and stable saints. Though the tuition is great and the schedule demanding, the design tends to produce resilient, disciplined and useful graduates.

I am not an exception to that rule. I have been a student in the school of suffering and the tuition of heartache has been incredibly costly. I didn't consciously sign up for classes, but a loving Father required me to study the curriculum of trouble nonetheless.

The content of these pages was born from my own personal valleys of affliction. I've known the foreboding feelings of helplessness concerning a grandchild's fragile and precarious health, a parent's haunting fears over the poor choices of teens trying to find their way, and the forlorn despair of a broken heart. I've wept profusely—tears that no one but the Lord knows—and agonized in prayer over a period of many years for God's mercy and grace. I've felt the self-doubt of unrequited love, the grief of love lost, the stabbing pain of gossip, the outrage of injustice, and the sadness of changes in my life occasioned by the choices of others and circumstances beyond my control. I've suffered the loss of reputation, of friendships, of intimacy with loved ones, and of familiar comforts. I've felt the physical effects of incessant stress, and struggled to overcome the kind of depressed feelings that unrelenting tension produces in the psyche.

I now understand why Asaph, in Psalm 73, struggled so with the apparent injustice of life: "Why do those who try to do the right thing suffer every day while those who do wrong seem to prosper?" I've prayed Jeremiah's prayer in Jeremiah 12, *"Righteous art thou, O Lord…yet let me talk with thee of thy judgments: Wherefore doth the way of the wicked prosper?"* and I've received Jeremiah's answer, *"If thou hast run with the footmen and they have wearied thee, then how canst thou contend with horses?"* (Jer. 12:1, 5). Oh, the inward wrestling and soul travail I've known!

In a word, I know suffering and heartache. Though the pain others have been called to face may be arguably more substantial than mine, yet my troubles were nonetheless big and life-impacting to me. But I also know God's mercy and what it means to hope. He is the God who makes all things new. I'm so thankful not only for His sustaining grace in the midst of my personal trials, but for His grace to deliver me from them and to grant me a fresh start, a Year of Jubilee.

He has lifted me from the miry clay, put a new song in my mouth, planted my feet on a solid foundation, and set me off on a new path (cf. Ps. 40:1). He has restored my soul…and my sanity…and my enthusiasm for life. He has answered my prayers and allowed me to feel what it is to be loved and admired and wanted. I still have scars to remind me, like Jacob's halting limp, of the struggle, but the wounds have healed. And I cannot thank Him enough. I've done the best I could under my trying circumstances. And He's done more than I expected or could have imagined. By His help, I've survived. By His grace, I'm revived.

So, I offer this volume as a fellow student in the school of affliction, not as a professor or expert on the subject, but as one who has traveled far enough to know that He is real, His promises are trustworthy, and His love is better than life. I have not yet arrived at the goal of spiritual maturity. I am not ready to graduate with honors. No doubt, many lessons remain to be learned and mastered. I am still learning, and I trust will continue to do so until my final breath, to fully trust in the Lord.

May these pages, however, convey my unhesitating conviction, forged and hardened on the anvil of personal experience, that God is faithful to sustain His believing children in their various trials, that He is enough for you, that His grace is sufficient, and that His purpose in chastening and training His child is not to crush (cf. Lam. 3:33-34), but to purify you, that you may reflect His glorious character (cf. Heb. 12:10b) and serve Him as a *"vessel meet for the Master's use"* (2 Tim. 2:21).

Be encouraged, then! And let not your heart be troubled.

Michael L. Gowens
Calabash, North Carolina

Part I

General Counsel

1
Where is God in My Pain?

"My brethren, count it all joy when ye fall into diverse temptaions; knowing that the trying of your faith worketh patience. But let patience have her perfect work, that ye may be perfect and entire, wanting nothing." James 1:2-4

N ever morning wore to evening but some heart did break."[1] It is true, isn't it? Ours is a world of pain. Broken dreams, the tragic loss of a child, a sudden disaster, unemployment, divorce, cancer, an illegitimate pregnancy, a handicapped child, the death of one's life companion, child abuse, bankruptcy, personal failure, loneliness, misunderstanding—these things intrude into our lives startling us with painful surprise like a blow in the solar plexus.

The pain, most of the time, seems to us indescribably savage and brutal. It is an unwelcome thief, come to steal our joy and rob us of our peace. We hate it. We despise it. We will do anything, virtually anything, to get away from it. We have a right, we are told, to a pain-free existence. No one should have to suffer.

We are living in the "aspirin age." It is an era in which the pursuit of personal comfort and pleasure is the supreme good, and the temporary alleviation of discomfort is valued above the radical cure of the disease. Hedonism, this "Disneyland mentality," produces a kind of short-term approach to life, a live-for-the-moment perspective that makes self-gratification the goal of existence.

Modern western man, in other words, is soft and overly sensitive to pain. As he has lost the Biblical emphasis on God's holiness and a personal sense of his own sins, he has come to expect VIP treatment from God all the time. He, in the words of J. I. Packer, cherishes "shockingly strong illusions about having a right to expect from God health, wealth, ease, excitement, and sexual gratification."[2] When he, on the contrary, receives pain, instead of pleasure, he reacts in

---

[1] Alfred Tennyson, "In Memoriam A.H.H." 1850
[2] J. I. Packer, *Rediscovering Holiness*, 1992, p. 250.

bitterness toward the Almighty, takes an aspirin to block the pain, and proceeds down the path in his own mad rush to pleasure and self-fulfillment. The result of this habit means that cause of the pain is seldom discovered. That would require too much time and effort. Instead, he opts for the quick-fix; then it's "back on the road again."

To minds conditioned to think in such pleasure-oriented terms, the words of James sound admittedly strange, maybe even convoluted and repugnant. James challenges his readers to welcome pain as a friend, rather than to resent it as an intruder: *"Count it all joy when ye fall into divers temptations."* He then counsels them further that once they have welcomed suffering, they should resist the urge to cut the process short, to escape the pain: *"But let patience have her perfect work, that ye may be perfect and entire, wanting nothing."*

Such advice goes cross-grain to our natural inclinations, doesn't it? By nature, the initial reaction to pain is the desire to escape from it. No one likes to hurt. Personal discomfort is not pleasant. But James encourages the Christian to allow the process to continue to completion, not asking the question "How can I get out of this trouble?" but "What can I learn from this trouble?"

On what basis would he advise a person to endure the pain? Was James some chirpy optimist, like Carlyle said of Emerson, who "standing well back out of the least touch of the spray, throws chatty observations on the beauty of the weather to a poor soul battling for his life in huge billows that are buffeting the breath and the life out of him, wrestling with mighty currents that keep sweeping him away"? Did James, like proponents of "mind over matter," suggest that pain was merely an illusion, a figment of the imagination? No, James is a realist—a realist whose realism springs from faith in God.

James does not deny the reality of pain and suffering. Real people who live in a real world have real problems. Neither does he minimize the troubles of those to whom he addressed his letter, attempting to convince them that suffering is pleasurable. It isn't. But neither does he lose sight of the reality of God, the God who stands in back of our pain and uses it as His school of spiritual maturity.

Undoubtedly, like James, the poet knew something of the spiritual benefit of suffering:

I walked a mile with Pleasure.
She chattered all the way,
But left me none the wiser
For all she had to say.

I walked a mile with Sorrow,
And ne'er a word said she;
But, oh, the things I learned from her,
When Sorrow walked with me!

As foreign as it sounds to our comfortable culture, pain may be beneficial. God is able to use it as a means to very valuable ends.

Even in a strictly natural sense, pain can be something positive. Pain is a human being's natural defense mechanism against potentially harmful external stimuli. It is a God-given signal that danger is near. What would happen to a little child who touched a hot stove, for example, if he could feel no pain? The sensation of pain triggers a reaction that literally spares the child from serious personal harm, maybe even death.

The pain of a scraped knee, fingers pinched in a door or cut by a knife, and a stumped toe all serve to promote caution and self-discipline in a child as he grows older. Head pain, muscle pain, joint pain, chest pain, and back pain are all signals of a more serious problem. The pain is intended to alert its victim to the unhealthy activity or harmful disease that is behind the pain so that steps can be taken to remove the stimulus.

Even emotional pain may be healthy. The pain of a failing grade is intended to help a child learn to complete his homework assignments. The pain of embarrassment and public exposure may halt a child's bent to mischief. All forms of godly and biblical discipline operate on the principle that there is such a thing as "healthy pain." Used properly, it can produce beneficial changes.

Maybe that's what my seventh grade track coach meant at the completion of each lap, when he said with unmerciful sarcasm, "Hurt's *sooo* good!"

Though we are tempted to cry out "Lord, take away pain," we need to ask ourselves, "Would we want a world devoid of heroes?" Were there no pain, there would be no hero rising from the desperation to triumph in faith. Would we want a world devoid of compassion? Were there no pain, there would be no pity that knit heart to heart in tender sympathy for the sufferer. Would we want a world without love? Were there no pain, there would be no need for self-sacrifice, the very essence of love. Would we want a world without hope? Were there no pain, there would be nothing better to hope for. Would we want a world without the cross of Christ? Were there no pain, there would be no need for the cross.

Granted, heaven will be a world without pain (Rev. 21:4 - Ah! wonderful prospect!), but until sinful mortals are glorified, we cannot conceive of glory except in contrast to suffering. The pain of life, consequently, "with its solemn, unsmiling, and sometimes deeply-lined face, is a great servant of God"[3] teaching us some of the most valuable lessons of life. Let's enumerate a few.

The Development of Christlike Character

James says a desire to endure rather than escape the trial produces spiritual maturity: *"But let patience* [i.e. patient endurance] *have her perfect work, that you may be perfect and entire* [i.e. fully mature], *wanting nothing."* Paul teaches the identical truth in Romans 5:3-4: *"And not only so, but we glory in tribulations also; knowing that tribulation worketh patience* [i.e. endurance or perseverance], *and patience experience* [i.e. character], *and experience hope."*

Grace, like the roots of a tree, grows best in the winter, albeit such character development is obscured from the observers gaze. Even so, the pressures of life provide an opportunity to persevere. In such

---

[3] William Clow, from a sermon entitled "Christ in a World of Pain," *Classic Sermons on Suffering*, p. 42

patient endurance under pressure, the roots of Christian character strike an equivalent beneath the soil to the visible portions of the tree on the topside of the earth. As character develops, so does hope.

The writer to the Hebrews explains this principle further in terms of the pain of Divine chastening: *"If ye endure chastening, God dealeth with you as with sons; for what son is he whom the father chasteneth not?...For they verily for a few days chastened us after their own pleasure, but He for our profit that we might be partakers of His holiness. Now no chastening for the present seemeth to be joyous, but grievous. Nevertheless, afterward it yieldeth the peaceable fruit of righteousness unto them who are exercised thereby"* (Heb. 12:7, 10-11).

Why would a parent allow a child to encounter pain? Because the parent was cruel? No, on the contrary, because of love. Parents who really love their children discipline them, that is, they train them to grow up to duplicate the parent's behavior. By the same token, the Father disciplines His children, both from a loving motive and in a loving manner, so that *"we might be partakers of His holiness."*

The parent/child relationship is essentially a discipling dynamic in which the parent not only tells the child what is expected but demonstrates that teaching by example, thus training the child to be like him. This is frequently a painful process, involving time, energy, ingenuity, exertion, sweat, tears, and correction. But the gain in the end is worth the pain: *"...nevertheless, afterward it yieldeth the peaceable fruit of righteousness"* to those who submit to the lesson. Sometimes a parent must be temporarily perceived to be cruel, e. g. saying "no," applying the rod of correction, etc., in order to be kind over the long-term.

Why does God permit His children to suffer pain? So that they might produce fruit: *"'Every branch in me that beareth fruit, He purgeth it that it might bring forth more fruit'"* (Jno. 15:2). It is through the sufferings of our lives and the occasion those sufferings make for the practice of the discipline of endurance (as well as through the other spiritual disciplines of Scripture intake, prayer, fasting, worship, etc.), that the Holy Spirit makes us into loving, joyful, peaceful, gentle, kind, faithful, self-controlled, and self-forgetful people (Gal. 5:22). It is in the school of suffering that we learn, like our Savior learned, obedience (Heb. 5:7).

Perhaps you wonder in what sense Jesus *"learned obedience by the things that He suffered."* He learned both the practice and the cost of it. Even so, we learn the value of obedience to God, making it the priority of our lives, through our pain: *"Before I was afflicted I went astray, but now have I kept Thy word...It is good for me that I might be afflicted that I might learn Thy statutes"* (Ps. 119:37, 71).

I maintain that the heart of every compassionate person was forged in the furnace of pain. Those who live without great pain are strangers to empathy, kindness, patience, and understanding. The "Greathearts" in Christ's kingdom were once in the ranks of the walking wounded whom they now serve. Perhaps A. W. Tozer had this in mind when he wrote, "I seriously doubt that God will ever use anyone greatly, until He has allowed that person to be hurt deeply." Pain produces character.

Pain Reminds Us of Our Weakness & His Strength

Someone once said, "Man's extremity is God's opportunity." Paul knew this fact firsthand: *"Because of the abundance of revelations, there was given unto me a thorn in the flesh, the messenger of Satan to buffet me, lest I should be exalted above measure"* (2 Cor. 12:7ff). That Paul was in some kind of pain (probably physical pain by virtue of the use of the word "flesh") is evident by the metaphor he selects – "a thorn in the flesh." If you were to ask Paul, "What does it feel like?" he would have responded, "It feels like a sharp thorn in my body."

What did Paul do about it? He prayed, not once, nor twice, but three times, that God would remove the pain. Did God remove the pain? No, but He gave Paul "grace sufficient" to bear his infirmity. Paul says, *"[His] strength is made perfect in my weakness...I will most gladly therefore glory in my infirmities that the power of Christ may rest upon me."*

It is admittedly strange that we need to learn and be reminded of our own frailty: *"Lord, teach me to know my end, the measure of my days, that I may know how frail I am"* (Ps. 39:4). That's an appropriate prayer. Why is it important to remember our own weakness? Because it is only in our weakness that God will demonstrate His strength.

Paul's pain was an opportunity for God to exhibit His power. Every time that He sustains someone under the burdens of grief, physical illness, family strife, financial reversal, or persecution, the cause of Christ is advanced.

It was in terms of the promotion of Christ's gospel that Paul viewed his own sufferings and imprisonments: *"Therefore I endure all things for the elect's sake, that they may also obtain the salvation that is in Christ Jesus with eternal glory"* (2 Tim. 2:10); *"But I would that ye should understand, brethren, that the things which happened unto me have fallen out rather unto the furtherance of the gospel..."* (Phi. 1:12-13). As others watch us under trial, they deduce either that Christ and His power to sustain is real, or that it is not, depending on how we react to our pain.

God seeks, through pain, to wean us from the tendency to cling to the earth, to seek our all in Him.

One by one He took them from me
All the things I valued most,
Til I was empty-handed,
Every glittering toy was lost.
And I walked earth's highways, grieving,
In my rags and poverty;
Until I heard His voice inviting,
'Lift those empty hands to Me.'
Then I turned my hands toward heaven,
And He filled them with a store
Of His own transcendent riches
Til they could contain no more.
And at last I comprehended
With my stupid mind, and dull,
That God cannot pour His riches
Into hands already full.

Pain Prepares Us to Minister to Others

In His providence, God frequently either brings or allows pain to touch His children, not only to correct yesterday's errors, but to prepare for tomorrow's role of ministry. Experience equips suffering saints to enter into the sufferings of others in a way that others of us cannot enter.

Second Corinthians 1:3 says, "*[God] comforteth us in all our tribulation, that we may be able to comfort others which are in any trouble, with the comfort wherewith we ourselves are comforted of God*." Those who have passed through the valley of suffering themselves command a right to be heard by those who are presently there.

Pain Drives Us to Seek Relief

As painful as it is to experience physical infirmity, financial collapse, social ostracization, or interpersonal conflict, perhaps the most acute kind of pain is the pain of a guilty conscience. To sense your own failure, the embarrassment of a public fall—to know to some degree that you disappointed those who trusted you and seriously impaired your credibility with them - to feel the weight of guilt before God and the awareness that you have despised his goodness and mercy to you through your blatant sin—the pain of this experience is unparalleled.

David describes it in Psalm 32: "*When I kept silence my bones waxed old through my roaring all the day long. For day and night thy hand was heavy upon me: my moisture* [lit. energy and vitality] *is turned into the drought of summer*" (vs. 3-4). Aching bones, a sense of heaviness every moment of the day, a lack of energy and sense of general fatigue—these are the kinds of things a guilty conscience feels.

How should we react to such pain? We should allow it to drive us to the throne of grace in confession and repentance: "*I acknowledged my sin unto thee...and thou forgavest the iniquity of my sin...Thou art my hiding place; thou shalt preserve me from trouble...*" (Ps. 32:5, 7). Notice the change of tone in the Psalm after verse five. Repentance brings wonderful relief.

Many people attempt to rationalize sin, or pretend that they did nothing wrong, or shift the blame on to someone else. Modern psychiatry frequently suggests that guilt is not good, that this kind of pain is harmful. But it is only harmful if you do not heed the warning.

Pain of conscience is God's alarm signaling that you have broken His law, and there is only one thing for you to do when you feel such inward pain. In the same way that physical pain drives the sufferer to seek relief, let the pain of a convicted conscience drive you to admit your sin and apply for forgiveness through the blood of Christ. Plead the promise of 1 John 1:9: *"If we confess our sins, He is faithful and just to forgive us our sins and to cleanse us from all unrighteousness."* You, my friend, will find unspeakable peace in His mercy.

Pain Makes Us Appreciate Heaven

Romans 5:4 affirms that tribulation leads to patience, which leads to experience, which issues in hope. Paul's point is that the pain of life here enhances our desire for the life hereafter.

Suffering has a way of helping us to see the transitory nature of earthly things, and the converse weightiness of eternal glory: *"For our light affliction worketh for us a far more exceeding and eternal weight of glory while we look not at the things that are seen but at the things which are not seen..."* (2 Cor. 4:18). Pain helps us to learn to live in the light of eternity, drawing present comfort from our hope of glory. It sharpens one's sense of the reality of heaven and the preciousness of living with Christ forever.

The whole creation is pictured in Romans 8:22 as *"travailing in pain, waiting for the adoption, to wit, the redemption of our bodies."* With disease and famine and war and death, our world writhes in pain under the curse of sin.

Notice the imagery of "travail" in this text. Travail is the pain of labor. Labor pain is a different kind of pain. It is a pain that is only bearable because of the expectation that something good will come from the pain. Labor pain is the pain of expectation. Likewise, the believer suffers severely here, but as he focuses on the glorious day of Christ's return, he is able to bear the pain of present travail in hope of a glorious outcome.

What basis do we have for hope? Is hope just a pipe dream, mere wishful thinking? No, says Paul: *"...and hope maketh not ashamed because the love of God is shed abroad in our hearts by the Holy Ghost which is given unto us*" (Rom. 5:5). The believer is not ashamed to look through his pain to a brighter day in the future, regardless of the hecklers and mockers who ridicule his faith. He is not ashamed because God has given him a witness within, a confirmation through the Spirit that he is loved by God, and that confidence that he is loved, despite the pain he must endure now, gives him the strength to persevere until the end.

One hymnwriter put it like this: "Our troubles and our trials here will only make us richer there." Another said, "Just one glimpse of Him in glory will all the toils of life repay." And Paul under the inspiration of the Holy Spirit said, "*I reckon that the sufferings of this present time are not worthy to be compared to the glory that shall be revealed in us*" (Rom. 8:18). I can't wait. Can you?

Summary

When Jesus came to this earth, he was moved with compassion at the pain and suffering he saw. He eased that suffering by healing the sick, cleansing the lepers, unstopping deaf ears, opening blind eyes, strengthening impotent limbs, and raising the dead to life.

Nevertheless, our Lord's primary mission was not to alleviate pain. He came to do away with the cause of the pain, not merely the symptoms. At the cross, he suffered the most excruciating kind of pain man or angel has ever known, the pain of separation from God, because of our sin. Through that pain, he conquered and removed our sin. Hence, the day is coming when God will forever shut the doors to His school of pain. But until then, He uses it to educate His children in holiness.

In a sermon entitled "Wearing the Thorns as a Crown," James S. Stewart summarized the proper reaction to pain in the following terms. May we all learn to think this clearly about our pain:

No, God knows best; and the true Christian reaction to suffering and sorrow is not the attitude of self-pity or fatalism or resentment; it is the spirit which takes life's difficulties as a God-given opportunity, and regards its troubles as a sacred trust, and wears the thorns as a crown.[4]

Do you have any thorns? Wear them as a crown to the glory of the One who did the same for you.

---

4 *Classic Sermons on Suffering*, p. 96.

2
Play the Man!
Recovering a Masculine Faith

"If thou hast run with the footmen, and they have wearied thee, then how canst thou contend with horses? And if in the land of peace, wherein thou trustedst, they wearied thee, then how wilt thou do in the swelling of the Jordan?" Jeremiah 12:5

What makes a minister? Martin Luther answered that question by citing three essential components in a minister's growth and development: 1) Prayer; 2) The word of God (or the discipline of study); and 3) Temptation.

By "temptation," Luther meant trials, afflictions, disappointments and heartache. He knew that it is in the valley of humiliation and affliction that God tempers the metal of usefulness for service. Not until a person has experienced the reality of God's sustaining power and grace in the midst of his own troubles is he then equipped to *"comfort others by the comfort [he himself] was comforted of God"* (2 Cor. 1:4).

It is for this reason, i.e. that trials and afflictions provide an opportunity for sanctification and spiritual growth, that most of God's servants have begun a ministry of public usefulness by spending private and personal time in the wilderness. That was true of Moses (Acts 7:29-30), Elijah (1 Kings 17:3-16), the Lord Jesus (Mt. 4:1-11), and the Apostle Paul (Gal. 1:15-17). It is in "Wilderness Seminary," that a minister, and every believer (for that matter), learns to *"have compassion on the ignorant and on them that are out of the way, for that he himself also is compassed with infirmity"* (Heb. 5:2).

Basic Training

I suppose that more than one recruit has been urged to survive the rigors of boot camp by a drill instructor's reminder "The more you sweat in training, the less you will bleed in battle." The military understands the principle that hardship and pressure is necessary to prepare a person to be a Soldier. One simply cannot learn to endure the harshness of combat if he never does anything but play video games, eat cupcakes and sleep on a comfort mattress. The whole purpose of "basic training" is built on this principle that success in handling minor adversity equips a Soldier to survive more major hardships and dangers.

Anyone who has endured basic training will likely take issue with my characterization of it as *minor* adversity. It is certainly no small feat to survive three months of estrangement from family and everything familiar, workdays beginning at 4:00 a.m., endurance marches, physical fitness tests, obstacle courses, eating MRE's, the loss of privacy, modesty, and personal identity, and hour upon hour of lectures and monotonous drills. The goal is to breakdown a recruit so he/she may be rebuilt as a stronger, more self-disciplined, wiser and better Soldier. The individual who survives the experience has certainly accomplished something that many others may never accomplish. He has earned an identity worthy of respect and honor.

The achievement of surviving basic training, notwithstanding, it is not an end in itself. Basic training, again, is intended to be preparatory for the even greater stress of real battle. As harsh as it may sound, the person who loses heart and succumbs to feelings of despair in boot camp simply will not be able to sustain the pressure of a real-life combat situation.

A Prophet's Perplexity

It is precisely that scenario described in the text that heads this chapter. *"If thou hast run with the footmen and they have wearied thee, then how canst thou contend with horses?"* means "If you have been brought to the point of physical exhaustion and emotional despair by long marches with your battle-buddies in basic training, then how will you be able to face an actual battle when the thundering hoof-beats of an enemy army invade the city?"

To whom did God speak these words? They were spoken in response to the prophet Jeremiah's complaint of the apparent injustice he had suffered: *"Righteous art thou, O Lord, when I plead with thee: yet let me talk with thee of thy judgments"* (Jer. 12:1a).

Jeremiah was hurting and perplexed. He knew that God was righteous and just and was careful to begin his complaint by acknowledging that fact, but it didn't seem to square with the way his abject circumstances as God's faithful servant compared to the relatively carefree circumstances of the rebellious people to whom he preached (cf. Jer. 12:1b-3).

Jeremiah had ample reason to be discouraged. His call to the ministry was no easy commission. God told him in advance that the people would reject him, resist his message, and proceed headlong down the path toward judgment. There would be no possibility of success.

Had such a negative prospect awaited me at my ordination to the gospel ministry, I doubt I could have survived. At least I had the prospect of a convert from time to time, or a sermon that touched someone's life in an encouraging way. But Jeremiah had no such positives in his prophetic career.

That the prophet experienced periodic moments of spiritual fatigue, weariness, and discouragement, then, is understandable. One can only endure for so long vicious slander, accusations of aiding and abetting the enemy, solitary confinement in a stinking dungeon, and terroristic threats on his life without losing heart. It is no wonder that Jeremiah decided to resign his prophetic ministry (Jer. 20:9). And he would have continued to enjoy a peaceful retirement, too, had God not put a "fire in his bones" that prohibited him from remaining silent.

When he complains to God, therefore, we expect the Lord to respond by saying, "I'm sorry! Bless your heart. You are justified to feel that you are on the short end of justice. I really appreciate all you are doing in my service." Instead, the Lord shocks our sensibilities by replying, in essence, "Jeremiah, you haven't seen anything yet. If you can't keep pace on a six-mile hike with periodic episodes of doing 'double-time,' then how will you be able to handle an actual combat scene?" "*If thou hast run with the footmen and they have wearied thee, then how canst thou contend with horses?*"

It seems especially harsh and unsympathetic, doesn't it? Why would the Lord tell the prophet to, basically, "toughen up"? Why would he challenge, not comfort, him?

The Sanctifying Value of Pressure

We learn from this that sometimes those who are weary need comfort and encouragement, and sometimes they need to be pushed and challenged. The personal trainer who knows that the client has not yet exceeded his/her capacities, or the coach who knows the particular level of challenge his team will face on the gridiron, may seem cruel to push the client to one more set of reps or to keep the team for an extra hour of conditioning. But there is method to the apparent madness.

That pressure may exercise a sanctifying effect on an individual is the point of the metaphor employed in Zechariah 13:8-9: "*And it shall come to pass, that in all the land, saith the Lord, two parts therein shall be cut off and die; but the third shall be left therein. And I will bring the third part through the fire, and will refine them as silver is refined, and will try them as gold is tried: they shall call on my name, and I will hear them: I will say, It is my people: and they shall say, The Lord is my God.*" Though we expect the Lord to comfort and coddle the remaining one-third, or remnant of the nation left after the Babylonian captivity, he intends to test and purify them in the furnace of affliction so that they are henceforth totally committed to Him. We might call this "sanctification by fire."

An old adage says, "Sometimes one must be cruel to be kind." Every parent who has applied physical correction to a child knows that though the child may perceive him as cruel, the discipline is really an expression of kindness and love, for it aims to teach the child obedience and self-discipline. Every emergency room doctor who has ever inserted a needle to deaden the nerves prior to suturing a wound knows that the patient may think this additional pain is especially cruel, but, in reality, it is perhaps the kindest thing the doctor could do, for it allows for an opportunity to stitch the wound and that is in the best interest of the patient. The long-term benefit must take precedence over the short-term comfort.

The point is simply that wisdom dictates that different people in different circumstances may need different tactics. One size does not necessarily fit all. *"And of some have compassion, making a difference: and others save with fear, pulling them out of the fire; hating even the garment spotted by the flesh"* (Jude 22-23; cf. 1 Ths. 5:14). The wise parent, or doctor, or coach, or pastor will tailor his/her approach to the particular needs and capacities of the individual. And our wise Heavenly Father knows how to measure pressure in the lives of His people so that they may best grow toward spiritual maturity.

Jeremiah thought he needed comfort, but God knew what the prophet needed more than he knew what he needed (cf. 2 Cor. 12:7-10). In His great wisdom, God urged him to "buckle-down" and to "man-up" because tougher challenges were on the way.

Quit Ye Like Men

We are living in a soft, pampered society. In such a day of affluence and indulgence, I fear the old masculine virtues of courage, firm resolve, delayed gratification, self-denial, hard work, perseverance and a long obedience in the same direction are increasingly rare. The tenacious grit of John Wayne has been replaced by the GQ sensitivity of Justin Bieber. It is a kinder, gentler age in which even Christianity has been recast into a bland message of tolerance and non-judgmentalism toward sin. Unlike John the Baptist, we wear "soft clothing," live in "palaces," and are as fragile as a "reed shaken with the wind" (Mt. 11:7-8).

In a word, we are emotionally wimpy. People like us who have never known what it is to suffer hunger, privation or persecution, consequently, find it difficult to handle the intrusion of pain and difficulty. It shakes us to the core, challenges our faith, and sends us spiraling downward in a freefall of despair.

I don't intend to minimize whatever trouble you, my reader, might face at this moment in your life. But I know that in my own experience, there have been occasions when, like Jeremiah, I thought I needed consolation and encouragement, but the Lord seemed intent to ratchet up the pressure and deny my request for a change in circumstances. Looking back with 20/20 hindsight on those experiences when relief seemed to languish, I see the wise, Divine intent of His methods of dealing with me. The stress on my spirit developed stronger spiritual muscles that I needed later when facing more severe trials.

Paul's imperative to the Corinthians is desperately needed in this spoiled age: *"Watch ye, stand fast in the faith, quit ye like men, be strong"* (1 Cor. 16:13). It is essentially the same message God gave to Jeremiah. "Toughen up! Act like men. Man up!"

Life in a world under the curse of sin is not for sissies. Although there is certainly a place for comfort and encouragement in the midst of trials and tribulations, there is also a need for endurance and confrontation and doing what you know needs to be done in order to deal with the particular problem you may face at the moment.

"Be strong in the Lord" (Eph. 6:10) is likewise an imperative. Paul is telling us to do something. He means, "Exhibit a manly faith. Get tough. Strain every nerve in resisting the enemy. Make a decisive, deliberate effort to show courage and strength in the face of every challenge." Again, I say, this message is especially pertinent to us at this late date in human history.

If this reading finds you in the valley of affliction, I trust these words will not sound too harsh and insensitive to you. Perhaps you do, in fact, need comfort and strength and a word of encouragement. Still, there is a place in every set of adverse circumstances for the assumption of personal responsibility, for doing what you know to do at the moment. Play the man, my friend. Do what needs to be done. Take control of your own attitude, get out of bed, read the Scriptures, wash the dishes, write the bills, get some exercise, make the difficult phone call, be charitable to the difficult people around you, and remind yourself that God is still on His throne, keeping watch upon His own.

When you determine to do the right thing, whether or not you feel like it, positive emotions have a way of catching up with the right behavior. So, never, never, never give up. Keep on keeping on. Quit ye like men! The strength you gain during basic training may very well be necessary in a greater battle down the road.

"And that's when this feeling came over me like a warm blanket. I knew, somehow, that I had to stay alive. Somehow. I had to keep breathing. Even though there was no reason to hope. And all my logic said that I would never see this place again. So that's what I did. I stayed alive. I kept breathing. And one day my logic was proven all wrong because the tide came in, and gave me a sail. And now, here I am. I'm back. In Memphis, talking to you. I have ice in my glass... And I've lost her all over again. I'm so sad that I don't have Kelly. But I'm so grateful that she was with me on that island. And I know what I have to do now. I have to keep breathing. Because tomorrow the sun will rise. And who knows what the tide could bring?"

- Tom Hanks, in *Castaway*

3
Christian Realism

"These things I have spoken unto you, that in me ye might have peace. In the world ye shall have tribulation: but be of good cheer; I have overcome the world." John 16:33

You have likely fielded the familiar question, "Are you a pessimist or an optimist?" I generally answer the question, "Neither. I'm a realist."

What is the difference? The pessimist says the glass is half-empty. The optimist says the glass is half-full. The realist simply acknowledges that there is water in the glass.

To the pessimist, nothing ever works out. His theme song is, "Nobody loves me; everybody hates me; I guess I'll go eat worms." To the optimist, everything is great and wonderful. His theme song is "Don't Worry, Be Happy." The realist, by way of contrast, sings as his theme song, "God has not promised skies always blue…but He has promised strength as our day, rest when we labor, light on the way."

The capacity to deal with reality is crucial to healthy-mindedness. We expect little boys to pretend they are superheroes, or little girls that they are beautiful movie stars. But we hope with maturity, they will learn to recognize that life in the real world doesn't always work out like they had once dreamed. For me, facing reality meant that my dream of being a professional football player would never come to fruition. Five feet eight inches and a heaping dose of want-to just didn't quite meet the minimum standards of the NFL scouts.

For someone else, facing reality may mean that your childhood goal of making it big as the next American Idol was circumvented by the fact that you had difficulty singing on key. A person may either spend his/her life railing at the way things are, or he may accept the situation as it is, cut his losses, and move on in pursuit of a goal that is more realistic. Healthy-mindedness largely depends on the ability to accept reality.

One of the most compelling apologetics for Christianity is that it is based in reality. It is neither pessimistic, like the ancient pagan religions that taught that man is the victim of fate and that the material world was evil, nor is it an exercise in positive thinking, denying human depravity or pretending that evil does not exist. The classic display in Scripture of this philosophical clash is the scene at Mars Hill, as recorded in Acts 17. The Stoics were the pessimists on the scene. The Epicureans were the optimists. But Paul was the Christian realist, preaching that the one Creator God made man for the express purpose of worshipping Him and holding him accountable for violations of that design.

Life is not a drudgery, as the Stoics taught; neither is it a party, as the Epicureans insisted. Instead notice how the Lord Jesus strikes a refreshingly realistic balance in the comments with which he closed his final sermon: *"These things I have spoken unto you, that in me ye might have peace. In the world ye shall have tribulation: but be of good cheer; I have overcome the world"* (Jno. 16:33). Three great realities may be gleaned from these words.

Reality One: In the World, Trouble is Inevitable.

Our Lord never pretended that His followers were exempt from problems. He did not promote the "prosperity gospel." *"In the world, ye shall have tribulation,"* Jesus said. It is a stunning admission from the Master. But it strikes me as refreshingly realistic. I need the reminder that life in this world will not be trouble- or hassle-free. I am not an exception to the rule. Trouble is just as inevitable as sparks flying upward from a bonfire (cf. Job 5:7).

No one will avoid problems in life. *"Man that is born of a woman,"* mused Job, *"is of few days, and full of trouble"* (Job 14:1). Though, comparatively, the wicked *"are not in trouble as other men"* (Ps. 73:5), yet even they do not escape flat tires, migraine headaches, job loss and relational stresses in life. Across the board, trouble is part and parcel of life in a world that is under the curse of sin.

The word "trouble" in this verse speaks of distress of every kind. It includes bodily weakness and weariness, physical ailments and disease, monetary losses, unemployment, dashed dreams and disappointments, relational crises, loss of loved ones, separation from friends, tragedies, emotional traumas, accidents, and heartaches. It also encompasses trouble from this world such as believers experience: persecution in the form of taunts, sneers, slander, rejection, threats, fines, imprisonment, and even martyrdom.

How many people struggle with life because they approach it with the optical illusion that difficulty is the exception rather than the rule? I'm thankful the Lord Jesus dealt with his people in realistic terms. His words remind us that trouble is inevitable; therefore we should not be surprised when difficulties arise.

Reality Two: In Christ, Peace is Available.

"In the world, ye shall have tribulation." That's reality number one. But the Lord doesn't stop there. Jesus says, *"In me, ye might have peace."* The peace available to the believer in Christ is just as much of a reality as the trouble that will come to us in this world.

Internal peace, in an external climate of trouble, is Christ's legacy to the church. In His final sermon, Jesus pledged, *"Peace I leave with you, my peace I give unto you: not as the world giveth give I unto you. Let not your heart be troubled, neither let it be afraid"* (Jno. 14:27). When our Lord left this world, he left behind a legacy. It was not a legacy of popularity or wealth, but of peace. *"Peace I leave with you."*

What kind of peace did He leave behind? The very same inner tranquility that He possessed during His public ministry in this world: *"My peace I give unto you."* What an incredible resource this is! Just as the Savior faced taunts and sneers and opposition with calmness of soul and poise of spirit, so His disciples have the same ability available to them through the ministry of the Holy Spirit.

I do not know of a more potent Christian testimony than a believer who faces daily afflictions with quiet peace and unflappable resolve. Like the calm waters beneath the turbulent ocean surface, the follower of the Lord Jesus Christ may experience genuine, spiritual tranquility in his heart though circumstances in his life are in turmoil.

This is not some mere pious platitude or Christian cliché. I am talking about something real, something true. The existential awareness that God is on His throne as the sovereign ruler of heaven and earth, that Jesus Christ is risen, never to die again, that the promise of His abiding presence is true and that it is true for me, and that He will return one happy day to vanquish every enemy of righteousness and gather His loved ones home affords real peace to the soul.

"Where," someone queries, "may I find this peace?" In Christ, by means of His word. *"These things have I spoken unto you that in me, ye might have peace."* This peace is not derived from a pill bottle or a cocktail or an escape to the mountains or beach. It springs from meditation on the truth of God's holy word.

Isaiah hits the proverbial "nail on the head": *"Thou wilt keep him in perfect peace, whose mind is stayed upon thee: because he trusteth in thee"* (Is. 26:3). Spiritual perspective is critical to spiritual peace. When your mind is fixed on the Lord, peace—perfect peace—will be the blessed by-product.

You may see, then, how important is the spiritual discipline of Scripture intake. Daily Bible reading coupled with ongoing meditation is the Great Physician's prescription for the malady of inward turmoil: *"Great peace have they which love thy law: and nothing shall offend them"* (Ps. 119:165). The word of God keeps the mind focused on the God of the word. There is no discipline more faith-building than time spent in Holy Scripture: *"Acquaint now thyself with Him, and be at peace: thereby good shall come unto thee"* (Job 22:21).

All of Scripture is profitable but the Psalms seem especially helpful to those who are walking through the valley of affliction. Whatever your particular circumstance at the moment, you may find companionship in the Psalmist's experiences penned in the Psalter. His words will sharpen your focus on the power, presence, mercy and faithfulness of God. With renewed perspective on your Lord, faith revives and heavenly peace floods the soul.

I suspect that many people think heart peace is something automatic, like some magical potion infused into the soul. They miss the fact that peace in the heart is inseparably connected to truth in the mind. God is certainly able to inject emotional peace directly into the heart of one of His little children, but that is not His ordinary habit. Peace in the soul is the result of faith: *"Now the God of hope fill you with all joy and peace in believing..."* (Rom. 15:13). It comes as a byproduct of a mind that understands and embraces certain truths as facts.

Because our minds, susceptible to distraction by the many cares and vicissitudes of life, tend to forget the truth of Scripture, we need regular reminders. Daily reading and meditation in the word of God, as well as regular attendance at public worship, then, is a spiritual necessity for the child of God. The more frequently a person avails himself of opportunities to be exposed to God's word, the greater peace he will have in his soul.

A pastor knows that the Bible is the believer's most important tangible resource. It is simply impossible to live a fruitful and productive Christian life without regular exposure to God's word. The words of Psalm 1 emphasize the synthesis between ongoing meditation in Scripture and spiritual vigor: *"But his delight is in the law of the Lord; and in his law doth he meditate day and night. And he shall be like a tree planted by the rivers of water, that bringeth forth his fruit in his season; his leaf also shall not whither; and whatsoever he doeth shall prosper"* (Ps. 1:3). There is nothing more important for the believer, therefore, than daily Bible reading and regular exposure to gospel preaching. The very peace of your soul depends on it.

The practice of spiritual disciplines, such as Scripture intake, is the means by which one stays connected to and in fellowship with the Lord Jesus Christ. Just a few sentences after pledging His peace to His disciples (and in the same sermon from which the text that heads this chapter derives), Jesus drew this familiar analogy: *"Abide in me, and I in you. As the branch cannot bear fruit of itself, except it abide in the vine; no more can ye, except ye abide in me. I am the vine, ye are the branches: he that abideth in me, and I in him, the same bringeth forth much fruit: for without me ye can do nothing"* (Jno. 15:4-5).

What does our Lord mean? He means that the fruit of the Spirit, one of which is peace, does not spontaneously generate itself. The branch that bears the fruit must stay connected to its life-source, i.e. the vine. Every nutrient necessary to produce fruit in the branch derives from the vine; likewise, the nourishment needed to produce peace in the heart depends on the moment-by-moment habit of personal fellowship with the Lord Jesus Christ by means of the practice of spiritual disciplines like Bible reading and meditation. Peace is (in a very real sense) available to you in Christ: *"These things I have spoken unto you that in me ye might have peace."*

Reality Three: By Faith, Victory is Possible.

In the third place, John 16:33 reveals a third glorious reality: By faith, victory is possible. Jesus says, *"Be of good cheer; I have overcome the world."*

"Be of good cheer" means, in Western vernacular, "cheer up." What an apparently unrealistic imperative! The Lord has just told the disciples that He is leaving. Further, He has warned them to expect persecution (cf. Jno. 15:18-25). Finally, He has informed them of the inevitability of tribulation in this life. On what realistic level could He possibly now turn to them and say, "Cheer up"? He could do so, and realistically so, on the very real premise that the Holy Spirit would come as Christ's agent to the church, empowering and enabling believers to live as Jesus lived (cf. Jno. 14:12).

While He was in the world, the Lord Jesus lived and ministered in the power of the Spirit (cf. Lk. 4:18; Jno. 3:34; Heb. 1:9). When He ascended to heaven, the Holy Comforter was dispatched in Jesus' name to minister to believers by mediating Christ's presence to the church (Jno. 14:16-18, 26). Today the church can say, in a very real sense, that the Lord Jesus is Himself with us as He promised (cf. Mt. 28:20) because the Spirit has been sent to abide with us forever (cf. Jno. 14:16; Eph. 1:14; 4:30).

What is the significance of the new covenant ministry of the Holy Spirit in the life of the believer? The new *Paraclete*, or Comforter, serves as the church's Teacher (interpreting the meaning and applying the truth of Scripture to the individual), Ally (befriending and encouraging the church by His presence), Advocate (defending them against opponents and interceding for them before the Father), Guide (leading and directing believers according to the will of God), Strengthener (enabling and equipping them for the tasks of ministry), and Sanctifier (helping them to mortify sin and to consecrate themselves to holiness). Each of these images is indigenous to the Greek title *Paraclete*.

In a word, the Comforter assists believers in Jesus Christ in the same way that Jesus assisted the original disciples to live and grow and understand truth. The Holy Spirit functions to fulfill precisely the same role to the church in each subsequent generation as the Lord Jesus did in His three-and-one-half year public ministry in this world.

That means that the prospect of living a victorious Christian life in this world is very real. If the Lord Jesus overcame the world, then we too, by faith in Him and through the energizing influence of the Holy Spirit, may do likewise.

Our Lord never succumbed to the world's temptations, deceptions, or distractions. He never lay down in despair, defeated by the world. He did not buckle beneath the world's pressure, give in to its sins, or fall in love with its enticements. He lived a perfect and faithful life from start to finish. Jesus conquered the world.

"But," some poor soul laments, "I'm not doing very well at overcoming the world. Life in this world beats me down. I feel intimidated by its frowns, flustered by its pressures, frail in the face of its enticements, frightened by the prospect of its troubles, and frustrated by the many obstacles to godliness it places in my path. I don't think it is possible for me to live as a victor. I feel more like a victim most of the time."

But God has equipped you with faith in regeneration. That faith, when put into action to lay hold on Jesus Christ, equips you to resist the world's relentless effort to defeat you: "*Whatsoever is born of God overcometh the world: and this is the victory that overcometh the world, even our faith*" (1 Jno. 5:4). You don't have to lay down in surrender before the pressures of life. You don't have to give in to the world's temptations. You needn't lose your sanity when the doctor informs you that you have some dreaded disease.

Cheer up, then, my brother! By faith in the Lord Jesus Christ, you too can overcome the world, with all of its lusts, carnal attitudes, discouragements, and allurements. You can practice holiness in your conduct. You can be loving and kind to others. You can be joyful. You can be faithful to God.

Yes, I'm speaking to you. Victory is possible, in spite of the troubles you now face. Whatever the nature of your current conflict, you can do things in a way that pleases and glorifies God. You don't have to give in to the flesh or give vent to your natural impulses. Without Him, you will be defeated. But through the Lord who strengthens you, you can do all things. I am not talking fantasy here. I'm talking reality. May God help you to prove it true in your own life.

Part II

Specific Counsel

4

Guard Your Heart
Resolving Inward Trials

"Teach me the struggles of the soul to bear;
To check the rising doubt, the rebel sigh;
Teach me the patience of unanswered prayer."
– George Croly (1780-1860)

The believer's own heart and mind is the primary theater in which spiritual warfare is waged. Victory in terms of healthy personal relationships, a powerful personal testimony, usefulness in Christian ministry and other more public areas of discipleship largely originate in the individual's own attitudes of heart and daily thought patterns. No doubt, the Holy Spirit had this "inside/out" dynamic in mind when He inspired Paul to write: *"Let the peace of God rule in your heart, to the which also ye are called in one body"* (Col. 3:15a). Peace in the heart of the individual believer will spill over into the promotion of peace in the local church. What an important principle to learn…and to remember!

It is because of the strategic role played by the heart and mind, or what Scripture calls the "inner man," that Solomon counseled his son to: *"Keep thy heart with all diligence; for out of it are the issues of life"* (Pro. 4:23). The inward man is the control center for every part of life, whether we are talking about a fulfilling marriage relationship, strength to resist temptation, the ability to bear burdens, an ethical and productive job performance, the maintenance of healthy friendships, the rearing of healthy (physically, emotionally and spiritually) children, or a life of service to others. Success in the public sector of life issues from a carefully nurtured and guarded heart.

This means that the most important thing any one of us may do for a relationship or in service to others is to keep our own hearts right. Attitude and mindset is everything when it comes to a productive and God-honoring daily life. Win the battle within and you have made great progress toward victory against the formidable enemy of your soul in every other dimension of life—relationally and ethically. Success in the public sector begins with vigilance to govern the private sector of the believer's personal attitudes and thought-life.

Psalm 73 is the record of a personal experience with "inward trials" in the life of a man named Asaph. According to 1 Chronicles 15:19 and 16:5, Asaph, the inspired writer of several Psalms (73 – 83), was a Levite appointed to serve as chief singer in Divine worship. His other Psalms consist of typical celebrations of Jehovah's glory, justice, power and deliverances, but the seventy-third is autobiographical. This is his story of how he lost and then regained his spiritual perspective.

He begins with a confession of God's goodness to His covenant people (v. 1), then immediately draws a contrast to that fact by acknowledging his own personal struggle: *"But as for me, my feet were almost gone; my steps had well nigh slipped"* (v. 2).

Why is Asaph so dangerously close to personal apostasy? His thinking is awry. Let's follow the stages of his slide down the slippery slope and subsequent rescue from the quagmire of total disillusionment.

Stage 1: Confusion (vs. 3-12)

The Psalmist's feet are slipping because he is standing precariously on the banana peel of confusion. He explains in verses 3 through 12:

> For I was envious at the foolish, when I saw the prosperity of the wicked. For there are no bands in their death: but their strength is firm. They are not in trouble as other men; neither are they plagued like other men. Therefore pride compasseth them about as a chain; violence covereth them as a garment. Their eyes stand out with fatness: they have more than heart could wish. They are corrupt, and speak wickedly concerning oppression: they speak loftily. They set their mouth against the heavens, and their tongue walketh through the earth. Therefore his people return hither: and waters of a full cup are wrung out to them. And they say, How doth God know? And is

there knowledge in the most High? Behold, these are the ungodly, who prosper in the world; they increase in riches.

What is the nature of his inner conflict? In a word, Asaph is struggling with his attitude. It is not that he vindictively wants to see the ungodly hurt. He does not wish misery upon them. Rather, it is the apparent injustice of it all that troubles him. It seems to him that evil is triumphant over good—that truth is on the scaffold while wrong is on the throne. He wonders why the nice guys always finish last.

When your thoughts are focused on the evil and wickedness of this world, it is easy to slip into confusion and perplexity. I know of nothing so effective to depress me as watching the talking heads on 24/7 cable news channels day after day. A steady diet of rumors of approaching war, threats of epidemic diseases, reports of corrupt politicians who win reelection, news of court decisions that perpetuate the moral freefall of society, and more is a fail-proof recipe for mental anguish and anxiety in my life. It produces such a dark frame of mind that I inevitably begin to lose my spiritual footing.

Stage 2: Complaint (vs. 13-16)

Next, Asaph looks at himself. A view of his own circumstances against the background of the relative hassle-free lives of wicked people leads to his complaint. Notice the contrast he draws between the prosperity of the ungodly in verses 3 through 12 and his own experience of relentless adversity in verses 13 and 14:

Verily I have cleansed my heart in vain, and washed my hands in innocency. For all day long have I been plagued, and chastened every morning.

To Asaph, the scales of justice do not appear to balance. While those who care nothing about God and righteousness seem to live relatively carefree and hassle-free lives, Asaph feels the pressure of daily trials and Divine chastening in his quest to live a clean and godly life. "I'm trying to do the right thing," he says, "and all I have are circumstantial problems and conviction of conscience every day." He concludes that it is just not worth it to try to live a holy life: "*Verily I have cleansed my heart in vain, and washed my hands in innocency.*"

Is he in a dangerous frame of mind? Yes, indeed! His "feet are almost gone; his steps have well nigh slipped." Again, it is not that he harbors malice toward or wishes ill upon nonbelievers. Neither is he seeking some sort of "pat on the back" or "attaboy" as a reward for righteous living. It is the apparent injustice of the circumstance that troubles him.

So troubled is he, in fact, that he is prepared to abandon his efforts to do the right thing. He is beginning to listen to the tempter's whisper, "It isn't worth it; you're beating your head against a brick wall; the wall hasn't moved and your head feels like it's about to split open. Why don't you just quit?"

As he thinks about the disparity between his relentless troubles and the relatively carefree lives of the ungodly, he recognizes not only how precariously close he is to personal apostasy but also how easily he might become a stumbling block to someone else:

> If I say, I will speak thus; behold, I should offend against the generation of thy children. When I thought to know this, it was too painful for me... (Ps. 73:15-16).

What is Asaph expressing here? He recognizes that if he verbalizes his inward trials—if he proceeds to talk about it publicly and to unburden his soul struggles to others—he risks becoming an impediment to them in their own respective commitments to the Lord.

Discouragement is infectious and discouraged people tend to spread the virus to others until an epidemic erupts. The discouragement generated by the unbelief of the ten spies within the camp of the Israelites is a classic example of this principle: "*Our brethren have discouraged our heart, saying, The people is greater and taller than we; the cities are great and walled up to heaven; and moreover we have seen the sons of the Anakims there*" (Deut. 1:28; cf. Num. 32:9). If good news spread as quickly as bad news, this world would be in much better shape. Sadly, however, few attitudes are as contagious as discouragement.

There are few things as helpful when the heart is heavily burdened than to be able to release that burden by talking about it to a wise and kind counselor. But such an option is not available to Asaph, as far as he is concerned. It's bad enough that he is fighting such a fierce inward battle; he certainly (and nobly so) doesn't want to express his innermost thoughts to someone else and be the cause of stumbling in his brother's life. So, he decides to internalize his soul struggles. "It is my own cross," he must have thought, "and I must bear it alone." Yet, the more he thought about the need to deal with his own inward wrestlings of heart in isolation, he despaired yet more: "*When I thought to know this, it was too painful for me*" (v. 16). The complaint seemed to be more than he could personally bear.

Stage 3: Comprehension (vs. 17-20)

Asaph's inward pain seemed unbearable. How could he possibly maintain the fight against the outrage of injustice? How could he resist the urge to blame the righteous Lord with unrighteousness? How might he retain his sanity when his mind was in such a whirl of confusion and his heart tangled in knots of conflicting affections?

This painful struggle continued...*until*... What sublime consolation I hear in that word! "*...It was too painful for me; Until I went into the sanctuary of God; then understood I their end*" (73:16b-17). A visit to the house of God to hear the word of God helped this struggling child of God by renewing his mind, once again, in the truth of God. Then, he understood. *Then, he understood!*

The importance of regular exposure to God's word in the believer's life cannot be overstated. Without daily Bible reading and regular church attendance to hear the word preached, the mind— and, in fact, every spiritual virtue—will atrophy. It is impossible to grow spiritually without the discipline of habitual intake of the truth of Scripture (cf. Ps. 1:2-3; 1 Pet. 2:2).

Paul said that the gospel will save the believer *if* he keeps it in memory (1 Cor. 15:2). "But, you see," someone objects, "that is just my problem. I don't have a very good memory." But the believer keeps the word of God in memory not by means of possessing a good memory but by being *reminded* of it on a regular basis. When the pure mind is stirred up by means of hearing the word taught again and again when the church assembles for public worship, the believer discovers the blessing of this gospel salvation.

The renewal of my mind by the preaching of the gospel has saved me, time and time again, from many pitfalls. It has saved me from despair on the sad occasion of a loved-one's funeral, from a bad attitude when pride or jealousy or self-centeredness raised its ugly head, from fear and anxiety when my problems had gained control of my mind, from discouragement when it seemed that nothing was working out as I had hoped. And it has saved me from the kind of confusion and perplexity that Asaph felt as he faced the apparent injustice of his own struggles in the context of the prosperity of the wicked. I need such gospel salvation every day that I live in this world.

When you find yourself in the kind of tailspin Asaph experienced, nothing is more important than attendance on public worship with the saints in the house of God. There you will be put back in touch with ultimate reality. Suddenly your mind will be renewed by the eternal verities revealed in God's word and every circumstance of your life will be put back in focus in the light of those sublime truths. Whatever problems you face will again assume their real size when you look, not at the things that are seen, but at the things that are unseen (cf. 2 Cor. 4:17-18). Then, you too will understand and your confusion will dissolve into restored comprehension and clarity.

"Far below the storm of doubt
Upon the world is beating,
Sons of men in battle long
The enemy withstand;

Safe am I within the castle
Of God's word retreating,
Nothing there can reach me—
'Tis Beulah Land."[1]

When Asaph retreated into the castle of God's word, what particular truth did he consider that brought clarity to his clouded mind? He found the answer to his perplexity when he considered the final end of the ungodly in contrast to that of the righteous: *"…then I understood their end. Surely thou didst set them in slippery places: thou castedst them down into destruction. How are they brought to desolation, as in a moment! They are utterly consumed with terrors"* (73:18-19).

I think it is safe to say that Asaph no more wants to see the ungodly suffer Divine wrath any more than he is jealous of their prosperity. He is not a psychopath who takes some kind of sinister pleasure in watching pain inflicted on another human being. His comfort, rather, is in the reassurance that justice will be served. The scales of justice will be balanced. All of the hard speeches that ungodly sinners have spoken against Christ and all of the ungodly deeds that have been done in dishonor to God's holy character will one day receive the justice they deserve (cf. Jude 15). To those who have labored to do right in a world that celebrates all that is wrong, the day when every wrong is made right will be incredibly jubilant.

Revelation 19 depicts the worship scene on that day: *"I heard a great voice of much people in heaven, saying, Alleluia; Salvation, and glory, and honour, and power, unto the Lord our God: For true and righteous are his judgments: for he hath judged the great whore, which did corrupt the earth with her fornication, and hath avenged the blood of his servants at her hand. And again they said, Alleluia. And her smoke rose up for ever and ever"* (Rev. 19:1-3). Note that the redeemed multitude is not here celebrating God's grace, but God's government. It is not his rescue of the righteous that elicits the Hallelujah chorus, but the judgment of the wicked. It is only as we increasingly understand the extent of Divine holiness

---

[1] C. Austin Miles (1868-1946), *Old School Hymnal Twelfth Edition*, No. 367.

and the heinousness of sin that this kind of worship scene will make any sense to us.

For Asaph, the reminder of the grand assize, i.e. the final judgment—a day when all wrongs will be righted—put everything he presently faced back into proper focus. He could see again that the ungodly may, in fact, prosper now but will not get away with sin forever. And though the righteous may presently suffer affliction and conflict, yet their best is yet to come. That Asaph has not mistaken the intended lesson is clear, for the same "now and later" idea is reiterated by the Lord Jesus Christ in the account of the Rich Man and Lazarus in Luke 16 (cf. Lk. 16:25).

Stage 4: Conviction (vs. 21-22)

Asaph's inward trials, however, were not yet gone. No sooner does he find peace from his initial confusion than his heart feels the sting of conviction of sin:

Thus my heart was grieved, and I was pricked in my reins. So foolish was I, and ignorant: I was as a beast before thee. (73:21-22)

Initially, he looked at the ungodly and compared their apparent prosperity to his relative adversity. This perspective produced confusion and complaint. Then he looked into God's word and considered the current state of affairs in the light of the final end of the wicked. Suddenly, his comprehension was restored. His initial struggles dissipated in view of the big picture. Now, however, he looks at himself and is ashamed for allowing himself to slide so precariously into such an unhealthy frame of mind.

It is as if Asaph has regained his spiritual sanity. Like the prodigal son who "came to himself" in the hog pen (cf. Lk. 15:17), and the king of Babylon when his understanding returned to him in the pasture (cf. Dan. 4:34), Asaph now realizes just how far backward he had slipped and just how close he was to allowing his bad attitude to destroy him. And it broke his heart.

He might have said, "What is wrong with me? I know better than this. How could I allow myself to sink so low? I am shocked at myself. I was acting just like an animal, as if I had no understanding whatsoever. What a fool I've been!"

Though it is seldom pleasant, a long, hard look at oneself, especially when fighting a battle within, is extremely important. "*Examine yourselves*," counseled Paul, "*whether ye be in the faith; prove your own selves*" (2 Cor. 13:5). It is so much easier to examine someone else, to scrutinize the life and conduct of another to see if it meets the standard, but Paul urges us to resist the temptation to audit our brother and turn our eyes inward in self-examination. Prove your own selves.

Walking in the light necessarily involves living honestly before God, not excusing or covering one's sins in dishonesty (cf. 1 Jno. 1:6-9). Indeed, it hurts to look in the mirror of God's word and to measure our attitudes, words, and actions by the perfect standard of Jesus Christ. But there will be no spiritual gain in godliness without the willingness to face that personal pain. "*He that covereth his sins*"— whether in terms of denying them, justifying and rationalizing them, or blaming them on someone else—"*shall not prosper; but whoso confesseth and forsaketh them shall obtain mercy*" (Pro. 28:13). How much better it is to deal with the Lord in the vulnerability of honesty: "*Search me, O God, and know my heart: try me, and know my thoughts: and see if there be any wicked way in me, and lead me in the way everlasting*" (Ps. 139:23-24)! The admission that "I was wrong" may very well be the turning point in the fight to overcome inward trials.

Stage 5: Confidence (vs. 23-26)

Although he feels deep conviction of his sins, Asaph now does something that every child of God must learn to do. He looks away from himself and looks toward the grace of God. And the view produces within him great comfort and confidence.

Nevertheless I am continually with thee: thou hast holden me by my right hand. Thou shalt guide me with thy counsel, and afterward receive me to glory. Whom have I in heaven but thee? And there is none upon earth that I desire beside thee. My flesh and my heart faileth: but God is the strength of my heart, and my portion for ever. (73:23-26)

He acknowledges that though he had strayed so very far, yet the Lord had not forsaken him: *"Nevertheless I am continually with thee: thou hast holden me by my right hand."* When his steps were slipping, the Lord was holding his hand to steady him.

How gracious is our God to sustain us, even in those seasons when we are waging a fierce warfare within our own hearts and minds! Hasn't that been your experience? As you look backward with 20/20 hindsight, can you not see how that the Lord has refused to abandon you to yourself in those experiences that now cause you to shake your head in embarrassment? I freely admit that this is my story. *"When I said, My foot slippeth, thy mercy, O Lord, held me up"* (Ps. 94:18).

It would probably surprise each of us to know just how many times the Lord kept us from falling to our own spiritual demise. His faithfulness to abide with us, even when we had wandered away from Him, is a testimony to His amazing grace. If you and I are thinking properly today, we must freely admit with the apostle Paul, *"I am what I am by the grace of God"* (1 Cor. 15:10).

Asaph's fresh sight of God's wonderful grace to him, even in his miserable state of personal apostasy, prompts the confession in verses 24-26: *"Thou shalt guide me with thy counsel, and afterward receive me to glory..."* He is not reluctant now to renew his confession of total confidence in the Lord: *"Whom have I in heaven but thee? And there is none upon earth that I desire beside thee."* Though he may not understand everything, He trusts implicitly in God's promise to guide him now and the rest of his days and then to take him home to heaven. He wants to live for this gracious God now and finds delight in the truth that the Lord is his heavenly helper. Though he feels weak and frail (*"My flesh and my heart faileth"*), yet God, he gladly owns, is his strength and portion forever.

Editorial Comment (vs. 27-28)

This autobiographical experience of Asaph's inward trials concludes with a word of application in Psalm 73:27-28:

> For, lo, they that are far from thee shall perish: thou hast destroyed all them that go a-whoring from thee. But it is good for me to draw near to God: I have put my trust in the Lord God, that I may declare all thy works.

The lesson learned from his experience concerned the necessity of a closer walk with God. He feels that had he stayed closer to the Lord, he would not have drifted into such an unhealthy frame. Distance from God leads to confusion of mind and personal apostasy. Nearness to God brings clarity of thought and personal strength for ministry.

It is good for me, as well, to draw nigh unto God. Under the shadow of his mighty wings, I discover peace and comfort and safety and courage. The best cure for inward trials is to draw near to Christ by means of daily communion with Him in prayer, the study of His word, and fellowship with His people. *"Draw nigh to God and He will draw nigh unto you,"* counsels James (Jas. 4:8a). Near to the heart of God, I find a place of quiet rest. You will too, friend. Draw nigh to Him today, and watch your inward trials dissolve into irrelevance in the light of His glory and grace.

These Inward Trials
by John Newton

I asked the Lord that I might grow
In faith and love and every grace;
Might more of His salvation know
And seek more earnestly His face.

'Twas He that taught me thus to pray,
And He, I trust, who answered prayer;

But it has been in such a way
As almost drove me to despair.

I thought that in some favored hour
At once, He'd answer my request;
And by His love's constraining power
Subdue my sins and give me rest.

Instead of this, He made me feel
The hidden evils of my heart;
And let the angry powers of hell
Assault my soul in every part.

Yea more, with His own hand He seemed
Intent to aggravate my woe;
Crossed all the fair designs I schemed,
Blasted my gourds, and laid me low.

'Lord, why is this?' I trembling cried—
'Wilt Thou pursue this worm to death?'
' 'Tis in this way,' the Lord replied,
'I answer prayers for grace and faith.

These inward trials I employ
From self and pride to set thee free,
And break thy schemes of earthly joy
That thou mayest seek thine all in Me.'

5
Cast Down, But Not Destroyed
Defeating Spiritual Depression

"Why art thou cast down, O my soul? And why art thou disquieted within me? Hope thou in God: for I shall yet praise him for the help of his countenance." Psalm 42:5

On September 11, 2001, Islamic terrorists hijacked four airplanes, steering them into economic and military symbols of Western civilization in what proved to be the worst attack on American soil since Pearl Harbor. Two thousand, nine hundred seventy-seven people died and over six thousand were injured. The trauma was so severe and mind-boggling that it made a permanent impression on practically everyone who witnessed the unfolding calamity. Most of us remember exactly where we were standing or sitting and what we were doing when the realization that America was under attack hit home.

It is true that life may change on a dime: "*Suddenly are my tents spoiled and my curtains in a moment*" lamented the prophet Jeremiah (Jer. 4:20). Ezekiel, likewise, experienced the sudden calamity of his wife's unexpected passing: "*Son of man, behold, I take away from thee the desire of thine eyes with a stroke...So I spake unto the people in the morning: and at even my wife died*" (Eze. 24:16, 18). Just the shock and surprise of a sudden change in circumstance, a trauma that you never saw coming, can shake the very foundations of emotional sanity to the core.

Personal 9-11's, events that are too big for us, are inevitable in life. How does a person survive when his savings for retirement are suddenly lost because the stock market bottoms out, or the man she loves suddenly breaks off the engagement, or the doctor tells you that you have some terminal disease, or the child you've anticipated is born with serious disabilities, or a spouse breaks his vows as well as your heart? What should you do when your world suddenly tumbles in on top of you?

The way forward in such times is not to collapse in despair but to maintain focus on Jesus Christ and triumph, by faith, over the negative emotions. The challenge to rule your own spirit, instead of being controlled by circumstances and the attending emotional response they engender, is essential to a sound, or healthy, mind. But that is easier said than done, isn't it?

David's Depression

Psalm 42 was composed by David during the ten year period in his life when he lived as a fugitive, fleeing before the jealousy and paranoia of King Saul. The caption reads *Maschil*, which indicates it was intended to be a *teaching* Psalm.

What lesson does it teach us? It records David's experience of spiritual depression and instructs us about how he found victory over the sad, sinking feelings of despair that invaded his heart and soul.

It is noteworthy that David, together with several other "larger than life" figures in the Bible, battled feelings of depression. I'm glad the Holy Spirit saw fit to record not only their triumphs and exploits but also their struggles and sins. I can identify with these men "of like passions as we are."

What were the circumstances that led to this episode of spiritual depression in David's life? Evidently, it was a "holy day" (42:4). David recalls happier times when he joined the multitudes of worshipers in Jerusalem at the house of God for Passover, or the Day of Atonement, or the Feast of Tabernacles. But now, a long way from home, he feels like a little deer chased by a predator, thirsty for a drink from the water brooks of spiritual fellowship with God. He wonders when the madness that requires him to miss Divine worship will be ended: "*...when shall I come and appear before God?*" (42:2).

Add to this sense of alienation the sting of discouraging remarks: "*My tears have been my meat day and night while they continually say unto me, Where is thy God?*" (42:3). He hears a waterfall in the distance and the roar resonates with the disquiet he feels in his own soul: "*Deep calleth unto deep at the noise of thy waterspouts: all thy waves and thy billows are gone over me*" (42:7). He cries out to God, "*Why hast thou forgotten me? Why go*

I mourning because of the oppression of the enemy?" (42:8). David is at a very low point in his life. He is sliding down the slippery slope into the Slough of Despond. He is depressed.

The Symptoms of Depression

It is important to distinguish between *spiritual* depression and *clinical* depression. That depression sometimes results from physiological causes is a well-established fact of medical science. Further, that prolonged stress, psychological trauma, or an old-fashioned "broken heart" may produce physical symptoms that accompany depressed feelings, is also common knowledge.

Obviously in both of these scenarios, a person may want to visit his family doctor. Despite the anti-medical views of non-Christian groups like Christian Scientism as well as a smattering of well-meaning, homespun folk who for one reason or another distrust alchemy, believers in the Lord Jesus Christ are not opposed to medical science and the use of a therapeutic regimen of medication to treat the physiological symptoms of depression. In fact, a mild anti-depressant may actually help someone to be able to regain sufficient mental clarity and calmness so that he may focus on addressing the essentially spiritual causes of depression.

Whatever the root cause of depression—spiritual or clinical—however, the symptoms of depression are generally the same from one case to the next. A depressed person, in contrast to someone who periodically gets a case of the "blues," generally presents:

- Pronounced feelings of hopelessness, sadness and despair;
- Irritability and frustration, even over small matters;
- Difficulty concentrating or making decisions;
- A sense of fatigue and general lack of energy;
- Loss of interest in normal activities;
- Difficulty with sleep and diet;
- A growing sense that life is not worth living.

Psalm 42 describes this kind of emotional distress in terms of feeling "cast down" and inwardly "disquieted." The expression "cast down" is a shepherd's term. It refers to a sheep that lay down in a soft spot of ground, causing it to inadvertently roll over on its back with its legs sticking straight into the air. It was in a cast position and unless the shepherd came along to rescue it, the sheep would certainly die. It was not able to rescue itself.

Perhaps the Psalmist David had this particular plight in mind when he wrote of the Good Shepherd, *"He restoreth my soul"* (Ps. 23:3a). How many times has your heavenly Shepherd lifted and restored your soul when you were in such a helpless, cast condition?

The other term he employs, "disquieted," means just what it says. David was experiencing the loss of inward peace and quietness of soul. His heart was filled with turmoil. He felt a tumultuous kind of chaos inside, like the sounds of the nearby waterfalls crashing on the rocks beneath (v. 7). Former days of calm and peace seemed but a distant memory.

There is another hint in this Psalm of the kind of symptoms presented by someone who is depressed. The repeated references to his "countenance," suggests that depression shows up in an individual's facial expressions. David acknowledges that his countenance needs "help" (v. 5) and is not "healthy" (v. 11). In a word, he suffers from a "fallen countenance" (cf. Gen. 4:6).

"Your face is as a book," said Lady Macbeth to her husband, "where men may read strange matters." Just as a person's words reveal what is in the heart (Mt. 12:34), so a person's countenance reveals his attitude and frame of mind (Gen. 31:2; Ps. 10:4; Pro. 15:13; Jer. 5:3). "What the heart feels, the face reveals."

The word "countenance" in Psalm 42 is translated from a Hebrew word (*paniym*) that is used some 2,100 times in the Old Testament. It is a plural term that refers to the many different expressions of thought, emotion and mood of which the face is capable. The face, for instance, may "shine," expressing joy and gladness (Ps. 104:15), or it may express anger (Pro. 25:23), or confidence and boldness (Ecc.

8:1). It may also display the emotion of intense sadness, or depression. Scripture refers to this as the "fallen countenance."

It is difficult for a depressed individual to hide his inward distress. It tends to show in his face. In such cases, a kind of spiritual face-lift is needed so the countenance is once again healthy.

The Causes of Depression

What are some of the reasons a person might sink into spiritual depression? What causes the countenance to fall? That is the very question the Psalmist asks himself in Psalm 42: "*Why art thou cast down, O my soul?*" There will be no progress made toward recovery from despondency until a person first analyzes and understands the particular dynamic that led to such an unhealthy frame of mind.

Life is sometimes described as a pressure cooker. That is certainly a pertinent metaphor. A pressure cooker builds tremendous pressure as heat is applied to the vessel. If it didn't have an escape valve to let off some steam from time to time, it would eventually explode. Likewise, the individual who does not take time to analyze the many different factors that have contributed to the pressure he now feels and to understand how each has contributed to the feelings of despair that presently grips his heart and mind will soon suffer complete emotional debilitation.

"Why art thou cast down?" is a question of paramount importance. Though it is not an easy question for the depressed individual to consider—for the tangled web of the present myriad of problems may seem so complex and chaotic that it cannot possibly be unraveled—it is nonetheless critical to attempt to sort through the various parts that make up the whole of crisis and to begin to address each one with a very specific plan of action. A pastor or wise friend may be of great help in this particular task.

In general, I think it is important to note, first of all, that in most cases the depressed individual has allowed *the trials and afflictions of life* to get on top of him. That was certainly the case in David's experience as recorded in Psalm 42.

Pursued by the insanely-jealous King of Israel, David spies a little deer (or 'hart') running away from some predator: "*As the hart panteth after the water brooks, so panteth my soul after thee, O God*" (v. 1). It's as if he says to the little deer, "I know how you feel."

Saul chased David from mountain to valley like a hunter might hunt for a partridge or quail flushed from safety. We don't know at what point in his approximate ten-year-long exile he writes these words, but, evidently, enough time has elapsed for the extremity of his circumstances, the uncertainty of his personal safety, and a sense of alienation and estrangement from his friends and family to wear on his ability to think rationally and calmly. His situation just seems too complicated to be resolved at any time soon.

When a person has borne up under a load of pressure for a long time, the least additional pressure tends to start the slide into despondency. The simple reminder in the Psalmist's case that this was a "holy day" back home and that the multitudes would be converging on Jerusalem for the festive occasion was the proverbial "last straw" that, added to the load he already carried, "broke the camel's back" in Psalm 42 (see v. 4).

The same was true in Elijah's case. This apparently indefatigable prophet had withstood a three-year famine living in obscurity, then an emotionally-charged confrontation with the prophets of Baal on Mount Carmel. It seemed that he was made of steel. But at Jezebel's threat to kill him, he fled like a scared puppy, sat under a juniper tree and requested to die (1 Kings 17-19).

Why did he flee from Jezebel's threat? He ran because he didn't want to die. What did he request from God as he sat under the juniper tree? He requested to die. He didn't want to die; then he wanted to die. Elijah exhibits a kind of hysteria on this occasion that can only be explained by the fact that the pressure finally got to him. Even the strongest of people become weary and fatigued in spirit when the pressure is relentless.

It is a challenge to stay on top of your problems and to keep them from getting on top of you. The first thing necessary in terms of resisting that feeling of being overwhelmed with the burdens of life is to maintain a realistic perspective on trials.

So many people approach life in this world with unrealistic expectations. They wrongly assume that life is basically trouble- and hassle-free and that trouble is the exception, rather than the rule. Peter's words to the persecuted church of God speak to this faulty assumption: *"Beloved, think it not strange concerning the fiery trial which is to try you, as though some strange thing happened unto you"* (1 Pet. 4:12). Don't be surprised, he urges, when you encounter opposition, pressure, and problems. That's good advice for everyone.

Perhaps such unrealistic expectations of a basically trouble-free life derive from a childhood that was inappropriately shielded from pain by an over-protective parent or from society in general. Popular culture, with its intention to give every child a trophy and to jettison the concept of winners and losers, contributes to this unrealistic softness and sensitivity to pain. I've known of parents that would not allow a child to play baseball because the danger of being hit by a forty mile per hour fastball was just too much of a risk. I've also encountered parents that never took a child to a funeral because they wanted to protect the child from the grief of loss.

I understand that desire to protect and concur that measuring the level of pain and suffering to which a child may be exposed is an essential part of the parent's responsibility to a child. Wisdom dictates that a parent consider a child's physical and emotional capacities at each respective stage of growth and development and measure the amount of pressure to which the child is exposed. But pressure is essential to psychological health.

A man once spied a butterfly attempting to free itself from its cocoon. In pity, he bent to assist the struggling insect, making tears in the cocoon so the butterfly would be able to escape with less stress. What he did for the butterfly, however, was no kindness. Though free from the cocoon without a struggle, the wings refused to unfurl and lacked the strength to lift the insect into the air. The butterfly needed the struggle to liberate itself from its former home if it was going to function and survive in its new form.

Likewise, measured pressure in a child's developmental years makes for tough-mindedness later. When an adolescent has been allowed to work through the emotions of not being chosen for the team, or failing a test at school, or suffering a skinned knee from a bicycle accident, he will be less prone to lose heart as an adult over an unexpected flat tire, leaking roof, or torn garment.

I don't intend, however, to give the impression of minimizing someone's problems. Perhaps you say, "I'm not depressed by a simple flat tire or tear in my new dress. I've suffered real trauma. My child is on drugs..." or "I've lost my job... My marriage is in shambles... I've been diagnosed with cancer... My phone rang in the middle of the night with news that my loved one was killed in an automobile accident... I live in an abusive relationship... My body is wracked with tremendous pain every day..." or any number of other traumatic scenarios. Maybe you are essentially tough-minded and tenacious of spirit, but in the aftermath of some traumatic event or series of events, you have found it difficult to rescue yourself from the emotional tailspin of spiritual depression.

When someone approaches me saying, "I'm depressed," I understand that the reasons they recite for depression, whether the ordinary problems of life or some trauma, merely constitute the presentation, or surface, problem. Behind the problem cited, the ultimate cause of depression generally has something to do with an unhealthy reaction to the problem. *Unbiblical thinking is usually at the root of spiritual depression.* If you trace depression back to its cause, it will have something to do with the individual's reaction to negative circumstances, not the circumstances themselves.

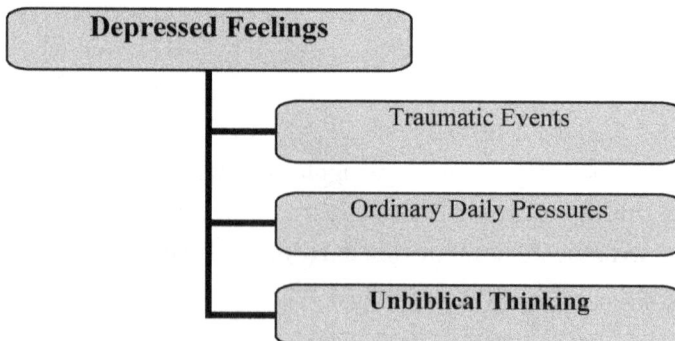

Depressed Feelings
Traumatic Events
Ordinary Daily Pressures
Unbiblical Thinking

Unless one deals with the issue of unbiblical response to the pressures of life, he will merely palliate the symptoms of depression without addressing the cause. The most that can be attained in such a scenario is some form of therapy, never a cure. Yet Scripture promises a cure. God's word indicates that the believer can live as an overcomer—a victor rather than a victim: *"This is the victory that overcometh the world, even our faith"* (1 Jno. 5:4); *"These things have I spoken unto you that in me ye might have peace; in the world ye shall have tribulation, but be of good cheer, I have overcome the world"* (Jno. 16:33).

What form does unbiblical thinking that leads to spiritual depression take? Sometimes a person is depressed due to ***an unhealthy focus on the past.*** He lives with vain regrets, thinking and moving in the realm of "if only." The celebrated poet John Greenleaf Whittier captured this point in his poem *Maud Muller*. The poem describes a summer day in which a wealthy Judge encountered a sweet-singing peasant girl as he rode his chestnut horse down the lane. But though the Judge is smitten with her simplicity, purity and genuine beauty, and Maud Muller dreams of his gentlemanly, stately manner, both made decisions to wed according to their respective stations in life. And both live long enough to bemoan their respective lot in dreams of "what might have been:"

> And the proud man sighed, with a secret pain,
> "Ah, that I were free again!
> "Free as when I rode that day,
> Where the barefoot maiden raked her hay."
> She wedded a man unlearned and poor,
> And many children played round her door.
> But care and sorrow, and childbirth pain,
> Left their traces on heart and brain.
> And oft, when the summer sun shone hot
> On the new-mown hay in the meadow lot,
> And she heard the little spring brook fall
> Over the roadside, through the wall;
> In the shade of the apple-tree again
> She saw a rider draw his rein.

And gazing down with timid grace
She felt his pleased eyes read her face.
Sometimes her narrow kitchen walls
Stretched away into stately halls;
The weary wheel to a spinnet turned,
The tallow candle an astral burned,
And for him who sat by the chimney lug,
Dozing and grumbling o'er pipe and mug,
A manly form at her side she saw,
And joy was duty and love was law.

Then she took up her burden of life again,
Saying only, "It might have been."
Alas for maiden, alas for Judge,
For rich repiner and household drudge!
God pity them both! and pity us all,
Who vainly the dreams of youth recall.
For of all sad words of tongue or pen,
The saddest are these: "It might have been!"
Ah, well! for us some sweet hope lies
Deeply buried from human eyes;
And, in the hereafter, angels may roll
The stone from its grave away!

"It might have been." For many people, those are, indeed, the saddest words of tongue or pen. And they live their lives with vain regret over opportunities lost, over the road not taken. But all such exercises in nostalgia are fruitless and vain.

Others live with regret over past sins. Someone speculated that memories of the days when he persecuted the church comprised Paul's thorn in the flesh, that he lived with the pain of regret for the rest of his days. Whether or not that is accurate, the fact that many people suffer depression because they live with lingering guilt over past failures is certainly true.

Still others struggle with depression because they continue to think of themselves and their lives in terms of some past hurt or heartache. Perhaps you suffered some trauma in the past. Maybe you grew up in the home of an abusive or absentee parent, or had a teacher or other authority figure that criticized you mercilessly. Does this mean that you are obliged to live the rest of your life with those words ringing in your head? Must you continue to think of yourself as the adult child of an alcoholic father?

May I suggest that you take Paul's words in Philippians 3:13 as your new motto: "...*this one thing I do, forgetting those things which are behind, and reaching forth unto those things that are before, I press toward the mark for the prize of the high calling of God in Christ Jesus*"? What a tragedy it is to forfeit the time you have remaining by opting to live in the past! It is not wrong to remember past blessings or even lessons learned from past errors and failures, but beyond that, a person cannot live in the past. It's gone. It happened. The check has been cancelled. It is what it is. The past cannot be changed or undone. The sooner an individual makes peace with that fact and accepts reality, the sooner he/she will be able to move forward. Nothing is accomplished by reliving every detail of some past struggle and wishing things had turned out differently. God has not predestined you to live the rest of your days as a victim of the past.

Unbiblical thinking that leads to depression also takes another form – *an anxious fear of the future*. Many depressed people are controlled by fear. They live in the realm of "What if?": What if I lose my job? What if I get cancer? What if my companion passes away?

Most people battle fear at some level. In fact, I think most of us would be surprised at just how much our actions are governed by fear. Fear of the unknown, fear of death, fear of tragedy, fear of rejection, fear of ridicule, fear of bad news...perhaps there is not a reader who, if he/she will be honest about it, cannot identify each form of fear in his/her own life.

Fear generally has to do with the loss of something you deem important to peace and safety. We fear the loss of a job because of the financial strain it will put on our families. We fear the loss of a child or spouse in death, or the loss of health, or the loss of reputation. To protect them against pain, people tend to adjust their present behavior so as to minimize the possibility of realizing the thing they fear.

For instance, the woman who fears the pain of a spouse's betrayal may exhibit extreme jealousy and suspicious behavior, even when the spouse gives little or no cause for accusation. And the individual who fears ridicule or the loss of respect from other people may simply withdraw into a shell of shyness and social insecurity. If he never speaks up or voices an opinion, he limits the risk of appearing foolish or attracting unwanted attention to himself. The examples could go on and on.

What inevitably happens, however, is that the suspicious spouse becomes depressed, because she creates an atmosphere of tension and polarization within the marriage due to her jealousy; and the shy student becomes depressed because the more he keeps to himself and refuses to engage in conversation for fear of ridicule, others assume that he either wants to be alone or cares nothing for them and they, in turn, leave him to himself.

It is a vicious cycle. Fear tends to create its own reality and kill the very thing it loves. It is a very subtle and insidious dynamic in which a person builds walls of psychological protection by attempting to control circumstances that will eliminate the risk of pain, but the very walls themselves become the individual's own prison.

The fact is that life involves risk and the person who ceases to risk, ceases to live. The woman who refuses to leave her home because of the risk of an auto accident or some other danger acts in that way in order to preserve life. But what kind of life is that, shut up in your own four walls without interaction with others? In the attempt to avoid risks with a view toward sparing life, she ironically ceases to really live.

To give a speech is to risk embarrassment; to compete is to risk defeat; to raise your hand in answer to the teacher's question is to risk ridicule; to try is to risk failure; but this is what it means to live. Everyone will be embarrassed at some point. No one wins every contest, or answers every question correctly, or escapes life without a few bumps and bruises. But those who try and fail, as Teddy Roosevelt said, at least fail while daring greatly. There's something to be said in favor of courage in a culture that has made self-protection one of its cardinal virtues.

David said, "*What time I am afraid, I will trust in thee*" (Ps. 56:3). The only way to courageously conquer fear is to learn to lean hard on the Lord Jesus Christ, to give your cares over to Him in prayer and to claim His precious promises as your own. Observe a mother holding an adoring child and ask yourself if that baby feels any fear. Of course, the child has no fear but is confident and at ease in the mother's faithful love. Then, meditate awhile on how much He loves you. He loved you enough to die for your eternal happiness. He loves you enough, therefore, to care for your temporal needs. Regular, steady reflection on His perfect love tends to dissipate residual fear in the believer's heart (cf. 1 Jno. 4:18).

Only God knows the future and He has promised never to leave nor forsake you. We are called to journey through this world one step at a time, one day at a time, looking to Him to lead and protect us at each juncture in the way. When you live by faith in a loving and capable God, you really have no occasion to be afraid.

Also, unbiblical thinking that leads to depression may present itself as ***an inordinate preoccupation with self.*** Now, we must be careful not to further discourage a reader here; nevertheless, there may be a case from time to time in which an individual has adopted an unhealthy self-interest and self-focus, a mindset that necessarily produces depressed feelings in a time of disappointment or some other adversity. Facing that issue squarely and honestly may very well prove to be a turning point toward victory over depression.

"Self" is the biggest problem I face in a day. Paul acknowledged, "*I know that in me (that is, in my flesh,) dwelleth no good thing: for to will is present with me; but how to perform that which is good I find not*" (Rom. 7:18). Because regeneration does not eradicate the old fallen nature with which each human being is born into this world—what Paul calls "the flesh"—daily experience for the child of God is comparable to walking, moving and breathing with a dead body attached to the back. How uncomfortable, unpleasant and exhausting would it be if you had to lug around the dead weight of a rotting, stinking carcass everywhere you went and whatever you did, day and night for the rest of your life? That is precisely the picture the Bible paints concerning the spiritual state of a sinner who has been born again. Two antithetical principles—the flesh and the spirit, the old man and the new—now coexist within the regenerate man, producing a "continual and irreconcilable warfare" for dominance in his/her life (cf. Rom. 7:15-25: Gal. 5:16-26).

By nature, sinful human beings are selfish. One of the first words a child learns is "mine," and it doesn't take long for that sweet little thing to reveal just how intent she is "to have and to hold" what is perceived as "mine." Further, we don't easily move beyond this innate tendency to think of ourselves as the center of the universe. Self-centeredness, self-concern, self-absorption, self-interest, self-pity, self-conceit, self-indulgence, self-consciousness, self-aggrandizement...these less-than-desirable vices of character seem to come very naturally to us.

It needs to be acknowledged that self-awareness is not fundamentally wrong. God created humanity *imago Dei*, in His own image, and part of what that means is that people, like the Creator, are inherently self-aware beings. But like every other part of the image of God stamped upon man, this innate awareness of one's own existence and search for meaning and significance has been deformed by sin's entrance into the world.

Adam and Eve were self-aware in the Garden prior to the Fall. But after Adam sinned, the virtue of self-awareness morphed into the vice of self-consciousness: "*And the eyes of them both were opened, and they knew that they were naked; and they sewed fig leaves together, and made themselves aprons. And they heard the voice of the Lord God walking in the garden in the cool of the day: and Adam and his wife hid themselves from the presence of the Lord God amongst the trees of the garden*" (Gen. 3:7-8). Mankind has been trying to hide from God and from one another ever since.

It has been observed that man's chief problem is that he is turned in upon himself and that his greatest need is to be turned outside himself in worship to God and service toward others. The happiest people I've encountered in life are those who live turned outside of themselves, loving and serving others. Likewise, the most miserable people I've ever met are those so wrapped-up in self that nothing or no one else matters. Is it any wonder that Jesus highlighted the path to blessedness in terms of self-denial in Christian discipleship: *"If any man will come after me, let him deny himself, and take up his cross daily, and follow me"* (Lk. 9:23)?

Early in my ministry, I possessed a healthy dose of ambition and egotism, masquerading as spiritual zeal. It's not, however, that my motives were entirely carnal. I genuinely loved the truth of God's sovereign grace and wanted others to come to understand and embrace this liberating gospel message. The problem was that my desire to be useful to God was sometimes indistinguishable from my personal ambition to be known, to be relevant, to be popular.

The Lord, however, was not nearly as impressed with me as I was with myself. Everywhere I turned, doors for greater usefulness in ministry were shut. God knew that I wasn't ready for any kind of larger success until I had learned to be content to serve Him in a more obscure setting. The problem was that *I* did not know it. And I began to lose heart. I wondered, *"Why is light given to a man whose way is hid and whom God hath hedged in?"* (Job 3:23). If I have a message to tell, why don't people want to hear it? I crouched in the corner of self-pity, licking my wounds in despair. Thank God for His longsuffering and mercy to deliver me from myself during those perilous days of pride and self-concern.

Looking back with 20/20 hindsight, it is evident that I did not truly understand my own heart. Though I thought my motives were pure and honorable, they were in fact essentially selfish and proud. I was depressed because I thought God and others had failed to give me the validation I deserved. The "I" key on my typewriter was stuck. I was, as the intellectual Malcolm Muggeridge expressed it, imprisoned "in the dark little dungeon of my own ego." Indeed, sometimes depression arises from thinking too much about and too highly of self. Victory over it may certainly arrive, as it did for Job, when we turn beyond ourselves and begin to live for others: *"And the Lord turned the captivity of Job when he prayed for his friends"* (Job 42:10).

And then, spiritual depression may frequently originate from *the habit of feeling-oriented living*. I use the word "habit" intentionally, for people develop habits by which they live their lives, and a life governed by the rising and falling tides of emotion or the lunar phases of daily moods is that way because of the force of long habit.

God calls upon His people to live by faith, not by feeling: *"Now the just shall live by faith"* (Heb. 10:38a). What does it mean to live by faith? The life of faith involves doing what God's word says in spite of feelings within us, circumstances around us, or consequences ahead of us. The individual who lives by faith moves ahead in obedience to God, doing the right thing, trusting God to provide and protect as well as to handle whatever fall-out may incur as a result of the action. In effect, to live by faith means to let the facts of Scripture guide you as you depend upon the God who wrote it to take care of you, regardless of how you may feel.

Many folk, however, live by feeling. First, there is the individual who constantly questions his/her feelings. Like a diabetic routinely testing his blood sugar, they regularly check their emotional state, asking, "Am I truly happy in life? Do I truly love God? I wonder if I said something to upset that person?" Though self-examination is an important biblical discipline, introspection and self-doubt is not. These sensitive souls make for thoughtful friends, but run the risk of depression because they can never quite attain the elusive feeling of satisfaction they seek.

Then, there is the individual who allows feelings to control him/her. Whatever mood is present upon awaking in the morning tends to set the pace for the entire day. "I can't help it; I'm just in a bad mood today" is a sure sign that this person thinks that emotions must have the final word. But feelings are not sovereign. In fact, emotions are an unreliable guide for life. Jeremiah 17:9 reminds us that self-distrust is basic and fundamental to godly conduct. No one can ever truly and completely know himself because the heart (or emotion) is naturally deceptive: *"The heart is deceitful above all things and desperately wicked; who can know it?"*

Perhaps depression is being fueled by the dishes piled high in the sink, or finances more tangled than the chaotic backlash of a fishing line. The situation looks hopeless. You lament, "There's no way I will ever resolve this problem." Should you just give in to the feelings of despair and decide to revisit the chaos tomorrow? If you do, in fact, permit feelings to dictate your present course, the challenge facing you will only be more difficult tomorrow as today's dishes are added to the pile, or today's transactions become a part of the ledger.

The disciplined person lives by a sense of responsibility, not feeling. When he does the right thing, regardless of how he feels about it at the outset, good feelings soon accompany the responsible behavior. For instance, I would never get out of bed to go to work if I lived by feeling, for sleep and comfort feel too good. At the sound of the alarm clock, however, I make a disciplined choice to do what I need to do (not what I want to do), arising from bed to prepare for the day. And it's not long before good feelings catch up to right behavior.

The individual who gives in to feelings, however, opts to live for the moment. He surrenders to the desire for personal comfort, and enjoys the feeling of comfortable rest. He enjoys it, that is, until he awakens two hours later and realizes that he is late for work. Once or twice a person gives in to this kind of behavior and he quickly finds himself unemployed. It felt good to sleep-in for the moment, but the long-term consequences of joblessness, embarrassment, a lazy reputation, and empty pockets don't feel nearly as pleasant.

Is there no place for personal comfort, relaxation and rest, then? Indeed! Personal rest inevitably follows responsible labor in terms of a kind of inner satisfaction and peace at the outcome of a task accomplished, a responsibility met, a job well-done. Further, the individual who prioritizes responsibility over personal comfort will necessarily enjoy the reward of his industry in terms of a well-deserved vacation, or some special privilege of time-off for good behavior. Solomon's observation *"The sleep of a laboring man is sweet"* (Ecc. 5:12a) conveys more wisdom than one might initially think.

The point I make is that spiritual depression may result from many and various unpleasant circumstances in life, but at its root, it is the product of unbiblical thinking, whether an obsession over vain regrets, fear of the unknown tomorrow, self-absorption, or allowing emotions to dictate conduct. Finding deliverance from the quicksand of depression begins when the sad individual courageously decides to ask himself/herself the hard question "Why art thou cast down, O my soul?", to squarely face the answer, and to tenaciously attack the problem in the strength of the Holy Spirit.

The Cures for Depression

The Lord Jesus' question to the lame man at the pool of Bethesda is especially *apropos* at this point. He asked, *"Wilt thou be made whole?"* (Jno. 5:6). Do you want to get well?

On the surface, the question sounds purely rhetorical. "Of course, he wants to get well," someone replies. "Doesn't everybody?" As a matter of fact, no. Although it sounds admittedly unkind to say, there are many people who have lived so long in an unhealthy state or under a debilitating problem that it has become a part of their identity. They cannot conceive of life in any other set of circumstances than they have previously known.

Perhaps you've heard of the bizarre psychological phenomenon called "Stockholm syndrome" in which the prisoner associates with the captor. Similarly, an individual whose malady has continued for a long time, such as the lame man at Bethesda pool whose infirmity had continued for thirty-eight years, may find it difficult to reset the parameters of daily function. The question "Do you want to be well?", then, is critically important.

If you can honestly answer "yes" to the question, then the following biblical principles and promises may help you to break free from this unhappy state. Break free? Yes, indeed. Jesus Christ can set you free. He can "make you whole."

Few would dare to use such language today. It is just too risky to talk about a cure for depression. Isn't it safer to discuss the possibility of making progress through long-term therapy and medication? If one defines the problem of depression merely in terms of the capacity of medical science to comprehend imbalances in the endocrine system, then I concur. The best case scenario is that a depressed individual may make progress toward control of the malady via a regimen of the right medication coupled with intensive psychotherapy. But if one defines the issue in terms of the omnipotence of the Lord Jesus Christ and his sovereign grace, together with an understanding that man is a spiritual as well as a physical creature, an immaterial soul as well as a material body, then it is not an exaggeration at all to talk about a complete cure.

I am not the least bit uncomfortable with the assertion that a cure is possible. "Ponder anew what the Almighty can do!" God is *able to do exceeding abundantly above all that we can ask or think*" (Eph. 3:20). The Holy Spirit is the best Physician of souls in the universe. He has a long track record of successes lifting up the downcast. What the Lord Jesus did physically for the lame man at Bethesda pool, He can do spiritually for you. So the first thing you need to know is that there is hope in God: *"When men are cast down, then thou shalt say, There is lifting up, and he shall save the humble person"* (Job 22:29).

Have Faith in God

Job 22:29 indicates that the solution to a downcast spirit is to look up, to refocus attention on the Lord. This may sound essentially simplistic, even superficial, but there is great wisdom here. The depressed individual is preoccupied with present circumstances. Like Peter, he sees boisterous winds and waves all around, and feels himself sinking in despair. What this person really needs is to look away from the present crisis and fasten his gaze once again on Jesus. Looking unto Jesus, you can do what appears to be, for all intents and purposes, impossible.

Renewing focus on the glory and greatness of God was the Divine counsel given to Abraham in his extremity: *"And Abram said, Lord*

God, what wilt thou give me, seeing I go childless....And He brought him forth abroad, and said, Look now towards heaven, and tell the stars, if thou be able to number them: and He said unto him, So shall thy seed be" (Gen. 15:2, 5). Abraham could only see his disappointment, but God urged him to look up. When the outlook is grim, try the uplook.

The uplook, likewise, proved to be the turning point in Jonah's sad case. As the disobedient prophet sunk into the depths of the Mediterranean Sea, his dire circumstances brought him to despondency: "*I said, I am cast out of Thy sight...*" (Jon. 2:4a). He feels to be a castaway, cut off from the mercy of God.

The certainty he felt that he would never preach again, that he had lost employment as God's prophet, must have been foreboding. But the inescapable sense that God's longsuffering with him had reached its end, that all of his blessings were behind him, that he was absolutely alone was, bar-none, the most frightening and forlorn place he had ever been. It was truly "the belly of hell." Jonah could not expect anything but death, unless God worked a miracle. And he dared not expect a miracle, for he had rebelled so audaciously against God. The haunting reality that he was, indeed, a castaway—that "it's all over now"—was unavoidable.

What did he do? Did Jonah give up? Did he lie down in defeat? No, he made one final resolve: "*I said, I am cast out of Thy sight; yet I will look again toward Thy holy temple*" (Jon. 2:4). He determined to look up: "Yet I will look again." One more time, he resolves, I will cast my eyes heavenward.

It was his only option. He could not look within himself to tap his alleged, indomitable human potential. Repeating "I think I can, I think I can, I think I can" would not help him with seaweed in his eyes, salt-water in his throat, and gastric juices from the whale attempting to digest his body. Neither could he look without to his friends or fellows for help. He had no means of communication with them. No one but God knew his dire circumstance and abject need. God was his only hope.

We need to emphasize, however, that this was not an act of desperation. It was an act of faith. "*Yet I will look again*" means "It may be the Lord will have mercy upon me, for all creature-helps are gone." Perhaps Jonah recalled words penned by his prophetic contemporary, Isaiah: *"Look unto me, and be ye saved, all the ends of the earth: for I am God, and there is none else"* (Is. 45:22). So he looked, in recognition that God alone was the source of his help and strength.

"*Yet.*" What a thrilling word! Jonah knows that God's child will never find himself/herself in a situation beyond earshot of the Almighty. We are never beyond hope, because we are never beyond the grace of God. There is hope for sinners and those who have miserably failed, because of grace. *"From the end of the earth,"* or from the ocean floor, sinners may *"cry unto Him when* [the] *heart is overwhelmed, Lead me to the Rock that is higher than I"* (Ps. 61:2). We are never beyond hope, because we are never beyond the power of God. There is nothing too hard for the Lord (Jer. 32:17, 27). We are never beyond hope, because we are never beyond God's love (Rom. 8:35-39). Whatever your circumstance at the moment, there is a "yet" for you.

Jonah looked again toward God's holy temple. He looked in repentance. He looked in faith. And the Lord mightily delivered him. On the banks of deliverance, Jonah exclaimed, *"Salvation is of the Lord!"* (Jon. 2:9). No man deserved the credit, neither did he have occasion to congratulate himself for his ingenuity or will-power. The fact that he was alive and on dry land was not due to his own survival-skills, or blind luck. It was the Lord alone who had saved him, and he was not tardy to acknowledge it.

God can do the same for you. But it will not happen unless you make it your priority to redirect focus upon Him. Yes, there is lifting up—help is available—but who is it that will experience that prospective deliverance? Job 22:29 answers *"...and He shall save the humble person."* It is only the individual who assumes personal responsibility to humbly "look up" in dependence on God who will be saved from despair. I am convinced from personal experience, as well as from years of encounters with depressed people in pastoral ministry, that the first and most basic need of a dejected spirit is a radical shift in focus.

In the Psalm with which we began this chapter—Psalm 42—
David illustrates the importance of reminding oneself who his/her
God is: "*Why art thou cast down, O my soul? ...Hope thou in God*" (v. 5).
Whatever the self-analysis reveals regarding the specific cause of
depression, the solution is always the same: "Hope in God."

David has learned, as the old Puritans liked to say, to "preach the
gospel to himself." He talks to himself, saying, "Now, David, you are
feeling quite hopeless at the moment. Lift up your eyes, man.
Remember who your God is. How has He blessed me in the past?
Hasn't He delivered me from some very precarious situations? Hasn't
God been faithful to care for me all the days of my life? Hasn't He
revealed His love for me? Then surely He is still mindful of my case.
There is nothing too hard for Him. None can stay His hand. His arm
is not too short to save, nor His ear to hear. He has promised never
to leave nor forsake me. I'm going to trust Him to help me now as
He has so graciously helped me until this very moment."

Hoping in God is precisely what David did as he stood in the
ruins of Ziklag (1 Sam. 30). Leading his make-shift army in battle,
David failed to leave a garrison to watch the women and children in
camp. While they were gone fighting, Amalekite raiders had invaded
the camp, kidnapping the families and taking their substance. When
David and his men arrived home from the battlefield, the camp was
in ruin. His own loyal soldiers, grieved at the loss of their families,
spoke of stoning him. "*But David encouraged himself in the Lord his God*"
(1 Sam. 30:6).

How did he do so? I don't think it is unreasonable to think that
the man who wrote so many of the Psalms reflected on some of the
same truths about God revealed in those Psalms. Perhaps he
reminded himself that the Lord was his very own Shepherd,
providing, protecting, leading and comforting him with His faithful,
abiding presence (cf. Ps. 23). Maybe he found solace in the
sovereignty of God, the great fact that "*The Lord reigneth*" (Ps. 97:1;
99:1). Possibly he repeated the words of Psalm 46, "*God is our refuge
and strength, a very present help in trouble*" (v. 1). Perhaps he repeated to
himself the words of Psalm 57: "*Be merciful unto me, O God, be merciful*

unto me: for my soul trusteth in thee: yea, in the shadow of thy wings will I make *my refuge until these calamities be overpast. I will cry unto God most High; unto* *God that performeth all things for me. He shall send from heaven, and save me* *from the reproach of him that would swallow me up. Selah. God shall send forth* *his mercy and his truth"* (vs. 1-3).

By shifting his focus from the present distress to reflect once more on who his God is, David finds hope and encouragement to go forward. With the courage of faith in God, David convinces his men to pursue the Amalekite marauders, to rescue their respective families and to recover their respective possessions.

Have you learned to encourage yourself in the Lord your God? Remind yourself what the Bible says about His sovereign power, His faithful promises, His wonderful works in the past, His amazing grace; then, trust him anew to work mightily in your present need.

> Sometimes I feel discouraged and think my life in vain,
> I'm tempted then to murmur and of my lot complain;
> But when I think of Jesus and all He's done for me,
> Then I cry, 'O Rock of Ages, hide thou me.'
>
> Sometimes it seems I dare not go one step farther on,
> And from my heart all courage has disappeared and gone;
> But I remember Jesus and all His love for me,
> Then I cry, 'O Rock of Ages, hide thou me.'[1]

Come Ye Apart and Rest Awhile

Secondly, it is crucial to remember that the individual who feels to be spiritually fatigued and exhausted has certain physical needs to be addressed. These include the need for rest, healthy eating, and physical exercise.

"Burnout" is the term coined in pop-culture to describe a phenomenon of mental exhaustion that presents itself in terms of a diminished interest in some task. Generally speaking, the person struggling with burnout shuts down, or crashes. The normal energy a

---

[1] L. R. Tolbert (1926), *Old School Hymnal Twelfth Edition*, No. 435.

person might exhibit who is engaged in a project is replaced by exhaustion; an attitude of cynicism replaces involvement; the capacity to be productive gives way to an inability to function. Burnout is generally marked by an inclination to disengage, to give up on a goal because of an inescapable sense of helplessness. The burned-out person suffers with a loss of motivation and hope.

This is an increasingly common problem among pastors. Some time ago, I saw a research study[2] that described some of the stresses of pastoral ministry. It stated that 1,500 pastors leave the pastorate each month and only 10% of the men who began on the road of ministry will retire as a pastor. It further revealed that 80% of pastors admit some level of discouragement, 78% feel to have no close friends, 97% have experienced false accusations and betrayal from close friends or family, and 90% report working between 55 and 75 hours per week. It makes one think of the old adage that "the bough that is always bent will eventually break," doesn't it?

What is so stressful about pastoral ministry, you ask? Take the serious responsibility of providing spiritual care for an entire congregation, coupled with the fact that he is always "on call," i.e. he cannot simply leave that responsibility "at the office" when he is at home with his family, and you have a circumstance tailor-made for potential burnout.

Add to that the burden of carrying secret confidences regarding individual and family struggles within the congregation together with the pressure of personal anxiety and worry about these problems; regular disappointment concerning the quality of his own pulpit efforts; a sense of responsibility concerning the health, vitality and growth of the church; the smart of periodic criticism; the incessant awareness that his efforts are being constantly evaluated to see whether he will be retained or asked to resign; the frustration of inconsistency in terms of church attendance; the challenges of moderating periodic spats between church members; the need to remain positive and upbeat in public and to internalize personal

---

[2] Source unknown.

discouragement; personal financial troubles coupled with the challenge of balancing time demands when the pastor is bi-vocational, as many pastors must be in order to provide for their families; an inescapable sense of falling short of living up to the expectations of the people as well as the work to which the Lord has called him; the pressure of trouble in his own marriage and family coupled with the fear that others will deem him unfit to lead because his kids are not perfect... Indeed, the list could go on and on.

Whether you are a pastor or not, a person may reach a point in which all he/she wants to do is lay down, curl up in a fetal position, pull the covers overhead, and cry. The pressures of ministry, and life itself, are enough to bring one to a point of wholesale mental, physical and spiritual exhaustion.

Depression, in other words, may simply be due to burnout. What should be done for the individual in such a case? One of the first and most basic things this person needs is a prescription for Sabbath rest. It is time to, as Jesus advised his disciples, *"come ye yourselves apart into a desert place and rest awhile"* (Mr. 6:31).

Someone remarked that the Lord knew that if the disciples didn't "come ye apart" for awhile then they would surely "come apart" at the seams. All work and no rest makes Jack a depressed boy. Interestingly, physical rest and a few good meals was also the remedy God prescribed for the prophet Elijah when the weary and exhausted man sat dejectedly under the juniper tree (1 Kings 19:4-8). God remembers that we are dust and we should remember it too (cf. Ps. 103:14).

The Lord Himself built the principle of a weekly sabbatical into His creation. By His own example, He established a rhythm of work and rest consisting of six days of labor and one day of rest (cf. Gen. 2:2-3), a rhythm that cannot be violated without serious negative implications. *"The sabbath was made for man,"* says Jesus, *"and not man for the sabbath"* (Mr. 2:27). He means that the practice of resting one-seventh of each week is intended for man's benefit. It is in man's best interest to get adequate rest. What a mercy that God established the principle of Sabbath rest for mankind!

And it is precisely at this point that we may gain some insight into the growing problem labeled "burnout" in Western cultures. Why is it that Americans, especially, suffer from this malady? What is it about us that makes us feel that we must "burn the candle at both ends," taking little to no time to recalibrate our spiritual focus and replenish our physical resources?

I suspect that the very things that have made America great—personal freedom, individual responsibility, and economic opportunity—have also created a climate in which there is a real temptations to become obsessed with success and prosperity. And perhaps here we are beginning to put a finger on the pulse of burnout. Driven, ambitious people seem especially prone to operate at a breakneck pace without taking the necessary time for adequate rest.

The desire to prove oneself and to establish one's place in an organization or the workplace may very well lead to neglect of family, friends, and personal health. Time spent walking the dog, or playing catch with the kids, or picnicking with your spouse on a Saturday afternoon at the park is seen as unnecessary, maybe even a distraction from what is truly important. A family meal may be tolerated, but only on the condition that your smart phone is beside your plate so you do not miss some important bit of information. Slowly and imperceptibly, relational tensions lead to alienation and a desire to isolate oneself more and more from others. The loss of the element of friendship and companionship in the home leads to the increasingly destructive habit of internalizing both personal frustrations and pressures from work, taking a toll on physical health and emotional happiness. The entire dynamic snowballs into a scenario in which the workaholic eventually crashes.

But what exactly caused the situation? The individual who feels to be so exhausted and spent may think the problem originated with a spouse who just didn't understand, or a child who acted out in anger because she felt neglected, or a boss who did not genuinely appreciate his hard work. In reality, the fault lay in the motives of the individual himself/herself. The cause of the current crisis was simply that this person thought himself exempt from the need to rest, relax, and recalibrate.

It has been said that the secret to success in life is finding the right master. Everyone serves some master. Your master may be societal standards, the desire for money or material things, a quest to be popular, the sense that you must prove yourself to a parent that never believed in you, or some subconscious egocentric need to feel that you are successful. If your master is any of the above, I guarantee that you are a candidate for burnout.

But Jesus said, "*My yoke is easy and my burden light*" (Mt. 11:29). If your aim in life is to "serve the Lord" (Rom. 12:11c) as Master, then you can be content to do your best then trust Him to take care of the rest. The driven man says, "I need more time in the day." No, dear friend; you don't need more time in the day. You need to find the right Master.

So, "*be still and know that He is God*" (Ps. 46:10). Work hard when it is time to work. Then set aside time for a sabbatical. Take a walk with your spouse. Smell the roses. Listen to the song of the whippoorwill and robin. Watch a children's movie with your kids on the television. Play a game of tennis with a friend. Read a novel. Listen to some classical music. Read your Bible. Spend twenty minutes in prayer. Go to church. Eat a square meal and drink lots of water. Take a nap. The world will not stop spinning if you rest awhile. And do it regularly, one entire day each week. You'll be amazed at the renewed sense of energy and optimism you feel.

Do What You Can

To the depressed person, every problem is exaggerated. The disorder in the heart matches the disorganization in the kitchen sink, or the laundry room, or the desktop, or the garage, or the bank account, and *vice versa*. Everything feels to be in a state of disarray—chaotic, confusing and impossible to unravel. "I don't even know where to begin," becomes the motto for daily life. Because the problem appears to be so overwhelmingly convoluted, it seems simpler to just ignore it for one more day and pretend the problem doesn't exist. But tomorrow, the scenario is even worse, for today's problems have been added to yesterday's, and the temptation to feel depressed is even more compelling.

Have you ever felt that you are in the lead car of a runaway locomotive on a downhill grade and the brakes have failed? I suspect that is precisely the sensation most disorganized folk feel as the problems of each day accrue like a growing snowball (if I may mix metaphors) into the next until the situation seems completely and hopelessly impossible to resolve. "How did my life become so chaotic?" you wonder.

It is no wonder you are struggling with depression. The disorder in your life is contributing to the disorganization you feel in your heart, and the chaos within is spilling over to your disheveled house, property, and appearance. What can be done to remedy this apparently hopeless case?

I suggest that you listen to the Lord Jesus' commendation of Mary of Bethany. When some indignantly questioned the propriety of wasting not only a valuable, alabaster container but also a pound of expensive spikenard perfume by means of breaking the box and pouring the ointment on Jesus as an act of devotion, the Lord silenced her critics and commended Mary, saying, "*She hath done what she could.*" (Mr. 14:8). She used what she had to show her love to the Savior. He was more valuable to her than this beautiful container and costly ointment. She did what she could.

Do what you can: that's all the Lord requires from any of us. He is not a hard taskmaster, requiring you to produce the regular quota of bricks without giving you the necessary straw with which to work. His service is reasonable (cf. Rom. 12:1); His commandments are not grievous, lit. *irksome* (cf. 1 Jno. 5:3b). He has promised to give His people "strength as their day" (Deut. 33:25b). His grace is sufficient for you (cf. 2 Cor. 12:9).

So, your kitchen is a disaster. You have visions of the apocalypse when you go near it. Every time you even think about it your feelings of hopelessness, failure and uselessness resurface. You cannot escape the thought that you'll never be able to solve this problem. You just want to lie down and forget about it. Here's my counsel to you: Do what you can today.

Maybe you say, "I can't do anything." Yes, you can, in the strength of your Lord and Savior Jesus Christ. Repeat these words to yourself, *"I can do all things through Christ which strengtheneth me"* (Phi. 4:13). Think about the text. Say it again. Write it on a scrap piece of paper or a post-it note and put it on the counter or cabinet. You can…through Him.

Now do it. Set the timer on the range or microwave oven to 15 minutes. Press "start." Now get to work. Unload the clean dishes in the dishwasher. You still have 5 minutes left. Begin reloading the empty dishwasher from the pile of dishes in the sink, one cup, one glass, one bowl at a time. The buzzer sounds. Time's up. Stop.

Tomorrow morning, repeat Philippians 4:13 to yourself again and claim it as something true for you. The Lord helped you yesterday; He will help and strengthen you again today. Now set the timer to 20 minutes. Press "start." Now tackle that pile of dishes in the sink. You can do it. You can accomplish this task today, through the strength of the One who has promised never to leave nor forsake you.

Do it again the third day. Once the dishwasher is loaded and the residual dishes that wouldn't fit are hand-washed, rinsed and placed on a clean towel on the counter to dry, use a clean cloth to wipe down the cabinets. Then stand back and look at your orderly kitchen. It's not perfect, but you've done what you could. The Lord has helped you. Give him thanks for helping you.

"But what about tomorrow?" you ask. Well, tomorrow, unload the dishwasher then load the dishes from today and run it through another cycle. It will only take a few minutes. Then, with the time you have remaining, tackle the wash, or the ironing, or the vacuuming.

It won't be long before you will begin to see evidence of an increasingly orderly world. And the outward order will do wonders for your inward sense of order as well. You may not be able to do much at first, but do what you can. God will bless it and bless you in the doing of it to feel that you have actually accomplished something important. Bite off a little at a time. Soon your appetite for efficiency will grow to what it should be to maintain your daily responsibilities.

God told an enfeebled Gideon, *"Go in this thy might, and thou shalt save Israel from the hand of the Midianites: have not I sent thee?"* (Jud. 6:14). He means, "Go in the strength you have." Gideon didn't feel to have much strength, just as you may not feel to have much strength at the moment. But do what you can. Use the strength you have. You will be amazed at how the Lord will multiply it with His might to help you accomplish your goal.

Give it a try, my friend. It will work. I've seen it work many times over. I've even proved it in my own life as well.

Lift Up the Hands that Hang Down

Finally, one of the best helps to the depressed soul is to get involved trying to minister to others who are in need. The saddest people I know are those introspective folk who cannot see past the end of their own noses. The happiest people I know are those who live to help and serve others.

Is it possible that someone else is in worse shape than you today? Perhaps your life is in a mess and your mind in a whirl. Your heart is heavy with the one-hundred-one knotty problems facing you and you don't even know where to begin to address them. Suddenly you remember that a precious sister from the church is having surgery today. Why don't you get dressed, drive to the hospital, inquire where she may be, and go to the waiting room to sit with her family. Perhaps you will arrive in time to see her for a minute before the procedure. You can hold her hand, let her know that you are praying for her, and tell her that she is dear to your heart.

You cannot imagine how it will encourage your own heart when you make the ministry of encouragement to someone else your life's work. How many times have I gone to a nursing home or hospital just to spend a few moments with a shut-in or someone on a sickbed, only to find myself flooded with peace and happiness when I depart. I went to be a blessing. I left that place as the one who received a blessing.

So you are not strong enough physically to make a personal visit? Then find an unused card or piece of notepaper around the house and write a message of encouragement to someone in need. Pick up the telephone and call a friend to inform them that you are thinking about them. Dispatch an email or text message to express your love. Be a blessing to someone else. It may very well prove to be the turning point in your own struggle with spiritual depression.

Summary

Depression is not a simplistic problem. There may be many reasons for it. But God is able to help you, so long as you refuse to give in to the devil's temptation to give up and quit. Be assured that you are not alone. So reach out to your pastor, your family physician, or your brothers and sisters in Christ. Ask for their prayers. And if you really want to be well, turn your eyes upon your loving Lord, going forward a step at a time, a day at a time, to do what you can so far as keeping up with your daily responsibilities. Rest when you need to rest and throw yourself into being a blessing to others. I'm confident that it won't be long before you will feel sunshine in your soul once again.

6
When God Says "No"
Defeating Disappointment

"But we trusted that it had been he which should have redeemed Israel: and beside all this, today is the third day since these things were done." Luke 24:21

Disappointment, the emotion generated when circumstances do not work out as we had hoped, is inevitable in this present world. No one is immune. Everyone who has ever stood in the charred remains of family heirlooms burnt in a fire; the person who has experienced the breakup of a marriage or the pain of rejection in a relationship; the individual whose hope of recovery from a dread disease was dashed by the grim report of an x-ray showing no improvement; the person whose aspirations of attending a special event were cut short by an unexpected illness; the athlete who has stood dejected on the field after losing an important game; the man nearing retirement who receives a termination notice after years of service; each knows all too well the emotional upset described by the word "disappointment."

I suspect that many of our disappointments in life arise from faulty and/or unrealistic expectations. It is unrealistic, in other words, to pin one's hopes on a fellow human being. Another person can not make me happy or solve my problems any more than a little girl's baby doll can meet her needs.

A four-year-old girl held a baby doll in each arm, weeping as she rocked. When her mother inquired the cause of her sadness, the little lady replied, "Momma, I love them and love them and love them, but they never love me back."

Of course, she did not yet grasp that they had eyes but could not see, ears but could not hear, and arms but could not hug. When a person pins his expectations on another human being, he will inevitably be as disappointed as the little girl was in her dolls, for people are just people. They are limited in what they can do.

The same goes for money. The late Robert Horton said the greatest lesson he learned in life was that people who set their hearts on money were equally disappointed, whether they had it or not. Money's capacity to satisfy someone's needs is, likewise, limited. Someone has remarked that money can buy a bed, but not sleep; it can buy books, but not brains; it can buy food, but not satisfaction; a house, but not a home; medicine, but not health; amusement, but not joy.

The best approach to life, of course, is to place our expectations only on the Lord. He alone is capable of satisfying every need and resolving every problem. David learned this important principle: *"My soul, wait thou only upon God; for my expectation is from Him. He only is my rock and my salvation: He is my defense; I shall not be moved"* (Ps. 62:5-6). When God alone is the focus of your hopes and expectations, everyone and everything around you assumes its proper shape and size.

But what about those situations when your expectations were, in fact, in the Lord—when you put your trust in Him and prayed for some desired blessing or hoped for some positive outcome—only to have circumstances turn out differently than you had hoped? What should you do when you thought you had found the person of your dreams only to discover that your love was unrequited? How could you handle the doctor's news that the cancer had returned after you had prayed so diligently for God's healing? How may we respond to disappointments in a godly way when God says "no"?

Critical Life Lessons

The mind and thought-life is the principal theater in which Christian people fight the good fight of faith. And perspective matters everything when you are faced with a disappointment in life. If you will defeat disappointment and resist the temptation toward disillusionment, it is crucial to remember four critical life lessons.

Lesson 1: You are not alone. First Corinthians 10:13 reads, *"There hath no temptation taken you but such as is common to man: but God is* *faithful, who will not suffer you to be tempted above that ye are able; but will with the temptation also make a way to escape, that ye may be able to bear it.*" The reminder that you are not the first person to travel down this path and that others have faced similar disappointments and survived is crucial to faith and healthy mindedness.

Paul prayed that God would remove his painful "thorn" on three separate occasions (2 Cor. 12:8). You can be sure that the man who exhorted others to pray believingly and fervently, with all supplication and thanksgiving, followed the same protocol as he made known his requests to the Lord. But the Lord said "no" and refused to remove the affliction.

He also yearned to preach the gospel to his own Jewish people, his kinsman according to the flesh (Rom. 9:2-3). To carry the good news to them was his "heart's desire" and "prayer to God" (Rom. 10:1). But God said "no" and sent him westward as the apostle to the Gentiles.

Moses' longing to enter the Promised Land was, likewise, met with Divine refusal, as was David's desire to build a permanent house of worship for the Lord (cf. Deut. 3:24-28; 2 Sam. 7:1-13). These requests were not, in any sense of the term, immoral or ungodly, but the Lord said "no" to these giants of faith and devotion.

Neither Paul, Moses, nor David, however, lost faith in God. Were they disappointed? Certainly! They would not be human if they did not struggle some with such emotions. But these men were able to face the emotional let-down without losing heart or wallowing in the mire of self-pity.

"But I take no comfort," someone says, "from another person's troubles. I am not looking merely for company in my misery. Why is it important to reflect on the fact that I am not the first person to ever experience a disappointment?"

These biblical examples of others who suffered disappointments are included in God's word for our benefit. They are written so "*that we, through patience* [the Greek word means 'endurance; perseverance'] *and comfort of the Scriptures might have hope*" (Rom. 15:4). We learn from them that disappointment didn't have the last word, that it is possible to move forward, and that God is still good.

Lesson 2: There is more to the story than you know. Secondly, it is crucial to remember that disappointment is often due to our failure to see the entire picture. There is more to the story than you may realize.

Jesus' words in John 13:7 speak poignantly to the individual reeling under the emotional waves of disappointment: *"What I do thou knowest not now; but thou shalt know hereafter."* Our Lord sees the big picture; we merely look through the lattice of circumstance. He knows what His children need better than they know what they need.

The text that heads this chapter, Luke 24:21, is a powerful illustration of this principle. The two disciples on Emmaus Road, Brother Cleopas and likely his wife Mary, have witnessed their hopes raised only to be dashed before their eyes: *"But we trusted that it had been he that should have redeemed Israel."* Do you hear the disappointment in their sad words?

It is obvious in their complaint that they were expecting the Messiah to bring political deliverance from the heavy-hand of the Roman Empire: "Our hopes were pinned on Jesus of Nazareth to deliver us, but now he has been crucified and our hopes and dreams have died with him." But there was more to the story than they knew.

God had something so much better than political deliverance in store for them. Jesus of Nazareth had, in fact, redeemed Israel, albeit not from Roman taxation. He had redeemed them from the curse of God's holy law. His death was not a tragedy, as it may have appeared on the surface, but a glorious triumph. He had procured spiritual deliverance for each of His elect—salvation from the bondage and penalty of sin.

Whether Cleopas and Mrs. Cleopas realized it, political liberation was not their greatest need. Their biggest problem was not economic or social; it was spiritual. They needed salvation from sin, not liberation from paying tax to Caesar. They were disappointed because they failed to realize that there was more to the story than it first appeared.

Sadly, people seldom recognize that God may say "no" because He intends to say "yes" to something better. He closes a window so He may open a door. And the present disappointment you feel, as painful as it may seem, may in fact be the means to keep you from going down the wrong path or save you from a much greater heartache later.

During my senior year of high school, I ran the first leg of a 400 meter relay team that had the distinction of never losing a race. Though we were only a small school, we boasted the second fastest 400m Relay time in the entire State of Texas, all classifications. We still, these three decades+ later, hold the school record in that event. Each of my relay teammates shared my aspiration to pursue a collegiate career as a sprinter. But an unforeseen and apparently tragic event occurred during the track meet that would have qualified us to compete at the State level that brought my dreams crashing down on top of me.

The sprint relay team of another school in our classification had posted times during the season that rivaled ours. To date, we had not competed against them in any of the other track meets. Their third leg of the relay, Victor Bugg, had already won the 100 and 200 meter sprints. Though we were confident of victory, there was, in our minds, a mild hint of intimidation at this boy's unusual speed; especially in the psyche of my buddy, Rod, whose task it would be to run against him.

By the time Rod took the baton, we were a good 20 meters ahead of the closest team. Rod was in top form and maintained our lead, even though he was matched against Bugg. But shortly before Rod reached the handoff zone to pass the baton to David, our anchor leg, curiosity got the best of him. He took a quick glance over his shoulder to see where Victor Bugg was in relation to him. That split-second glance interrupted the finely-tuned handoff to the final runner. Rod couldn't quite catch the anchor leg before the exchange zone expired. He lunged to pass the baton to David, but it fell to the track, rolled from our lane, and we were disqualified. Suddenly, all of my dreams and aspirations about a State Championship and a collegiate track career rolled off the track with that baton.

It was my first real experience with disappointment. My world was in chaos. I felt completely lost. Within an hour or two, I departed the meet with my parents to attend a worship service at the church my dad pastored. Although I was truly despondent when we arrived, I felt much better when we left. The singing of faith-building hymns together with the power of the gospel to lift my thoughts to nobler themes than a track and field competition genuinely lifted my spirits.

Now, these three decades later, I can see, with the clarity of 20/20 hindsight, that the Lord used that experience to redirect my focus, and, indeed, my path of life. I had already started speaking some in the church before that disappointing episode on the oval. The loss of my dream gave me the incentive necessary to redirect my energies toward God's calling on my life. He had something better in store for me. He took away the first, that he might establish the second (cf. Heb. 10:9). Who knows what sin and misery I was spared? What He did, I didn't understand at the time; but I did understand it afterwards.

In the aftermath of that personal experience, I have often thought of Joseph's disappointment at the loss of his family and his freedom. Though it is certain that he did not comprehend God's providence at the time, he came to see that his losses and crosses had, indeed, been amply compensated by the Lord.

When his wife bore his firstborn son, Joseph named him "Manasseh" meaning "forgotten," *For God, said he, hath made me forget all my toil, and all my father's house*" (Gen. 41:51). It was as if he breathed a deep sigh and said, "It's okay now; the sorrows of the past now pale into insignificance in the light of the blessings of God." Looking into the face of baby Manasseh, Joseph knows that all the disappointments of the past are worth the singular joys of the present. If you had offered him the opportunity to go back and change the course his life had taken, he would have declined the offer. His initial disappointment, no doubt, could be directly traced to his inability to see the whole picture, as God did.

Norman J. Clayton captures this powerful point in his beloved poem, *If We Could See Beyond Today*:

> If we could see beyond today
> As God can see,
> If all the clouds should roll away,
> The shadows flee;
> O'er present griefs we would not fret,
> Each sorrow we would soon forget,
> For many joys are waiting yet
> For you and me.
>
> If we could know beyond today
> As God doth know,
> Why dearest treasures pass away,
> And tears must flow;
> And why the darkness leads to light,
> Why dreary days will soon grow bright,
> Some day life's wrongs will be made right,
> Faith tells us so.
>
> If we could see, if we could know,
> We often say,
> But God in love a veil doth throw
> Across our way;
> We cannot see what lies before,
> And so we cling to Him the more,
> He leads us 'til this life is o'er,
> Trust and obey.

How thrilling to know that we trust a God of providence! Though His presence may not be evident in the midst of a disappointing circumstance, He, nonetheless, stands "somewhere in the shadows keeping watch upon His own." Perhaps He suffered the disappointment to touch you, not because He takes some sinister pleasure in afflicting the children of men (Lam. 3:33), but because He treasured some grander plan for you.

John Warburton (1776-1857), an English Strict Baptist minister, is best remembered for his autobiographical sketch titled *The Mercies of a Covenant God*. In that account, he tells, with uncommon vulnerability, of "a few providential trials and deliverances which have happened to me since I was called to the work of the ministry, which have driven me to…despair at times…but when deliverance has come, it has been a fresh song of praise to God…"[1] One such experience concerned a titan struggle with disappointment concerning a pastorate. Warburton writes:

> About this time I was invited to go and preach at Pool Moor, in Yorkshire, and I believe the Lord went with me, and blessed the word to many of them. My very soul fell in love with the people and the chapel…Indeed, I was so taken up with the people and the place that I thought I must die if the Lord would not grant me the situation. I thought that it was just the very spot that God had designed for me, and believed it was the case, because my heart was so knit to it.
>
> At that time, the people were without a pastor, and many of them were very fond of me. "O," said I, "it will come to pass in the Lord's own time;" for I was sure that there was nothing impossible with Him, seeing that He had so many times answered my prayers, and had never failed me in all my straits…So I set to work with all my might to pray for the place. For, thinks I, the Lord says, "Whatsoever ye shall ask in my name it shall be given;" and, "Open thy mouth wide, and I will fill it." I could bring in plenty of Scriptures if I could but persuade the Lord to perform it in the way that I wanted. And I thought there was no other way but to keep on crying for it night and day…
>
> I went several times to supply at this chapel, and every time I went I was more and more in love with the situation. O, thinks I, it is just the very spot for my large family. So again I cried and prayed from week to week, and, to my views at that time, I had such

---

[1] John Warburton, *The Mercies of a Covenant God*, p. 79.

assurances from the word of God and my own feelings, that I believed at times I was as sure to have it as that there was a God.[2]

Warburton then makes note that the church was also using another minister, a Mr. Webster from Liverpool, to supply pulpit duties. And although some in the church seemed to favor this other minister, John was confident that God would honor the "many cries and tears [he] had put up" toward heaven in prayer. He states:

> The next Lord's day for my supply was…three weeks from this time, and some of the people hoped it would be my last. And, O, what a three weeks' cry I had! …When the Saturday came for me to go…I verily believed…if it were settled for Mr. Webster to be their pastor that it would kill me.
>
> I arrived in the evening at the house of one of the members…and as soon as I got in: "Well, by this time," said I, "I suppose you are settled with a minister…?" "Why," answers the man, "it was settled for Mr. Webster to come; some of us indeed did not wish it, but numbers overpowered us, and we must submit."[3]

Warburton was overwhelmed by the news. He grabbed his hat, exited the house and ran to a little valley between two hills, where he knew he was alone. There he "roared like a raging bear bereaved of her whelps." He reports, "I roared and wept while I had power to weep. Then the devil set on with all his hellish spleen, and worked up such infidelity in my heart that I never can express a thousandth part of it." He recounts how the devil tempted him with hard thoughts of God:

> "Now," says he, "what do you think of the Bible? Do you think it is true? Have you not prayed for this place hundreds of times, and have not floods of tears flowed from your eyes for it? And does not the Bible say, 'He that soweth in tears shall reap in joy?' But you have sowed in tears and [now] reap in sorrow. And does not the Bible tell

---

[2] Ibid. p. 89.
[3] Ibid. p. 90.

you that whatsoever you asked it should be given you? But you have asked and you believed that you should have the place, and have been denied. There is no God, and the Bible is nothing but priestcraft, and all your preaching and religion is nothing but an empty farce.[4]

The disappointed preacher continued in this condition even after he returned to the church members' home. He refused to take supper, grabbed a candle and locked himself in his bedroom:

And the tossings to and fro! Sometimes in bed and sometimes walking the room till about four or five o'clock in the morning, till I verily thought that my natural senses were going, and felt quite confident that a mad-house would be my place. But as to pray, to hope, or ever think it possible for me to preach again, I could as soon blot out the sun with my hand as do any of them.

And then, Warburton's covenant God, faithfully and mercifully, condescended in blessing upon the miserable man:

But I shall never forget the sound of those words that dropped like rain, and did indeed distil like the dew: "What I do thou knowest not now; but thou shalt know hereafter" (John xiii. 7). O the softness these words produced in my heart in a moment! The beasts of the forest all gathered themselves into their dens, my soul sprang up like a bird that had broken out of the snare, and I cried out, "It is the voice of my Beloved." O how my poor soul was melted down at His blessed feet! I covered my shameful face, and could neither look nor speak for wonder and astonishment at what it could all mean...

...My soul was so drawn out and encouraged that I went down on my knees, and felt just like a child. "Lord, how is it, and why is it that my prayers are not answered? O, dear Lord, do show...Thy poor ignorant, sinful and helpless child: do, my dear Jesus, show me." And O with what light, life, and power did He speak these words into my heart that settled the thing in a moment, and showed me the why

---

[4] Ibid.

and the how: "Ye ask, and receive not, because ye ask amiss, that ye may consume it upon your own lusts" (James iv. 3).

O how clearly did I see it was all my own fleshly planning and contriving, and that it was to gratify my own fleshly pleasure. O how sweetly could I give it all up into the hands of my covenant God!

The narrative concludes with an account of the freedom he felt in preaching the next day, and his heart-felt attitude of quiet submission to the will of the Lord and genuine concern for the good of the church. He then proceeds to tell how the Lord opened the door for him to a pastorate at the Baptist Church in Rochdale within the next year. The attendants on his ministry increased so steadily under his pastoral labors that the congregation, under the blessing of God, constructed a new building which they named "Hope Chapel." Were he to speak today, Warburton would say that though he was initially disappointed by the Pool Moor situation, there was more to the story than he knew.

Lesson 3: A fresh dose of gospel preaching is the best cordial for the malady of disappointment. To the two sad travelers on Emmaus Road, Jesus met their expression of disappointment ("*We thought that it had been he that should have redeemed Israel*") with a reminder of the good news of Messiah's victorious sufferings, death and resurrection: "*Ought not Christ to have suffered these things, and to enter into his glory? And beginning at Moses and all the prophets, he expounded unto them in all the scriptures the things concerning himself*" (Lk. 24:26-27).

Nothing so effectively lifts a dejected countenance as a reminder of the sweet, old gospel story. "Jesus Christ and him crucified" is the best news poor sinners have ever heard. Like a drink of cold water revives a thirsty man on a hot summer's day, so a fresh view of the Lamb for sinner's slain renews every latent spiritual grace in the soul.

Why is the glorious gospel such a boon to flagging faith? Because it reminds the disappointed believer that Christ has already purchased for him the best gift of all. How could a temporal loss of some personal desire or perceived happiness here, whatever it may be, possibly compare with the unsearchable riches of God's grace purchased for His elect in Christ? Does not the experience of having a job application rejected appear as a mere trifle in light of the truth that you belong to the God whose name is *Jehovah-jireh*? What if you were not chosen for the team? God chose you as His very own in Jesus Christ before the foundation of the world. And though the one you perceived to be the love of your life left you feeling unwanted and unloved, yet no one and nothing can separate you from the love of God which is in the Lord Jesus Christ.

When dejected souls avoid church attendance because, as I've heard on more than one occasion, "I was too depressed to come to church," I say, "You are neglecting the only thing that can help you." Nothing so animates and reinvigorates the spiritually fatigued believer as a fresh reminder of the old, old story of Jesus and His love. To see life with all of its various disappointments in the light of the cross is to put it all, once more, into perspective (cf. Rom. 8:32). Finally, it is critical to remember a fourth life lesson:

Lesson 4: Disappointment fades into obscurity in light of the resurrection. At the moment Mr. and Mrs. Cleopas recognized the unique, but mysterious, visitor in their home, Jesus vanished from their sight. They immediately returned to Jerusalem, found the disciples, and reported, *"The Lord is risen indeed!"* (Lk. 24:34). The fact of Christ's resurrection made them forget about their initial disappointment. Because He lived, they could now face tomorrow!

Are you disappointed by some current circumstance in your life? May I point you, then, to the empty tomb. The resurrection of Jesus Christ means that you have a bright future. Because He lives, there is hope, both for this world and the next (cf. Jno. 14:19b; 1 Cor. 15:19-20). It means that when this brief parenthesis of present life and existence is over, you will at once awaken in a paradise of unmitigated joy and unalloyed bliss. And there will be no disappointments in heaven: *"As for me, I will behold thy face in righteousness: I shall be satisfied, when I awake, with thy likeness"* (Ps. 17:15).

Be still, my soul, the hour is hast'ning on
When we shall be forever with the Lord;
When disappointment, grief and fear are gone,
Sorrow forgot, love's purest joys restored;
Be still, my soul, when change and tears are past,
All safe and blessed, we shall meet at last.[5]

You Can Defeat Disappointment

Let's look a bit more closely now at three real-life examples of people who successfully defeated disappointment. We have already hinted at each of these Biblical cases, but perhaps you may find yourself and your current case in one or more of them.

Example 1: Moses denied entrance into the Promised Land.

Since the inauguration of the Abrahamic Covenant, the children of Israel yearned for the day they would inhabit the land that God had promised to them. The exodus from Egypt and march through the wilderness toward Canaan would be the final chapter in the realization of that four-hundred-year hope. Moses was God's chosen man for the monumental task.

Shortly after Moses led the nation out of Egyptian bondage, he commissioned twelve spies, one from each of the twelve tribes, to do reconnaissance of the land. They returned with a report that discouraged the people: *"We came unto the land whither thou sentest us, and surely it floweth with milk and honey; and this is the fruit of it. Nevertheless the people be strong that dwell in the land, and the cities are walled, and very great: and moreover we saw the children of Anak there"* (Num. 13:27-28). Only Caleb and Joshua believed God: *"And Caleb stilled the people before Moses, and said, Let us go up at once, and possess it; for we are well able to overcome."* But the other ten replied, *"We be not able to go up against the people; for they are stronger than we...and there we saw the giants, the sons of Anak, which come of the giants: and we were in our own sight as grasshoppers, and so we were in their sight"* (Num. 13:30-31, 33).

---

[5] Katharina von Schlegel (1752), *Old School Hymnal Twelfth Edition*, No. 173.

Discouraged by the report of the ten spies, the congregation of the children of Israel succumbed to unbelief. They wept and murmured against Moses, crying, "Why have you brought us out into the wilderness to be slain? We wish we had never left Egypt" (cf. Num. 14:2-4). The Lord was so displeased that He, for the second time on their journey, determined to disinherit the nation and start over again with Moses (Num. 14:11-12). How could they fail to believe Him after He had demonstrated time and again His power to save?

Had Moses not "stood in the gap" as intercessor for the nation, again for the second time (see Ex. 32), God would have annihilated them all. Though He spared them, He did swear in His wrath that only Caleb and Joshua, among the people twenty years old and upward, would enter the Promised Land. The rest of the adult Israelites would fall in the wilderness (Num. 14:27-35). Within hours, the ten spies were smitten with a plague and died, as an object lesson to the rest of the nation that God was provoked to judgment by their unbelief.

In the aftermath of this mutinous episode, Moses' impatience with the rebellious nation escalated. It peaked when they came to the desert of Zin and the people again murmured against Moses for water (Num. 20:1-6). Moses evidently struggled with his temper anyway—*vis a vis*, he previously broke the tablets of testimony in a fit of rage when he descended from Sinai. Now, again, his frustration with the nation has reached a fevered pitch.

God, in mercy, prescribed a remedy for the people's thirst: "*Take the rod, and gather thou the assembly together, thou and Aaron thy brother, and speak ye unto the rock before their eyes; and it shall give forth his water, and thou shalt bring forth to them water out of the rock: so thou shalt give the congregation and their beasts drink*" (Num. 20:8). But Moses, not yet as merciful as the Lord, was livid: "*Hear now, ye rebels; must we fetch you water out of this rock? And Moses lifted up his hand, and with his rod he smote the rock twice: and the water came out abundantly, and the congregation drank, and their beasts also*" (Num. 20:10-11).

God said "speak to it;" Moses struck it...twice! Yes, God still provided for the people, but Moses was in trouble: "*And the Lord spake unto Moses and Aaron, Because ye believed me not, to sanctify me in the eyes of the children of Israel, therefore ye shall not bring this congregation into the land which I have given them.*" (Num. 20:12).

I can almost hear the thoughts in Moses' mind: "Oops...I'm sorry...I didn't mean to do that...Wait!...What?...What did He say?...Is He serious?...It was a mistake...I mean, I didn't mean to disobey...I just...I just got mad and made a mistake...But it's not that big of a deal, is it?...C'mon, Lord...Please, give me another chance...I'm sorry..." But God had spoken and his sentence was just. Moses, after all, had disobeyed a clear command from his "Commander-in-Chief."[6]

This raises a very uncomfortable yet extremely important observation: *Sometimes the disappointments we face in life are due to our own poor decisions.* Every action carries with it an inescapable consequence. It's a harsh reality, but a reality nonetheless. And healthy-mindedness demands we face it.

Consider the High School Senior not permitted to graduate with her class because she ended up two credits shy of the required standard. The disappointment she feels is significant, and the temptation to blame the situation on another, be it a teacher or administrator or legislature that passed the bill into law, is strong. But in the final analysis, her disappointment, as harsh as it may sound in our pampered and permissive age, is likely a consequence of her own choices.

---

[6] Interestingly, the military metaphor of Israel as Jehovah's army is a principal motif in the book of Numbers. Numbers 1:1-10:10 describes the constitution of the army and the regulations it must observe as it marched toward conquest. Chapter 10:11 through chapter 25:18 catalogs the actual march from Sinai to the plains of Moab with the army's attendant failures and successes. Numbers 26-36 describes the organization of a new army and its preparations for invasion of the land of Canaan. For a more complete development of this military motif, see my title *Understanding Your Bible: An Old Testament Survey*, Copyright © 2005, Sovereign Grace Publications.

The young lady really has two options in this scenario. She may give up in despair, adopting (or continuing, as the case may be) a victim mentality (e. g. "Everybody is against me") and railing at the establishment—an attitude that will guarantee repeat performances in the future. Or she may accept responsibility, repent of past, sinful habits and commit herself to a changed attitude and more disciplined conduct in the future.

Will the present, disappointing consequence be reversed if she repents? Probably not, but it is not wrong to ask; however, if she is truly penitent, she will not expect it. The pledge to change toward a more positive course may simply be, so far as the school's administrators are concerned, a manipulative tactic to get what she wants. Only time will demonstrate whether or not she is sincere in her repentance. But until she faces the fact that she is responsible for her own disappointment, no positive change will be made in her life or personal development.

God did not reverse Moses' sentence, and the sovereign God has the right to do as He pleases. That didn't deter Moses from appealing the sentence and asking for the favor, however: *"And I besought the Lord at that time, saying, O Lord God, thou hast begun to show thy servant thy greatness and thy mighty hand: for what God is there in heaven or in earth, that can do according to thy works, and according to thy might? I pray thee, let me go over, and see the good land that is beyond Jordan, that goodly mountain, and Lebanon"* (Deut. 3:23-25). But the appeal met with denial: *"But the Lord was wroth with me for your sakes, and would not hear me: and the Lord said unto me, Let it suffice thee; speak no more unto me of this matter"* (Deut. 3:26).

If the lack of mercy surprises you, then keep reading: *"Get thee up into the top of Pisgah, and lift up thine eyes westward, and northward, and southward, and eastward, and behold it with thine eyes: for thou shalt not go over this Jordan. But charge Joshua, and encourage him, and strengthen him: for he shall go over before this people, and he shall cause them to inherit the land which thou shalt see"* (Deut. 3:27-28). Though God did not reverse the verdict, he did make a concession, in His great mercy, for Moses to see the land. That was no small kindness.

Four observations need to be made concerning a right response to disappointment before we leave this example from Moses' life. The godly way he accepted the verdict is an example to every person to whom God says "no."

First, *Moses corrected any perceived sense of personal entitlement he might have harbored.* He needed to be reminded that this was not about him; it was about God's glory. The disappointment he felt when God refused to permit him entrance into Canaan served to remind Moses that he wasn't the only player in the story. He was just a servant, as was Joshua who would succeed him, in a greater cause. It was the glory of God, not the servant's personal privilege, that ultimately mattered. Though God buries His workman, He carries on His work. There are, indeed, many blessings in the service of God, but there are no entitlements. The sovereign Lord is not obligated to bless any man, even a Moses.

Secondly, instead of pouting or stomping his feet in a tantrum, *Moses responded in humble submission to the will of God.* He did not bring the subject up again. He found peace in acquiescence to the Lord. Like Eli, he might have said, "*It is the Lord, let Him do what seemeth Him good*" (1 Sam. 3:18). He was dumb, opening not his mouth, because the Lord did it (Ps. 39:9). He refused to complain in the face of Divine chastening (Lam. 3:39). He "*behaved and quieted himself, as a child that is weaned of his mother*" (Ps. 131:2). To bow in quiet submission before the Lord is the proper posture for every disappointed soul. There is freedom in the grace to sing, "Thy way, not mine, O Lord."

Thirdly, *Moses relished the mercy that permitted him to at least look over into the land from Mt. Pisgah's lofty heights.* In every disappointment, there will be a mercy: "*But though He cause grief, yet will He have compassion according to the multitude of His mercies*" (Lam. 3:32). Look for it. Avail yourself of it. Enjoy it. It may be something as apparently small and insignificant as a kind word of encouragement from a stranger, but still, what a blessing in a heartless world that is! In Moses case, it was no small mercy that God suffered him to, at least, see the land. You can be sure that he enjoyed the view.

Finally, ***Moses received a better blessing than the one for which he had longed.*** Though he was not permitted to enter Canaan, he did, in fact, enter Heaven that very day. Just one glimpse of Christ in glory more than adequately repaid him for any perceived loss or disappointment he felt in this world.

Example 2: David prohibited from building God's house.

Second Samuel 7 records David's serendipitous thought to build a permanent place of worship for Jehovah: "*And it came to pass, when the king sat in his house, and the Lord had given him rest round about from all his enemies; that the king said unto Nathan the prophet, See now, I dwell in an house of cedar, but the ark of God dwelleth within curtains. And Nathan said to the king, God, do all that is in thine heart; for the Lord is with thee*" (2 Sam. 7:1-3).

What a noble desire—to build God a house so that the symbol of His presence did not have to live any longer in a temporary tent! Even the prophet saw nothing wrong with this worthy objective. But God said "no."

God was not, in fact, "with him." The Lord spoke to the prophet that night, commissioning him to dispatch the message that God did not approve (2 Sam. 7:4-11). No doubt, David was disappointed.

Why would God refuse to allow this noble gesture? It makes us shake our heads. The Divine refusal stuns us. What David wanted to do was not immoral, in any sense of the term. On the contrary, it was an expression of gratitude, of honor, of worship to God. What could possibly be wrong with David's desire?

The answer is that there was nothing wrong with David's desire. Yet, God was not capricious; He had a reason for denying the request. The Chronicler explains, "*But the word of the Lord came to me, saying, Thou hast shed blood abundantly, and has made great wars: thou shalt not build an house unto my name, because thou hast shed much blood upon the earth in my sight*" (1 Chr. 22:8). David was a warrior king, and his reign was characterized by strife and conflict. Though such tensions were necessary in order to establish the kingdom and root out the enemies, yet the worship of God would be characterized by peace, not war. David, consequently, would not be the one to construct the house of Divine worship.

But the disappointment he must have felt at this rejection was not the end of the story. After informing him of the negative response to his request, God adds, *"Also the Lord telleth thee that He will make thee an house. And when thy days be fulfilled, and thou shalt sleep with thy fathers, I will set up thy seed after thee, which shall proceed out of thy bowels, and I will establish his kingdom. He shall build an house for my name, and I will stablish the throne of his kingdom for ever"* (2 Sam. 7:11b-13).

Solomon, David's son and successor, would be given the privilege of constructing a permanent temple to house the ark of God. It wasn't that the Lord was opposed to the idea; He simply disallowed David from spearheading the project. Further, the Divine prohibition was not due to any displeasure with David, but rather, the nature of his reign as a warrior king.

How do we know that God did not forbid the plan to see fruition because He was displeased with David? Because the Lord said, "You want to build me a house? No, I'm sorry. But I'm going to build you a house" (cf. 2 Sam. 7:11b). What a gracious, encouraging promise!

What does it mean? Two things, really...It means, first, that God intended to establish David's dynasty, i.e. that his sons would rule in his place for many years hence. That is the immediate, historical application of the promise. But there is another, more long-term, prophetic application. It points toward the coming Messiah, who would be David's greater son. Through Him, God would establish David's kingdom and throne "for ever" (7:16). Second Samuel 7, in other words, has as much to do with the Lord Jesus Christ as it does with Solomon.

Peter's explanation at Pentecost may clarify the passage: *"Men and brethren, let me freely speak to you of the patriarch David, that he is both dead and buried, and his sepulcher is with us unto this day. Therefore being a prophet, and knowing that God had sworn with an oath to him, that of the fruit of his loins, according to the flesh, he would raise up Christ to sit on his throne..."*

(Acts 2:29-30). Peter clearly understands the fulfillment of the Davidic Covenant outlined in 2 Samuel 7 to be Jesus Christ, not Solomon. The "house" that God intended to build David is an everlasting kingdom ruled by David's descendent, according to human lineage, the Lord Jesus Christ. What a magnificent thought! It was the reality of this everlasting covenant that brought David comfort even on his death-bed (cf. 2 Sam. 23:5).

Was David initially disappointed when God closed the door on his noble dream to build a house for the Lord? I'm sure he was. But the Lord redirects his focus from himself and his own plans to God's great plan of the ages, reminding him that it is impossible to out-distance the Lord in giving or to repay the Lord for grace. Though he wanted to do something magnificent to show his gratitude to the Lord, yet God turned the situation around, as if to say, "I'm the Benefactor here; you're merely the beneficiary." If you are disappointed today, dear friend, nothing will redirect your focus like a fresh reminder of all that God has graciously given to you in Jesus Christ.

David's disappointment quickly transformed into humble worship: *"Then went king David in, and sat before the Lord, and he said, Who am I, O Lord God? And what is my house, that thou hast brought me hitherto? And this was yet a small thing in thy sight, O Lord God; but thou has spoken of thy servant's house for a great while to come…Wherefore thou art great, O Lord God: for there is none like thee, neither is there any God beside thee…"* (2 Sam. 7:18-22). He does not sound disappointed in the least, any longer.

"But it is still sad to me," someone replies, "that David was not permitted to witness the fulfillment of his desire." He did see it. He saw it when he went to heaven. Furthermore, he was blessed to participate in Solomon's project of constructing the temple by making preparations in advance. First Chronicles 29 records how David, before he died, gathered building materials and readied the site for later construction. Like the widow with two mites, David did "what he could."

Was he saddened to be relegated to the "supporting cast" rather than the "lead actor"? Well, read 1 Chronicles 29 and ask yourself if he sounds sad. He is anything but sad. Once the materials have been gathered and preparation for Solomon to build have been made, David breaks forth into one of the most sublime worship scenes recorded in Scripture.

> Thine, O Lord, is the greatness, and the power, and the glory, and the victory, and the majesty: for all that is in the heaven and in the earth is thine; thine is the kingdom, O Lord, and thou art exalted as head above all. Both riches and honor come of thee, and thou reignest over all; and in thine hand is power and might; and in thine hand it is to make great, and to give strength unto all. Now therefore, our God, we thank thee, and praise thy glorious name. But who am I, and what is my people, that we should be able to offer so willingly after this sort? For all things come of thee, and of thine own have we given thee (1 Chr. 29:11-14).

No. Whatever disappointment he had once felt, it had dissipated in lieu of the great privilege of serving such a worthy King as Jehovah.

Example 3: Paul's thorn not removed. In 2 Corinthains 12:8-9, Paul talks about the "thorn in the flesh" God gave to him to keep him humble after his unique third-heaven experience. The particular nature of his problem is not specified but it was evidently something physically painful, as the metaphor "thorn in the flesh" indicates. Perhaps he struggled with migraine headaches or gout or rheumatoid arthritis or something similarly agonizing, but whatever it was, he wanted it gone so that he may be free from the incessant pain. I can understand his desire to be free from the misery.

To this end, Paul prayed three times. We can be sure that the man who had so much to say about acceptable prayer in his epistles prayed fervently, importunately, and with all supplication in the Spirit with thanksgiving. But the Lord said "no." God did not grant Paul's passionate petitions for relief.

Was he disappointed? The Bible does not say it, but Paul, like
every Bible character, was "a man of like passions" as us. I know that
I would feel a certain level of dejection to know that I would have to
live with debilitating pain the rest of my life. I'm sure Paul, likewise,
was disappointed, at least momentarily, by God's response to his
request.

Relief from his painful problem would have been a mercy. But
God knew Paul better than Paul knew Paul. He knew that in Paul's
life and temperament, afflictions could exercise a sanctifying effect.
He knew that Paul may be lifted up in pride because of the
abundance of revelations that he had witnessed. He knew that Paul
needed a reason to remember his need of grace and to empathize
with others who likewise suffered.

Were the thorn removed, I can just imagine the scene. Some one
audaciously crosses the line of protocol, challenging Paul's teaching
or questioning his apostolic authority. He might very well then say,
"Who do you think you are? I've been to heaven itself and seen
things you've never even imagined. How dare you challenge a giant
of the church like me!" *"Lest I should be exalted above measure through the
abundance of the revelations, there was given to me a thorn in the flesh, the
messenger of Satan to buffet me, lest I should be exalted above measure"* (2 Cor.
12:7).

To give him pause before flexing his apostolic muscles in
intimidation of less experienced and less mature believers, God gave
him the affliction. "God gave him the affliction" someone replies?
Yes; the Lord alone is concerned to keep his servant humble. The
devil is the king of pride; he seeks to cultivate pride in men. "But,"
someone objects, "if God gave him the affliction, why does it say that
the thorn was "the messenger of Satan to buffet" him? Because the
devil took occasion from the affliction to tempt Paul to think hard
thoughts of God, to sow seeds of doubt in Paul's mind about God's
goodness and love; but the Lord gave the affliction for Paul's benefit.
To take it away would be to remove something that was actually
conducive to Paul's sanctification. Paul could now understand, in a
personal and experiential way, the meaning of the Psalmists words,

"Before I was afflicted I went astray: but now, I have kept thy word" (Ps. 119:67).

God, however, did not simply deny Paul's request. He gave him something better. He said in answer to Paul's repeated request, *"My grace is sufficient for thee: for my strength is made perfect in weakness"* (2 Cor. 12:9). He means, "Paul, you feel that you cannot handle this pain? I understand, but I can handle it. My grace is adequate. My grace is enough for you. Though you do not feel 'up to the task,' I am and I will help you."

When you think of grace, resist the urge to think of some kind of heavenly potion in a container with a piece of masking tape bearing the letters "Grace" to identify the contents within. Grace is not some magical concoction that God pours out in some kind of mystical, paranormal way. Grace speaks of Divine favor bestowed on an unworthy object. It is simply a word to speak of God's blessings.

What does the Lord mean, then, by the reply, *"My grace is sufficient for thee"*? He means, "I will bless you with the resources you need to bear your infirmity. I will grant you physical stamina, moments of relief from pain, and seasons when the suffering is lessened. I will give Dr. Luke, your traveling companion, special insight into treatments for your case. I will bless you with friends to encourage you, to pray for you, and to love you in the midst of your afflictions. I will give you moments of special communion with Christ through the ministry of the Comforter and particular blessing in Divine worship that you may rejoice in me. I have the resources to help you bear the affliction, one step at a time, one day at a time. My grace is enough for you, Paul."

Though he was probably disappointed, at least initially, by the rejection, Paul was encouraged by the promise of sufficient grace. He responded to the prospect of a life riddled with pain in an attitude of humble dependence on the Lord: "*Most gladly therefore will I rather glory in my infirmities, that the power of Christ may rest upon me. Therefore I take pleasure in infirmities, in reproaches, in necessities, in persecutions, in distresses for Christ's sake: for when I am weak, then am I strong*" (2 Cor. 12:9b-10).

In your weakness, and mine as well, dear friend, Jesus Christ is strong. Your extremity is His opportunity to demonstrate His sufficient grace and His ability to sustain you. What a gracious privilege to be used by the Lord as a witness to others of His power to sustain a person in the midst of affliction! How blessed to be a broken vessel that showcases His sufficient grace! May we live with humble submission before Him in every disappointment, saying *"Not my will, but Thine be done."*

7
Never Alone
Living with Loneliness

"I am like a pelican of the wilderness: I am like an owl of the desert. I watch, and am as a sparrow alone upon the house top." Psalm 102:6-7

Several of David's Psalms were composed during that ten-year period in which he lived as a fugitive, running and hiding from jealous king Saul. To go from the momentary celebrity status of a giant slayer to a decade of humiliation as a perceived revolutionary who sought to overthrow the king must have proved an incredible shock to David's faith and sanity. Yesterday he was a hero. Today, he is a traitor and a villain.

Psalm 102 is one such Psalm. Can you see him wandering alone in the desert, sitting solitarily in a cave like "a sparrow alone upon the house top"? He feels keenly the pain of isolation from family and friends and a sense of remoteness from everything familiar. No man cares for his soul. As far as he knows, the whole world is against him in the solitary confinement of his present trial.

Psalm 56, likewise, was written during this difficult period in David's life. The caption to Psalm 56 includes an interesting notation:

To the chief Musician upon Jo-nath-e-lem-recho-kim, Mich-tam of David, when the Philistines took him in Gath.

The curious term *jo-nath-e-lem-recho-kim* literally means "silent dove in distant lands." Using the lonely bird metaphor[1] again (just as he does in Psalm 102), David has an intense feeling that he is a long way from home with no one to know or to care for his case. A sparrow alone on the house top...a silent dove in distant lands.

---

[1] David frequently employs the image of birds to describe his spiritual experience. See Psalm 11:1, 55:6, 57:1, 61:2-4, 84:3, 91, 102:6-7, 103:5, 124:7, etc.

I've been there. I'm sure you have too. In fact, I suspect that loneliness is an experience with which most people can identify. The author Thomas Wolfe said, *"The whole conviction of my life now rests upon the belief that loneliness, far from being a rare and curious phenomenon, peculiar to myself and a few other solitary men, is the central and inevitable fact of human existence."* The deployed Soldier feels the pain of it, as well as his family at home. The grieving widow or widower knows the haunting silence of it every day, but especially during the holidays. The little child sitting by herself in the school cafeteria or playing by himself on the playground knows the sadness of it. The single mom trying to make a life for herself and her children in a little apartment in the middle of town feels keenly the void of loneliness deep in her heart. In fact, I suspect that few people will complete their respective life journeys without experiencing loneliness to some degree.

Society is not necessarily the solution to the problem of loneliness. Even in a crowd of people, it is possible to feel very much alone. Sir Francis Bacon wrote: *"Little do men perceive what loneliness is, and how far it extends. For a crowd is not company, and faces are but a gallery of pictures, and talk but a tinkling cymbal, where there is no love."* Neither is fame the answer to this universal dilemma. In an introspective moment, the celebrated scientist Albert Einstein mused about the inability of fame to satisfy the need for loving companionship: *"It is strange to be known so universally and yet to be so lonely."* If a person is not careful, the lonely soul may drift precariously into the rip-tide of cynicism. In a surprising turn of phrase, comedian Lily Tomlin captures the sentiment of many a lonely heart: *"We are all in this…alone."*

Loneliness Not Synonymous to Solitude

It needs to be noted, however, that loneliness is not necessarily the same as solitude. Loneliness suggests the pain of being alone, but solitude, the joy and pleasure of it. Even Jesus practiced the discipline of solitude: *"And when he had sent the multitudes away, he went up into a mountain apart to pray: and when the evening was come, he was there alone"* (Mt. 14:23; cf. Mr. 1:35). The practice of solitude is essential to discipleship. In fact, I am bold to say that if you don't have a time and place to spend some quiet time with the Lord and His word every day, away from the noise and chatter of society, the sense of loneliness you feel will be necessarily aggravated. Fellowship with the Lord in solitude is essential to every part of spiritual health, especially when addressing the problem of loneliness.

No, solitude and loneliness are not synonyms. Solitude is a good thing, but loneliness may prove to be a very perilous condition of the mind. General Lew Wallace, the author of *Ben Hur*, wrote of one of the more particular dangers of loneliness: "*When people are lonely, they stoop to any companionship.*" How frequently have we heard stories of lonely hearts who suspend judgment in the interest of discovering companionship in the first person to come along? Perhaps this danger of compromising conviction for the sake of company is the idea behind the old Irish proverb: "*Even strife is better than loneliness.*" Indeed, strife does not pose the same level of peril to the soul as loneliness.

It may surprise you to know, however, that in spite of the dangers associated with the feeling of loneliness, the experience may also be beneficial to the child of God. Wolfe made the astute observation that loneliness is the surest cure for vanity. Nothing abases the pride of man like the overwhelming sense that the rest of the world is oblivious to him and could get along just fine without him.

Perhaps Moses learned the important lesson of humility between the ages of forty-one and eighty when he kept Jethro's sheep on the backside of the lonely desert. The man who once took matters in his own hands to deliver a Hebrew from an Egyptian needed to learn that he was inadequate, in and of himself, for the task and that God alone was able to affect deliverance. Such a lesson may only be learned in seclusion.

You Are Not Alone in Feeling to be Alone

In fact, I maintain that loneliness is a required course in the curricula of God's seminary. Scripture records the case of one servant after another who traveled the remote path of loneliness. David, as noted previously, learned the lesson of dependence on the Lord during the lonely years of his isolation. Job certainly knew the experience of feeling abandoned by every relation and friend. In his extremity, he asked, *"Why is light given to a man whose way is hid, and whom God hath hedged in"* (Job 3:23). How many ministers without a pastorate or field of labor have asked that very question! When circumstances are such that doors of opportunity appear shut to you, the temptation to loneliness can be strong.

When, on the other hand, the times call for an unflinching stand for truth and righteousness, the servant of the Lord may again feel to be very much alone. Elijah took such a stand against wicked king Ahab and the idolatrous people of the northern kingdom. As far as he was aware, Elijah was the only prophet standing for Jehovah and truth against a tidal wave of opposition. The rigors of a three and one-half year famine, the public rumors that he was to blame for the drought, and a showdown with the 800 priests and prophets of Baal on Mount Carmel took a toll on his spirit. When Jezebel threatened his life, he fled and requested God to relieve him from the pressure. Sitting under a juniper tree, the miserable man gives every sign of spiritual fatigue.

Listen to his weary acknowledgment: *"Lord, the children of Israel have forsaken thy covenant, thrown down thine altars, and slain thy prophets with the sword; and I, even I only, am left; and they seek my life, to take it away"* (1 Kings 19:10). He feels to be completely alone. The man is completely spiritually exhausted and emotionally spent. The pressure under which he has labored for the past four-odd years has been tremendous. It was indeed a heavy load for one man to bear.

But Elijah was not alone. Though he thought he was the only one who cared about the glory of Jehovah, Elijah did not see the complete picture. In fact, as the Lord informs him, God had reserved to himself "seven thousand men who have not bowed the knee to the image of Baal" (Rom. 11:3-4; cf. 1 Kings 19:18). Elijah was not a one-man-army after all, neither did the outcome of the battle depend completely on him. How comforting it was to learn that there were others—many others—who cared as much about the true worship of God as he did!

Perhaps the epitome of loneliness is the Son of God himself. The Lord Jesus said, "*Foxes have holes and birds of the air have nests; but the Son of man hath not where to lay his head*" (Lk. 9:58). Have you ever compared the last verse of John 7 with the first verse of John 8? John 7 ends by saying that the disciples left Jesus and went to their own homes. John 8 begins by saying that Jesus went to the Mount of Olives. There is something quite sad to me in that thought.

Never in history has there been a lonelier figure than the Lord Jesus Christ as he neared the cross. In Gethsemane, he left the disciples to "watch and pray" as he went a little further to agonize in prayer with the Father. How subtle, yet how profound, is the lesson here! No man could go where the Savior must go. The work before Him must be done without human assistance. Christ alone must redeem sinners. He must tread the winepress alone, with no man to help (cf. Is. 63:3, 5).

Then, on the cross, he was both ostracized by men and forsaken by heaven. See the holy Lamb of God suspended on crossbeams between heaven and earth, the one Mediator between God and men, rejected by His own (Jno. 1:11) and crying out as He felt the agonies of separation from God, "*My God, my God, why hast thou forsaken me?*" (Mt. 27:46). He is there because He alone could accomplish this work. How wonderful to know that "*when He had by Himself purged us from our sins*" (Heb. 1:3), the Savior was exalted to the right hand of Divine Majesty! And how equally salutary to consider that because He knows the experience of loneliness better than anyone else, He is able to empathize with those who travel the path of loneliness in this world (cf. Heb. 2:17-18; 4:15-16)!

Others, even the blessed Lord Jesus, have walked this path before us. Though you may feel to be very much alone at this moment, you are not alone in that experience. Their testimony reminds us that "this too shall pass," and that it is possible to be faithful to God until the sun shines through the gloomy clouds once again. Further, your great High Priest in heaven knows what it is to be lonely. Go to Him in prayer; pour out your soul before Him. He knows. He understands.

You are Not Alone in the Causes of Loneliness

Why do people feel to be alone? It seems to me that feelings of loneliness derive from five basic categories: *grief, rejection, isolation, guilt, and godliness.* Whatever the peculiar circumstances a person may face, the sense of loneliness will generally fall into one of these five areas. Let's develop each one.

First, loneliness frequently derives from *grief.* The person who has suffered some loss, perhaps of a life mate, a child, or a friend, will inevitably experience the emotions associated with that loss, one of the most powerful of which is loneliness. Sir Walter Scott wrote "When thinking about companions gone, we feel ourselves doubly alone."

Secondly, sometimes feelings of loneliness frequently surface in those who have experienced some form of *rejection.* Mother Teresa astutely observed that *"Loneliness and the feeling of being unwanted is the most terrible poverty."* Though she had witnessed indescribable poverty among the poor people of Calcutta, she noticed that economic poverty was nothing compared to the inescapable sense of being unloved. My, how true that is! Whether we are talking about the little handicapped child rejected by his parents, the husband or wife replaced by another, or the aging parent left to fritter the remaining days of life away secluded from loved ones and friends, the feeling that one is unwanted and unloved is a kind of poverty worse than want of shelter, food and clothing.

Then, there is yet another reason people feel to be alone. Feelings of loneliness sometimes spring from physical or relational *isolation,* whether that isolation is due to someone else's decision or by virtue of a personal choice. A Soldier called to leave family and friends for a lengthy deployment to some foreign assignment will necessarily encounter a significant sense of loneliness and deep longing for the return of familiarity. The sheer physical distance between him and the comforts of home coupled with the unfamiliar circumstances of his new life makes his sense of isolation intense.

Not every experience of isolation, however, is physical. There is a kind of relational isolation as well. Sometimes a person makes a choice to isolate himself/herself from others, cutting off communication and withdrawing into a cocoon of fellowship with the unholy trinity of me, myself and I.

I've seen it in pastors who, for some reason, could not seem to get along with other preachers in their extended fellowship and systematically withdrew from society with other churches until they were alone. Indeed, there are essentials of the faith that cannot be negotiated or compromised. But when a man makes every issue and interpretation a test of fellowship, he will effectively exclude everyone that doesn't agree with him until his circle of influence is narrowed to his own little "us four and no more."

I've also seen it in preachers who adopted some unconventional view of a fundamental doctrine. Once he begins to publicize his position, the brother attracts criticism for it. As efforts to convince him of his error meet with resistance, increasingly more and more of his colleagues withdraw and distance themselves from him, leaving him essentially to himself. Though he complains that no one will fraternize with him any longer and that he is isolated, the fault is his own. He has "painted himself into a corner" by virtue of his own recalcitrance.

Solomon said, "*If thou scornest, thou alone shalt bear it*" (Pro. 9:12b). He means that an individual may produce his own condition of loneliness by harboring a bad attitude. Common sense demands that one keep his distance from a skunk; likewise, wise folk tend to avoid someone who exhibits traits of internal anger and sinful behavior. "*Ephraim is joined to idols: let him alone*" counsels the Lord (Hos. 4:17). Though it is not easy to consider, the lonely individual who feels isolated from others needs to ask himself/herself if he may, in fact, be responsible for creating his own reality.

Fourthly, sometimes loneliness is caused by *guilt*, or the conviction of sin. Jeremiah felt keenly a lonely sense of God's displeasure as he walked in the smoking ruin that was the city of Jerusalem: "*He sitteth alone and keepeth silence, because He hath borne it upon him*" (Lam. 3:28). Few experiences make a person feel more forlorn and lost as the sense that he has offended the Lord. A guilty conscience senses isolation from God, the same kind of isolation (in terms of quality, not degree) that Jesus suffered when he bore our sins on the cross and that the wicked will experience in the God-forsakenness of eternal punishment. The feeling of isolation is not indicative of the reality, for God will never forsake His people for whom Jesus Christ died (cf. 1 Jno. 3:20). The relationship will never be broken, but the fellowship may be interrupted and breached. The Lord draws back, in terms of the manifestation of His presence and favor, when His child disobeys Him, and He draws near in their obedience (cf. Jno. 14:21, 23; Jas. 4:8). When He hides His face in response to sin, the child of God feels to be very much alone (cf. Is. 59:1-2).

Finally, God's people may experience a sense of loneliness simply by virtue of their commitment to the Lord Jesus Christ, or because of *godliness*. Mark Twain wrote, "*Be good, and you will be lonely.*" Every young adult who resists the pressure to conform to the crowd knows that faithfulness to Jesus Christ frequently comes at the cost of personal popularity.

In his authorized biography of the late Dr. D. Martyn Lloyd-Jones, Iain Murray tells of the Doctor's overwhelming sense of loneliness in ministry. It was the 1960's and the ecumenical movement was in full swing. Lloyd-Jones was virtually a lone voice in evangelicalism for the importance of doctrine. Everyone else, it seemed, was quick to jump on the bandwagon of unity, regardless of doctrinal consensus, as promoted by the World Council of Churches. When a colleague in the ministry commented on the loneliness of the work of the ministry, the Doctor responded, with feeling, "You speak of loneliness! I am the loneliest man in this room…I am alone in this world." One of the preachers who heard him commented that it was not loneliness for any personal reasons but rather by virtue of standing for the word of the gospel.[2]

The apostle Paul suffered extreme loneliness as a consequence of his commitment to the Lord. His words in 2 Timothy 4:9-15 tug on my heart-strings:

---

[2] Iain Murray, *The Fight of Faith: Vol. 2 of the Authorised Biography of D. Martyn Lloyd-Jones*, p. 461.

Do thy diligence to come shortly unto me: for Demas hath forsaken me, having loved this present world, and is departed unto Thessalonica; Crescens to Galatia, Titus unto Dalmatia. Only Luke is with me. Take Mark, and bring him with thee: for he is profitable to me for the ministry. And Tychicus have I sent to Ephesus. The cloak that I left at Troas with Carpus, when thou comest, bring with thee, and the books, but especially the parchments...At my first answer no man stood with me, but all men forsook me: I pray God that it may not be laid to their charge.

It is generally agreed that 2 Timothy is Paul's "swan song," the final letter he wrote before he was beheaded under Nero in A.D. 68. Cold and alone in Rome's Mamertine Prison, Paul longs for his coat, books, parchments, and the fellowship of Brother Timothy, his son in the faith of the gospel.

Why is he there? He is in this lonely circumstance because he refused to compromise his Christian confession. Like Jeremiah of old (Jer. 15:15-21), Paul suffered persecution in the form of seclusion from society as a result of his commitment to godliness. If you and I are likewise committed to the integrity of the truth of Jesus Christ, we may also suffer loneliness in one form or another.

How much better it is to feel to be alone because you have done the right thing, than to suffer loneliness because you have been so obnoxious and uncouth! *"If ye suffer for righteousness' sake,"* says Peter, *"happy are ye...for it is better, if the will of God be so, that ye suffer for well doing, than for evil doing"* (1 Pet. 3:14a, 17). There are lonely people in both camps. If you are lonely today because you are committed to the Lord Jesus Christ, you may bear the painful circumstance as a badge of honor, identifying you with the Savior, for your Lord likewise suffered the stigma of the cross for you when he had done nothing amiss.

Some Cordials for the Lonely

How may a person endure the painful circumstances of isolation and loneliness? They may address the situation and overcome the accompanying temptation to despair in the same way these various Bible characters did: by recalling the truths and promises of God's word and appropriating the resources God in mercy has made available to His people in this world.

First, the Bible confirms the soul-cheering truth of *the love of God*. What a cheering theme! Though every creature-help may fail you, God's love will never let you go. How long has it been since you have pondered—seriously and deliberately meditated upon the meaning and significance, as they apply to you—Paul's words in Romans 8:35-39?

> Who shall separate us from the love of Christ? Shall tribulation, or distress, or persecution, or famine, or nakedness, or peril, or sword? ...in all these things we are more than conquerors through him that loved us. For I am persuaded, that neither death, nor life, nor angels, nor principalities, nor powers, nor things present, nor things to come, nor height, nor depth, nor any other creature, shall be able to separate us from the love of God, which is in Christ Jesus our Lord.

It is helpful in personal Bible study to read passages like this existentially. Change the collective pronouns to first person pronouns. "Who shall separate *me* from the love of Christ? *I* am more than a conqueror in each of these trying circumstances through Him that loved *me*. For nothing shall ever be able to separate *me* from the love of God in Jesus Christ *my* Lord." It is surely not wrong to claim, by faith, this great Bible truth as your own. To meditate on the fact that the Lord loves me (miracle of miracles!) and that nothing that I could ever do or that may ever happen to me could change that fact is a precious cordial to soothe my lonely soul.

George Matheson (1842-1906), the blind Scottish hymnwriter, found sweet comfort in the unfailing love of God toward him. During his studies for the ministry, Matheson learned that he was losing his eyesight. His fiancé, concerned about the challenges of caring for a blind husband the rest of her life called off the engagement and broke George Matheson's heart. His eldest sister took the dejected seminarian into her own home, caring for him as his eyesight quickly degenerated and assisting him in the completion of his studies for ordination. With her assistance, George graduated, was ordained, and assumed a pastorate. She read the Bible to him, transcribed his dictated sermons, assisted him in the memorization of his weekly pulpit fare, and listened reverently as one of his congregants during the delivery of his Sunday sermons.

In time, his sister was married, leaving Matheson bereft of care. Though he did not begrudge her the joys of living her own life, he felt, undoubtedly, very much alone in this world. On the eve of her wedding, Matheson began to meditate on the unfailing love of God for him. He sat down to record his meditations, writing the words that have meant so much to Christian people for the past century and one-half:

O Love, that will not let me go,
I rest my weary soul in Thee,
I give Thee back the life I owe,
That in Thine ocean depths its flow
May richer, fuller be.

George Matheson said of the composition of this beloved hymn-poem, "I am quite sure that the whole work was completed in five minutes, and equally sure that it never received at my hands any retouching or correction. I have no natural gift of rhythm. All the other verses I have ever written are manufactured articles; this came like a dayspring from on high."

No doubt, the Lord gave him a special gift that day. In the comfort of God's love for him, Matheson lived and ministered for over four more decades. He was one of Queen Victoria's favorite preachers, preaching at Balmoral upon her request on more than one occasion. She even had his sermons on the Book of Job published.

Like George Matheson, lonely souls may also find sweet consolation in the knowledge that God will never stop loving His own. No circumstance or deed will ever cause the Lord to cease to love one of His dear children. He will keep them all as the apple of His eye.

Further, there is sweet comfort to be found in the Biblical reality of *the friendship of the Lord Jesus*. The lonely soul feels to be friendless. He is like the impotent man by Bethesda's pool who had no man to help him into the healing waters. *"I have no man"* (Jno. 5:7) is the doleful refrain of the lonely. Ah, but he did, in fact, have a man. The impotent man had an omnipotent Man, the man Christ Jesus. Though he thought he had no friends, Jesus proved himself a true friend, saying, *"Rise, take up thy bed, and walk"* (Jno. 5:8).

Jesus is that *"friend that sticketh closer than a brother"* (Pro. 18:24b). He is not a fair-weather friend—one that stands beside you only when the way is smooth—but faithful and true, in sunshine and in shadow. He has "shown himself friendly" at the cross, voluntarily humbling himself to assume the place of sinners in order to rescue the elect from their sins. In Him, we have forgiveness of our sins according to the riches of His grace (Eph. 1:7). Sensible sinners, like the lonely woman of ill-repute who wept at Jesus' feet (Lk. 7:37ff), still find Him to be a true Friend and rejoice in His salvation.

I've frequently found comfort in loneliness from Grace Gordon's hymn, "Never A Friend Like Thee." She writes of the many ways that Jesus shows himself to be the best Friend a poor, struggling sinner will ever have:

> *Loving me ere I knew Him,*
> *Calling with voice so sweet,*
> *Burdens of life I brought Him,*
> *Knelt at His wounded feet;*
> *Naught from that love can sever,*
> *Wonderful, changeless free,*
> *Master, I'll serve Thee ever,*
> *Never a Friend like Thee!*

Sing of a Friend so loyal,
Sing of a Friend so true,
Giving His gifts so royal,
Blessings that aye are new.
King of the heavenly glory,
Lowly of earth was He;
Master, we sing Thy story,
Never was One like Thee.

Thirdly, you may find *the word of God* to be a companion to you in times of alienation and estrangement. The Psalmist affirmed, *"Thy statutes have been my songs in the house of my pilgrimage"* (Ps. 119:54). A pilgrimage is a lonely journey. To keep them company as they wend their way homeward, God has given His people His special revelation in Scripture. What companionship I've found in Jeremiah, and David, and Peter, and Joseph! These men have become my friends as I've reviewed their respective life narratives and experiences. God's word has never failed to occupy my mind with healthy meditations and to lift my spirits beyond myself.

In the fourth place, *the fellowship of the saints* may prove a real help to the lonely heart. I believe the church of the Lord Jesus Christ is the greatest support group in the world. To cast in your lot with a congregation of believers means that you are no longer alone in this world but surrounded by many brothers and sisters in Christ. *"Two are better than one,"* says Solomon, *"...for if they fall, the one will lift up his fellow"* (Ecc. 4:9-10). Are there self-serving people who lack hospitality? Of course; but by and large, genuinely loving people who reach out to others in love far outnumber the insincere. Here, you may find a true friend and loving encouragement. And here you will find opportunities to reach out in ministry to others. Above every secular friendship, I value the friends of my Master, the children of God. I am glad to claim with the Psalmist, *"I am a companion of all them that fear thee, and of them that keep thy precepts"* (Ps. 119:63).

Finally, *the abiding presence of the Lord* is a sweet cordial to the lonely soul. The thrice repeated refrain in Genesis 39, *"But the Lord was with Joseph,"* reveals the secret of his capacity to persevere beneath the many distresses he faced. Though Joseph was estranged from family, unjustly incarcerated by his master, and forgotten and left to languish in prison by the butler, yet the Lord never abandoned the lonely man. God was with him.

Previously, we mentioned Paul's experience at his initial hearing before Caesar. The believers at Rome had told him that when his court date arrived, they would be there to provide moral support and perhaps speak in defense of his character. Yet, he says, "*At my first answer, no man stood with me, but all men forsook me*" (2 Tim. 4:16a). How lonely he must have felt in that critical hour! Yet, amazingly, he is not bitter against his friends. With magnanimity reminiscent of the Savior on the cross, he responds, "*I pray God that it may not be laid to their charge*" (4:16b).

On what basis could Paul be so generous of spirit? How could he resist the natural temptation to anger in the wake of such a let-down? No doubt, Paul knew very well that people are just people at best, with good intentions albeit feet of clay. His expectations were in the Lord, not in his fellow mortals. And the Lord did not let him down: "*Notwithstanding the Lord stood with me and strengthened me; that by me the preaching might be fully known, and that all the Gentiles might hear: and I was delivered out of the mouth of the lion*" (2 Tim. 4:17).

The abiding presence of Jesus Christ with His servant Paul was the reason for Paul's courage, spiritual strength, and inward peace in that lonely hour. And God has promised that same abiding presence to you and me in our lonely hours as well.

Years ago, I committed to memory several precious promises concerning the presence of God. I love to remind myself of these Divine pledges in moments when I feel to be alone. Promises like Hebrews 13:5, "*...I will never leave thee nor forsake thee. So that we may boldly say, The Lord is my helper, and I will not fear what man shall do unto me,*" and Isaiah 41:10, "*Fear thou not; for I am with thee: be not dismayed; for I am thy God: I will strengthen thee; yea, I will help thee; yea, I will uphold thee with the right hand of my righteousness,*" and Isaiah 43:2, "*When thou passest through the waters, I will be with thee; and through the rivers, they shall not overflow thee: when thou walkest through the fire, thou shalt not be burned;*

neither shall the flame kindle upon thee," have proved salutary to my lonely soul on more than one occasion in my life.

Even when the Christian's path leads through the cold dark valleys, there is no need to fear, for our Heavenly Shepherd is with us, both to protect from dangerous predators and to guide us forward in the way (Ps. 23:4). Though you may be tempted to think of these promises as nothing more than religious rhetoric, I assure you they are real and that He is good for His word. You can trust Him today to be near you, to manifest His presence to you, and to help you, though a sparrow alone on the housetop, to sing, "He promised never to leave me, never to leave me alone."

The world's fierce winds are blowing,
Temptations sharp and keen,
I feel a peace in knowing,
My Savior stands between;
He stands to shield me from danger
When earthly friends are gone;
He promised never to leave me,

Never to leave me alone.
When in afflictions valley,
I'm treading the road of care,
My Savior helps me to carry
My cross when heavy to bear;
My feet entangled with briars,
Ready to cast me down,
My Savior whispers His promise:
"I never will leave thee alone."

No, never alone,
No, never alone;
He promised never to leave me,
Never to leave me alone.[3]

---

[3] Anonymous.

8
Suffering for Well Doing
A Christian Response to Mistreatment

"For it is better, if the will of God be so, that ye suffer for well doing than for evil doing." 1 Peter 3:17

A cliché, if repeated enough, eventually assumes the force of law. People tend to repeat it without a second thought of scrutiny regarding its veracity. "If it is meant to be, then it will happen" is a popular one. "God helps those who help themselves" is another in the long list of trite, superficial efforts to mentally process the vicissitudes of life.

One of the worst clichés, in my opinion, resurfaces in almost every case of setback, injustice, or even tragedy. Inevitably, some well-meaning soul will try to comfort a stunned or grief-stricken friend by saying, "Well, everything happens for a reason."

Sadly, many folks simply accept such statements as if they had been scientifically verified or prominently documented in Scripture. Rare is the person who scrutinizes one of these simplistic explanations of life's circumstances in terms of the particular philosophy it promotes. Even rarer is the individual that challenges the assertion.

What philosophical school of thought underlies the assertion that "everything happens for a reason"? This idea derives from a philosophy called *determinism*. Determinism teaches that all of life is prescripted, predetermined and unalterably fixed by some superior force, whether destiny, the fates, or even God. Ancient Greek dualism, like its oriental predecessor, was deterministic. It suggested that the two eternal forces of good and evil, or light and darkness, competed against each other for dominance, using the natural world and its inhabitants like a chess player moves his pawns, bishops, knights and queen to achieve his goal.

According to the deterministic model, every human action, whether good or evil, is simply an involuntary response to the will of a superior power. We may never know the reason things happen, this school suggests, but there is a reason nonetheless. Somehow, this trite explanation of life and its painful circumstances is supposed to console the spouse who has just discovered the infidelity of his/her mate, the parents whose teenager has died of a drug overdose, or the young lady who has been the victim of a sexual assault. Everything happens for a reason, huh? Do you mean the gods are toying with us, or worse, that the true and living God orchestrated the immorality for my good and His glory? Sorry, it doesn't work for me.

Some years ago when a friend used the cliché on me as we discussed some tragedy, I had finally had enough. I respectfully replied, "You know, you're correct…everything happens for a reason, and most of the time, the reason is *sin*." He looked at me quizzically, surprised that I would challenge what he thought was a truism. I explained, "You say that everything happens for a reason. I agree, but I don't believe the reason is necessarily a Divine one. Many of life's circumstances are simply the result of the fact that we live in a world that is under the curse of sin. If I drive around a hair-pin turn on wet roads at ninety miles per hour, it is not God's fault when I lose control, roll the vehicle, and wrap it around a tree. To impute the consequences of my recklessness to God is to evade personal responsibility and to impugn His moral character, regardless of the verbal gymnastics one employs to try to avoid doing so. God is certainly able to use the event to enforce a lesson I need to learn or to mercifully intervene so that my life is spared from death, but the wreck *happened* for the express reason that I was acting irresponsibly and unwisely."

Nowhere is this point more important than when dealing with the painful experience of mistreatment. Try the cliché "everything happens for a reason" on a teenage boy who is bullied every day on the school bus, or the secretary who loses her job because she refused the inappropriate advances of a supervisor, or the single mom who cannot make ends meet because of a deadbeat dad, or the man "phased out" of a company just months before retirement, or the victim of vandalism or robbery. Everything happens for a reason?

Perhaps, but more often than not, the reason is someone else's sinful conduct.

It is impossible to live in this sinful world without suffering mistreatment at the hands of another at some point. I know the "victim card" is overplayed in popular culture, but that doesn't change the fact that victimization is real and that everyone will be victimized, at some point, by the misdeeds of another. I don't know any exceptions to this rule.

It may be something as seemingly insignificant as an unpaid personal loan, or borrowed equipment never returned. Or it may be something as traumatic as physical abuse, or theft of your property, or gossip and slander against your good name, or the infidelity of a spouse. The fact is that none of us will get out of this world without suffering mistreatment at some level.

Love Covers a Multitude of Sins

Indeed, mistreatment is part and parcel of living in a world under the curse of sin. We need to distinguish, however, between minor mistreatment and major mistreatment. A periodic harsh word from one's spouse because he/she just doesn't feel well that day or is under some particular stressful deadline is not typically what one should consider major mistreatment.

There are many situations in daily life, in other words, that do not rise to the level of a real injustice. Though an occasion in which you feel momentary disrespect from another person may feel, at the time, like an injustice, it is generally best to just let the issue slide without response. If I demanded justice at every point in daily activity when I felt that some other human being had done me wrong—whether a surly clerk at the grocery store, an angry motorist riding my rear bumper because I was traveling too slowly, or a friend that failed to return my phone call—I would never get anything else done.

"*Charity*," says the apostle Peter, "*shall cover a multitude of sins*" (1 Pet. 4:8). In fact, we might be surprised just how many minor mistreatments might be borne patiently if we extend to others the same kind of love that Christ has extended toward us. Without a generous, daily application of the oil of grace to the gears of relationships, the engine of happiness will soon lock-up and progress in life will be severely impacted.

Solomon puts it like this: *"The discretion of a man deferreth his anger; and it is his glory to pass over a transgression"* (Pro. 19:11). A wonderful word exists to describe this kind of gracious response to mistreatment: *magnanimity.*

Magnanimity might be defined as "great-heartedness; the ability to rise above insult and injury; the refusal to be petty." A magnanimous person is noble, exhibiting a lofty generosity toward perceived slights.

A few anecdotal examples of magnanimity in action may be helpful.

1. One day when Professor Booker T. Washington was walking to work at the Tuskegee Institute, he passed the mansion of a wealthy widow. She didn't recognize him and called out, "Come here, boy; I need some wood chopped." At once, Washington removed his jacket, split a load of wood, carried it into the house and stacked it neatly. After he left, a female servant said to her, "That was Professor Washington, ma'am." The widow woman was so embarrassed that she went to the Institute, sought out the Professor, and apologized. He replied, "There's no need to apologize, ma'am. I'm delighted to do favors for my friends." Moved by his ability to rise above pettiness, the woman became one of Tuskegee Institutes most generous supporters for years to come.

2. Edward Stanton was not an admirer of President Abraham Lincoln. He called Lincoln a "fool," "a low and cunning clown," and said that he looked like "the original gorilla." Yet Lincoln appointed Stanton to the position of Secretary of War because, as the President said, he was "the best man for the job." At the slain President's bedside, Stanton was heard to say through tears, "There's lies the greatest ruler of men the world has ever seen."

3. Shortly after the Civil War, a former slave entered the Episcopal church in Richmond, Virginia during communion. He walked

down the center aisle and knelt at the altar as a rustle of shock and anger swept through the congregation at such an apparently presumptuous act. Suddenly, a distinguished gentleman arose from the crowd, made his way to front and knelt beside the man. Tension was at once diffused. The man's name was General Robert E. Lee.

But what about those situations in which mistreatment is so severe that life is in danger? What about serial infidelity, physical and emotional abuse, or school bullying? What about persecution for righteousness' sake? What about those situations in which magnanimity is impossible?

Inevitable Persecution

Jesus said, *"Woe unto the world because of offenses! For it must needs be that offenses come, but woe to that man by whom the offense cometh"* (Mt. 18:7). Our Lord pronounces a Divine malediction, or curse, on the world because it inevitably offends, or trips-up, his children. It does, doesn't it? This vile world is not a friend to grace to draw us closer to God.

On the contrary, it is extremely challenging to live a faithful Christian life when the world bombards us with distractions, delusions, diversions, and discouragements. The life of discipleship is essentially a matter of spiritual combat, and this world is enemy territory to the Christian. It *must needs be*, i.e. it is inevitable, that the world will mistreat those who follow the Lord Jesus Christ.

In fact, the Bible teaches that persecution for righteousness' sake, the epitome of mistreatment, is every true Christian's lot: *"Yea, and all that will live godly in Christ Jesus shall suffer persecution"* (2 Tim. 3:12). This fallen world system despises the believer, simply by virtue of the fact that he belongs to the Lord Jesus Christ: *"If the world hate you, ye know that it hated me before it hated you. If ye were of the world, the world would love his own: but because ye are not of the world, but I have chosen you out of the world, therefore the world hateth you"* (Jno. 15:18-19; cf. 1 Jno. 3:13).

True discipleship is by definition a counter-cultural lifestyle (cf. Rom. 12:2a) in which societal values are rejected in favor of God's word (cf. 1 Jno. 2:15-17). Such an approach to life does not set well with the world. Ask John the Baptist how much Herod appreciated the preacher's call to repentance.

Because mistreatment is inevitable in this life, especially in terms of Christian persecution from this unbelieving world, we must not be surprised when we are called to suffer for the sake of doing the right thing: *"Beloved, think it not strange concerning the fiery trial which is to try you, as though some strange thing happened unto you, but rejoice, inasmuch as ye are partakers of Christ's sufferings, ye may be glad also with exceeding joy"* (1 Pet. 4:13). The very fact of identification with Christ means that persecution is inevitable for every true believer (cf. 2 Tim. 3:12).

In fact, the early Christians deemed persecution for Jesus' sake an honor and privilege. When the disciples were beaten and threatened not to speak any more in the name of Jesus, they *"departed from the council, rejoicing that they were counted worthy to suffer shame for his name"* (Acts 5:41).

Paul's great passion to "know Christ" included not only the quest to experience, on the positive side, "the power of his resurrection" but also, on the negative, "the fellowship of his sufferings" (Phi. 3:10). If discipleship aims to make the student as the teacher (cf. Mt. 10:24-25), or as Thomas a'Kempis expressed it, at "the imitation of Christ," there is no greater honor than to share the Master's life experience, both in victory and in suffering. Those who know the experience of his glorious love are called by the gospel to ally themselves to him, with others of like precious faith, in the commitment of gospel discipleship: *"Let us go forth unto him without the camp, bearing his reproach"* (Heb. 13:13).

The Lord Jesus did not conceal the inevitable prospect of persecution from his followers. Over and again, he transparently disclosed the fact that identification with him would necessarily produce suffering: *"And she shall be hated of all men for my name's sake..."* (Mt. 10:22a); *"If the world hate you, ye know that it hated me before it hated you. If ye were of the world, the world would love his own: but because ye are not of the world, but I have chosen you out of the world, therefore the world hateth you. Remember the word that I said unto you, The servant is not greater than his lord. If they have persecuted me, they will also persecute you...*" (Jno. 15:18-20).

Likewise, the apostles minced no words regarding the cost of discipleship. Suffering on Patmos Island for the sake of the gospel, the apostle John wrote to the persecuted saints in Asia Minor, calling them his "companions in tribulation" (Rev. 1:9). The apostle Paul encouraged beleaguered Christians by modeling an attitude of privilege in suffering persecution for Jesus' sake (cf. Acts 20:24; Col. 1:24; 2 Tim. 1:8) as well as a resolute commitment to faithful discipleship, come what may (cf. 2 Tim. 2:9-10; 3:10-14).

Taking his cue from the eighth Beatitude (cf. Mt. 5:10-11), the apostle Peter reminds persecuted believers that it is a "happy" thing to "be reproached for the name of Christ," (1 Pet. 4:14), for the Holy Spirit helps those so mistreated to *"rejoice, inasmuch as ye are partakers of Christ's sufferings; that, when his glory shall be revealed, ye may be glad also with exceeding joy"* (1 Pet. 4:13). He then issues an important warning: *"But let none of you suffer as a murderer, or as a thief, or as an evil-doer, or as a busybody in other men's matters"* (4:15). Suffering for being obnoxious is not persecution, but suffering for righteousness' sake, or for being a true follower of the Lord Jesus Christ, is a badge of honor and incentive to glorify God.

Rare is the person today who stands for principle, regardless of the personal cost. Why is that the case? It is likely due to the fact that popular culture tends to deify the slick-talking politician trafficking in obfuscation, evasiveness, and double-speak. Though there are exceptions to the rule, the politician offers us an object lesson on the silencing effect that ambiguity and equivocation have on the conscience. How many men of conviction have promisingly achieved public office, only to pay the price of compromise necessary to assimilate into the *status quo*! It makes one wonder how some of these folk can sleep at night.

Someone once said that a belief is what you hold, but a conviction is what holds you. If you are a person of conscience and conviction, you will be tested. Some circumstance will necessarily surface to challenge those convictions. It is not a question of "if" but "when."

It may be something as seemingly harmless as the temptation to succumb to peer pressure at school, to talk as the popular crowd talks, to experiment with recreational drugs, or to cheat on a test. Or it may be something as intimidating as a legal requirement to, as some early Christians encountered, "burn a pinch of incense before the bust of the emperor and swear by the genius of Caesar." Whatever form it takes, real-life tests challenging the believer's values are inevitable.

My point is simply that some battles are worth fighting, some values worth protecting, some principles worth defending. Taking a stand for Christ and His truth in a culture of compromise is a Christian imperative: "*Stand fast in the liberty wherewith Christ hath made us free, and be not entangled again with the yoke of bondage*" (Gal. 5:1; cf. 1 Cor. 16:13; Eph. 6:11f). The primitive Christians valued the gospel of grace as a conviction, refusing to compromise it for the sake of personal ease and comfort. Christ was more precious to them than life itself, and to act against conscience they deemed neither right nor safe. Like Paul, they did not count life dear unto themselves if it meant the furtherance of the kingdom of God (cf. Acts 20:24). And like the apostle, again, they deemed the scars on their backs a badge of honor, "the marks of the Lord Jesus" (Gal. 6:17).

Narrative accounts of Christian persecution, both past and present, make for heart-wrenching reading. But to those who dearly love the Lord Jesus Christ and His church, the stories of Christian commitment and loyalty to the gospel in the face of tremendous personal recrimination are tales of triumph, not tragedy.

I frequently think of Martin Luther's humble yet courageous defense at the Diet of Worms. When the Imperial Diet called upon the youthful monk to recant his books challenging the magisterial church, Luther replied, "Unless I am convinced by sacred Scripture or by evident reason, I cannot recant; for my conscience is held captive by the word of God, and to go against conscience is neither right nor safe. Here I take my stand; I can do no other, so help me God."

Is your conscience held captive by the word of God? Then, necessarily, your conviction will run counter at some point to this fallen world in which we live. Conflict is inevitable, but Christ is worthy of your best esteem. If and when you are called to suffer for righteousness' sake, count it all joy, my friend. Count it all joy.

Setting Boundaries

Now, it needs to be said that the Christian should not court persecution or passively subject himself/herself to abusive treatment. The imperative to be "harmless as a dove" is preceded by another imperative equally as important: *"Be wise as serpents"* (Mt. 10:16). A serpent will wisely avoid potential danger whenever possible; likewise, the believer is not only justified but also charged to take necessary steps to protect himself from harm, if at all possible.

Consider Paul's narrow escape from Damascus in Acts 9:23-25. After his dramatic encounter with the risen Christ on Damascus Road (9:1-9), Paul stayed for awhile with the disciples in Damascus. For many days, he preached Christ in the Jewish synagogue, *"confounding the Jews…*[and] *proving that this is very Christ"* (9:22). Then *"the Jews took counsel to kill him: but their laying await was known of Saul. And they watched the gates day and night to kill him. Then the disciples took him by night, and let him down by the wall in a basket"* (9:23-25).

Why didn't he stay in Damascus and trust God to protect him? Why was it necessary to make his getaway under the cover of darkness? Wouldn't the Lord shield him from any physical harm if Paul was indeed doing the Lord's work? And why, on other occasions such as Paul's visit to Lystra when the people stoned him and dragged his apparently dead body outside the city gates, did the revived preacher arise and return straight back into the heart of the city to preach again (Acts 14:19-20)?

The answer to the apparent discrepancy between his actions at Damascus and Lystra is simply that he made a rational judgment, using what old folks once called "common sense." Obviously, he reasoned at Damascus that to stay would not be an act of trusting but of tempting God. Just as Jesus recognized that to cast himself down from the pinnacle of the temple in the confidence that God would dispatch angels to protect him from harm would be an act of tempting, not trusting, God (Mt. 4:5-7), for it would occasion a set of circumstances in which the Father had to perform a miracle to rescue him, so Paul recognized that to stay in Damascus, or to try to walk through the city gates in broad daylight, when the plot to kill him was already at the point of a mobilized plan would be foolhardy and reckless.

At Lystra, on the contrary, the people assumed that Paul was truly dead. To return to the city after supposing him deceased would exercise a kind of "shock and awe" effect on the superstitious populace. It would also demonstrate uncommon valor and conviction of the truth of his message. Though we cannot be sure, it seems plausible that this was the tone of his thinking.

At any rate, it seems obvious that Paul used his head and thought the various situations through. The point I make, again, is that it is not unspiritual to employ the mind that God Himself gave you when facing a potentially dangerous set of circumstances.

People in an abusive relationship, whether physical or psychological, may need this reminder. It is not unchristian to set boundaries for the sake of your own safety. Simple "common sense" tells us that in a sinful world, it is wise to put locks on doors and take other safety precautions to protect oneself against robbers, vandals, identity thieves, rapists, kidnappers, terrorists and murderers. I cannot stress strongly enough that Christianity does not encourage a pacifistic approach toward the protection of personal property. The Framers put the Fifth Amendment in the United States Constitution because they understood that God's moral law teaches the sanctity of private property (cf. Ex. 20:15) as a "self-evident truth," the unalienable right of which has been conferred on every human being by the Creator.

But, someone objects, doesn't Jesus encourage Christian pacifism in the Sermon on the Mount? How does the exhortation to "turn the other cheek," "go the extra mile," "settle out of court," and "give the coat off your back" square with my claim that it is appropriate, and even necessary, to set boundaries in terms of the kind of treatment one will accept from another person?

Is it ever appropriate for a Christian to tell another person "no"? Is there ever a case in which a believer is justified to defend himself against a bully, or challenge a harmful rumor, or refuse a call soliciting donations to a charity? If Jesus intends by these sayings to teach that His disciples observe an unqualified pacifism, as some people believe, then we must answer in the negative. It would never be permissible in that case to press charges against a thief, or answer a critic, or protect oneself against an abusive spouse, or object to an unjust law. The individual who accepts full-blown pacifism is obliged to say that the American Revolution, justified as an act of civil disobedience against religious oppression, was, in fact, fundamentally ungodly. Further, one would have to admit that Christianity allows for no legal recourse in any case of injustice. Pacifism is certainly a slippery-slope, one I daresay our Lord never commanded.

What, then, does the Sermon on the Mount mean when it urges us to "turn the other cheek," etc.? It means that in most cases, a believer should be ready to deny personal ease and comfort for the greater good of the kingdom of God. Consider the actions of the meek and lowly Lamb of God when he went to the cross.

When our Lord stood before false accusations and was condemned to death, He meekly went *"as a sheep to the slaughter and like a lamb dumb before his shearer, so He opened not His mouth"* (Acts 8:32). Though the Lord Jesus had every right to defend Himself, yet He never spoke a word in His own defense, for He aimed for a goal greater than self-protection and self-preservation.

That is really the key to understanding the admonition to "turn to [the man that smites you on the right cheek] the other also" and the other similar statements. Christian people should be so committed to the greater good of the kingdom of God that they are willing to endure personal inconvenience, loss, and even mistreatment for sake of the gospel of Christ.

No doubt, this is the context in which we are to interpret the exhortation concerning interpersonal conflicts we may face with unbelievers: "*Agree with thine adversary quickly, whiles thou art in the way with him; lest at any time the adversary deliver thee to the judge, and the judge deliver thee to the officer, and thou be cast into prison. Verily, I say unto thee, Thou shalt by no means come out thence, till thou hast paid the uttermost farthing*" (Mt. 5:25-26). The Lord means, "Settle disputes with your neighbors quickly before it goes to court and before anger has the opportunity to intensify to volcanic strength, because once it reaches that point, your entire life may be preoccupied with the attempt to resolve the conflict, distracting you from the greater business of the kingdom of God."

Paul likely has this same principle in mind when he scolds church members in the Corinthian Church for pursuing litigation with other believers: "*Why do ye not rather take wrong? Why do ye not suffer yourselves to be defrauded? Nay, you do wrong, and defraud, and that your brethren*" (1 Cor. 6:7b-8). The greater good in view is the church of Christ. It is even more important than a personal slight or injustice. When responding to mistreatment, a Christian must always weigh this issue of the potential harm that may come to the cause of Christ as a result of defending personal rights. That is the thrust of our Lord's teaching in the Sermon on the Mount.

Does that mean, however, that it is wrong to impose boundaries, protect oneself, or speak in one's own defense? No. Even Paul the apostle spoke in his own defense before Felix, Festus and Agrippa (cf. Acts 24-26), as well as Nero's court (cf. 2 Tim. 4:16). Further, when the Roman centurion proceeded to beat him, Paul took steps to circumvent such unjust treatment, asking, "*Is it lawful for you to scourge a man that is a Roman, and uncondemned?*" (Acts 22:25). It wasn't lawful, and because he spoke up, the beating didn't happen.

David, likewise, fled from jealous King Saul when he discovered that Saul planned to kill him. He did not respond in kind, for this young man of godly integrity would not dare lift his hand against God's anointed, but he still took steps to avoid the mistreatment.

These Biblical examples suffice to establish that the Lord does not intend for His followers to set themselves up as a punching bag for abuse. Believers should never court persecution, but should use sound judgment to avoid putting themselves in a position of threat or danger. Though we may not control the actions of other people, we are responsible to control the degree to which they might hinder us from serving Jesus Christ and doing what He has called us to do.

Someone has wisely quipped that "the triple A" recipe for healthy-mindedness involves avoiding, accepting, and adapting. It begins with the need to *avoid.* There are some situations, and people, in this life that simply need to be avoided. Avoiding conflict and occasion for trouble, as much as possible, is a biblical principle, by the way (cf. 2 Ths. 3:6; Titus 3:10; Rom. 16:17; 1 Pet. 2:11; 1 Ths. 5:22). Notice that the Holy Spirit does not encourage us to persecute these people or to seek to harm them in any way, but simply to back away and refuse to participate.

Next, we must *accept.* Some circumstances cannot be altered and mental health springs from acceptance. But what about those inevitable situations in life where mistreatment is inescapable? How should a Christian respond? He must *adapt* and adjust to the difficult circumstances. Two particular Psalms speak poignantly to this matter of adaptation to personal mistreatment.

Psalm 37 – Meekly Wait on the Lord

Psalm 37 is written for people who feel to be on the wrong side of the scales of justice. When it seems that "truth is on the scaffold and wrong is on the throne," this precious passage offers wise counsel in the form of several negatives and positives. We might entitle Psalm 37 "The Do's and Don'ts When Wrong is Winning."

Interestingly, the tone of the Psalm is one of calmness, not panic or hysteria. It is written by David in his mature years: "*I have been young, and now am old,*" he says, "*yet have I not seen the righteous forsaken, nor his seed begging bread*" (v. 25). He writes words of calm wisdom, ripened by long experience. It is evident that the many changes and challenges of life have not soured him. To all who feel to be mistreated as a victim of injustice; to those who sense that wickedness is the rule and righteousness the exception, David's seasoned, steady advice in this Psalm speaks with unique relevance.

What counsel does the Psalmist offer you? Negatively speaking, he points to three particular attitudes to avoid. He says, first, ***Don't Get Uptight***. *"Fret not thyself because of evildoers, neither be thou envious against the workers of iniquity* (v. 1). He repeats the imperative again in verses 7 and 8: "*…fret not thyself because of him who prospereth in his way, because of the man who bringeth wicked devices to pass…fret not thyself in any wise to do evil."*

"Fret not" means "do not be frustrated, agitated, or irritable." The term means "to be vexed in spirit" or "to chafe with inner turmoil" and speaks of a kind of gnawing or eating away. In Leviticus 13, a "fretting leprosy" is a kind of contagious disease that ate away at human flesh or structural component.

Public enemy number one to the individual who is suffering some form of injustice is the temptation to become so preoccupied with the occasion of distress that it completely overwhelms the thought-life and destroys inner peace. Christ alone has exclusive rights to my heart and no one or nothing else has authority to displace Him from that place. The admonition to *"Sanctify the Lord God in your hearts"* (1 Pet. 3:15) is given in a context of biblical counsel to people who are being persecuted for righteousness' sake, and means to make sure that He and He alone occupies the central place in your soul. To the extent that the believer is obsessed with inner turmoil, the Lord Jesus Christ has been unseated from the throne of the heart.

Secondly, David counsels, ***Don't Panic***. The imperative to "wait patiently" in verse 7, coupled with the reassurance that God "will bring it to pass" in verse 5 suggests that it is important to resist the urge to panic when injustice appears to prevail.

It has been my experience that impulsive action fueled by the sense that "I need to do something and I need to do it now" has proved to be an occasion of serious regret. Paul counseled Timothy to "watch thou in all things," or literally, "keep your head" when the time of apostasy comes and men no longer endure sound doctrine (2 Tim. 4:5). He says, in essence, "Timothy, when other people are losing their minds and embracing every new idea that comes down the pike, do not lose yours. Keep your head. Stay cool. Remain calm. Think things through. Do nothing rashly."

Interestingly, Peter offers the same Divinely-inspired counsel in the 1 Peter 3 passage on persecution for righteousness' sake: *"But and if ye suffer for righteousness' sake, happy are ye: and be not afraid of their terror, neither be troubled"* (1 Pet. 3:14). Don't be intimidated with fear or allow your persecutors to agitate you heart, he says. Take a deep breath, calm down, remember who your God is, and think the situation through.

Thirdly, he advises, ***Don't Lose Your Temper.*** *"Cease from anger, and forsake wrath: fret not thyself in any wise to do evil"* (v. 8). It is true that injustice inevitably occasions feelings of anger, and one would have to be subhuman to avoid the emotion. It is not wrong to be angry (in fact, anger at sin is justified), but it is dangerous to allow anger to seethe and simmer to the point that it leads you into sinful behavior yourself.

Ephesians 4:26 makes the same point: *"Be angry and sin not: let not the sun go down upon your wrath."* I admit, in all candor, that it is impossible for me to think about the ungodliness of the modern world and the unjust laws passed by politicians without feeling righteously indignant. What bible believer does not experience the anger of injustice when men turn biblical values topsy-turvy, calling good evil and evil good, putting darkness for light and light for darkness, and bitter for sweet and sweet for bitter (cf. Is. 5:20)?

But what if I allowed that righteous anger to simmer to the point that I exploded in some form of volcanic, vigilante rage? What if I took matters into my own hand to right perceived wrongs? Would I be justified, as a follower of the Lord Jesus Christ, to allow someone else's wrong to lead me to do wrong myself?

Both David and Paul answer negatively. And James agrees: *"The wrath of man worketh not the righteousness of God"* (Jas. 1:20). Each would warn, "Do not allow your anger over someone else's indiscretion to tempt you to commit a similar sin. Fret not thyself in any wise to do evil." Instead, Paul says, keep short accounts with God when you feel angry. Deal with it by sundown and refuse to pick it up again tomorrow. Anger accrued from day to day becomes a spirit of bitterness that negatively affects both the person who harbors it and everyone with whom that individual comes into contact (cf. Heb. 12:15).

So, the Psalmist David offers counsel to the mistreated individual in terms of three "don'ts." But what does he have to say in positive terms? What are we to "do" when wrong appears to be winning? We may glean at least four positive directives from Psalm 37. These comprise the "how" of the three "don'ts" previously detailed.

First, he says, ***Make up your mind to do the right thing and leave the consequences to the Lord.*** "*Trust in the Lord, and do good; so shalt thou dwell in the land, and verily thou shalt be fed*" (v. 3). Regardless of the other party's audacity, arrogance and apparent impunity, you continue to do what is right. Though you may be tempted to query, "*Lord, what shall this man do?*", His reply to you is what it has always been, "*What is that to thee? Follow thou me*" (cf. Jno. 21:21-22). Do right, even if no one else is doing it. That's God's holy call upon your life.

Secondly, David counsels, ***Find your joy and happiness in the Lord.*** "*Delight thyself also in the Lord; and He shall give thee the desires of thine heart*" (v. 4). Though you have no cause for delight in your current circumstances, you have every reason to find delight in the Lord. Shift focus for a moment off the current distress and reflect on His glorious character and the wonderful works that He has done. Is He your heavenly Father who delights to hear your voice in prayer? Is Jesus Christ the Lamb for sinners slain, the Savior of your soul? Is He your Great High Priest who at this very moment intercedes at the Father's right hand on your behalf? Has He promised to be with you always, even to the end of the world? Is He the Creator of the universe, the sovereign Ruler of the skies, the God with whom nothing is impossible? Does He hold the king's heart in his hand, turning it as rivers of water, whithersoever He wills? With such a God and Savior, the believer can live in this dark world with sunshine in his soul.

I suspect that when we make the Lord the object of our desire and delight, the desires of our hearts soon become the desires of His heart for us. There are a thousand inexhaustible delights to be found in the Lord Jesus Christ, in the wake of which joys every earthly dream disappears into the fog of insignificance. The hymnwriter put it best:

Turn your eyes upon Jesus,
Look full in His wonderful face;
And the things of earth will grow strangely dim,
In the light of His glory and grace.[1]

Thirdly, he urges the mistreated soul, **Entrust your future to your capable God** *"Commit thy way unto the Lord; trust also in him; and he shall bring it to pass"* (v. 5). Though any hope for the immediate future may look bleak and grim, Christ is able to part the dark clouds of circumstance and restore your soul. He is the God who makes all things new (Rev. 21:5). Inward fretting and fear dissipates when the Christian stops attempting to control every circumstance and rests in the knowledge that "my times are in His hand" (cf. Ps. 31:15).

Is He trustworthy? Absolutely. Paul knew that Christ was faithful to keep His promise, wise to precisely what was needed in each situation, powerful to defeat every problem, and loving, having His child's best interest at heart at all times. In confident faith, he exclaimed, *"For I know whom I have believed and am persuaded that He is able to keep that which I have committed unto Him against that day"* (2 Tim. 1:12). Do you trust Him with your future?

Finally, the Psalmist counsels, **Wait patiently upon the Lord to work** *"Rest in the Lord, and wait patiently for him..."* (v. 7a). In the knowledge of Jehovah's sovereign character, gifts of grace and precious promises, there is rest for the weary: *"Thou wilt keep him in perfect peace whose mind is stayed upon Thee, because he trusteth in Thee"* (Is. 26:3). In such a state of sweet repose, we may trust Him to work in answer to the prayers and petitions of His beloved child in a way that will be to our good and His glory.

---

[1] Helen H. Lemmel, 1922.

Know, however, that His timing is always best. He may not answer your need immediately. He is never in such a hurry as we are. If he tarries to respond to you, be sure that He does so in order to demonstrate an even greater blessing as the need grows greater: "*And therefore will the Lord wait, that He may be gracious unto you, and therefore will He be exalted, that He may have mercy upon you: for the Lord is a God of judgment: blessed are all they that wait for Him*" (Is. 30:18).

Be careful, then, not to rush before Him to manufacture your own solution or you will only complicate the problem: "*Who is among you that feareth the Lord and that obeyeth the voice of His servant, that walketh in darkness and hath no light? Let him trust in the name of the Lord and stay upon his God. Behold, all ye that kindle a fire, that compass yourselves about with sparks: walk in the light of your fire, and in the sparks that ye have kindled. This shall ye have of mine hand; ye shall lie down in sorrow*" (Is. 50:10-11). Just ask Abraham and Sarah how their hasty conspiracy to help God fulfill His promise complicated not only their life, but all subsequent history.

In another Psalm, David remembers such a season of waiting on the Lord. With 20/20 hindsight, he reflects on the fact that patient waiting for God to work brought an incredible blessing: "*I waited patiently for the Lord; and He inclined unto me, and heard my cry. He brought me up also out of a horrible pit, out of the miry clay, and set my feet upon a rock, and established my goings. And He hath put a new song in my mouth, even praise to our God: many shall see it, and fear, and shall trust in the Lord*" (Ps. 40:1-3). Indeed, every trial and unpleasant circumstance is merely temporary (cf. Ps. 37:2, 9a, 10, 35-36). This, too, shall pass. When the Lord is pleased to work to relieve your distress, you too will sing a new song and others will be drawn closer to Him by virtue of His mighty deliverance in your life.

Psalm 37 counsels the victim of injustice and mistreatment to be focused on the Lord (v. 4), be content with your circumstances (v. 16), be godly in spite of the apparent fact that others seem to get away with wrongdoing (v. 27), and trust a Just God to right every wrong in His time (vs. 12-13, 14-15, 20, 28, 32-33, 38). In a word, **meekness** is the right response to mistreatment.

What is meekness? Meekness is self-effacing non-aggression. It is that virtue that resists the fallen tendency to "look out for old number one," pursue self-interest or assert oneself above others. Instead, the meek person is content to occupy a place of humility because he/she has found peace in the Lord and learned to trust Him to meet every need according to His wise and loving heart.

Is the meek person a pushover, then? No. Meekness is strength under control. The picture is of a wild stallion whose energy has been harnessed so that it may now be used productively. Moses, who was anything but weak, was called the meekest man on earth because he calmly and submissively obeyed the Lord, doing what was right, trusting in Him to work His will in His perfect time.

But, someone objects, won't the self-assertive individual take advantage of the meek individual? No; Psalm 37 promises that the meek individual will not be the loser, victimized forever by injustice. Instead, *"the meek shall inherit the earth; and shall delight themselves in the abundance of peace"* (v. 11). In the end, the individual who does what is right even when others seem to be getting away with sin, will be the winner, not the loser (cf. v. 37). So, keep on doing the right thing, finding your joy in your God, and trusting Him to balance the scales of justice in His time and His way. That's the wise counsel offered every one who feels to be the victim of injustice in Psalm 37.

Psalm 35 – Leave Vengeance to the Lord

One more word of divine counsel to the individual who feels to be on the short end of justice is necessary. Simply put, it is "leave the execution of any justice to the Lord." You will find this important principle spelled out in Psalm 35.

Psalm 35 is an imprecatory Psalm. An imprecation is a curse, the antithesis of a benediction. Other imprecatory Psalms include Psalm 5, 58, 64, 69, 79, 82, 83, and 94. In each of these Psalms, the sacred writer appeals to the justice of God against his enemies, praying for God to vindicate the righteous and judge the wicked.

I must admit that for the longest time, I did not understand these passages of Scripture. In fact, the tone of biblical imprecations sounded very foreign to the spirit of the New Testament, the spirit of love and mercy and grace. Several personal experiences in which I have felt to be unjustly wounded by the sins and indiscretions of other people, however, together with a keener awareness of many circumstances in the broader world in which it seems that "wrong is on the throne while right is teetering on the scaffold," have served to open the eyes of my understanding to the appropriateness of these biblical passages.

Would it surprise you if I said that an appeal to God for justice is not inconsistent with a proper understanding of His grace and mercy? In fact, God never extends mercy at the expense of His justice. He does not violate His own law in the process of forgiving sinners. The cross is the ultimate proof of this principle.

Someone asked why Jesus had to die on the cross. Why didn't God just forgive the sins of His elect saying, "I'll just forget about it and pretend it never happened?" The answer is that God must act contrary to His own character to do so. He would be unrighteous to simply "wipe the slate clean" and let the guilty go free.

We understand this principle when we witness it on the human level. When a judge, perhaps on a legal technicality or an undercover bribe, permits a guilty man to walk free, a general consensus that a travesty of justice has occurred ripples through the populace. There is a public outcry that the law has not been upheld.

Likewise, if God had simply said to guilty sinners "I forgive you," He must do so at the expense of His own law. This is one of the dominant motifs of Paul's letter to the *Romans*. The New Testament book of *Romans* is a classic example of a literary genre called *theodicy*, a justification, or defense, of God against the charge of injustice. The key verse for this motif is Romans 3:4: "*Let God be true, but every man a liar; as it is written, That thou mightest be justified in thy sayings, and mightest overcome when thou art judged.*"

Over and again, Paul addresses the question, "Is God unrighteous?" and answers with a resounding "no." Is God unrighteous to take vengeance on sinners? He answers no, *"for how [then] shall God judge the world"* (Rom. 3:5-6). Is God unrighteous to forgive the sins of His people who lived prior to the actual legal payment for sin on the cross? Again, he responds no, for God made a covenant and cannot break His word (Rom. 3:24-26). Is God unrighteous to choose some and bypass others in the covenant of grace? He replies in Romans 9:14, "God forbid," for God is sovereign and not obligated to any man. In Romans 10, the question is "Is God unrighteous to grant gospel blessings to the Gentiles but judge the Jews with judicial blindness?" Paul, again, replies in the negative, for God was very longsuffering to give the Jews opportunity after opportunity to receive the message and they rejected it (Rom. 10:20-21).

But, far and away, the primary question Paul addresses in *Romans* is this one: "Is God unrighteous to count ungodly sinners righteous?" How could He do so without violating His own righteous law? Paul's reply is simply, "Yes, God is righteous to forgive sinners because He satisfied the legal demands of His justice by means of the substitutionary sacrifice of the Lord Jesus Christ." Romans 5:8-9 expresses the good news poignantly: "*But God commendeth his love toward us, in that, while we were yet sinners, Christ died for us. Much more then, being now justified by his blood, we shall be saved from wrath through him.*"

That means that because the Lord Jesus took the place on the cross that belonged to each of God's elect, bearing the punishment due to their sins, the wrath of God against them has been satiated, and the law of God has been satisfied. They are now justified, declared to be righteous, by virtue of the imputation of Christ's righteousness to their account.

The two antithetical principles "mercy and truth" (or justice), then, "are met together" and now live in perfect harmony in and through the finished work of our Lord Jesus Christ (cf. Ps. 85:10). God did not violate His own law in order to extend mercy to sinful people.

Likewise, the imprecatory prayers of the Bible, such as Psalm 35, are not inconsistent with the spirit of the gospel, any more than the triumphant song of the saints in Revelation 19 is inconsistent with the spirit of the gospel. The redeemed throng in Revelation 19 are singing the "Hallelujah Chorus" not in praise to God for salvation from sin but for His holy justice: "*Alleluia…for true and righteous are his judgments: for he hath judged the great whore, which did corrupt the earth with her fornication, and hath avenged the blood of his servants at her hand*" (Rev. 19:1-2). Those who love righteousness will also despise the opposite of righteousness and rejoice when the scales of justice are balanced (cf. Ps. 5:4-5; 11:7; 33:5; 45:7; 139:22). The antipathy toward sin and evil we feel is not a personal malice or some psychotic desire to watch people suffer, but a yearning for the vindication of God's righteous name and law. What a happy day it will be when every enemy is trampled beneath the feet of King Jesus (cf. 1 Cor. 15:25-26)!

When we suffer mistreatment in our lives, therefore, it is not wrong to appeal to a just God for justice. That is precisely what the Psalmist David does in Psalm 35: "*Plead my cause, O Lord, with them that strive with me: fight against them that fight against me…Let them be confounded and put to shame that seek after my soul: let them be turned back and brought to confusion that devise my hurt*" (Ps. 35:1, 4). He takes his angst to the Lord in prayer, enlisting a just God in his righteous cause.

He complains that "*False witnesses did rise up; they laid to my charge things that I knew not. They rewarded me evil for good to the spoiling of my soul*" (35:11). Then David adds, "*But as for me, when they were sick, my clothing was sackcloth: I humbled my soul with fasting; and my prayer returned into mine own bosom.*" He sincerely felt the burden in his heart for this individual's wellbeing, praying for God's mercy. Yet his kindness was rewarded with perjurious slander aimed to destroy him.

When did David suffer such an injustice? No doubt, he refers to that period in his life in which he lived as a fugitive, chased like a hunter hunting a quail by jealous King Saul. People he once deemed his friends now turned against him, making him the subject of rumor and hearsay, assuming the worst about him, i.e. that he was a revolutionary attempting to overthrow Saul as king and that he had made an alliance with Israel's enemies, and repeating the gossip to others. And it grieved him in his heart.

Where could he go but to the Lord? Only a just God could repair the damage done to his reputation by such vicious slander. Confident that he was righteous and that he had done nothing wrong, David now appeals to God to rise to his defense. He cries, "*Lord, how long wilt thou look on? Rescue my soul from their destructions, my darling from the lions...let not them that are mine enemies wrongfully rejoice over me: neither let them wink with the eye that hate me without a cause...This thou hast seen, O Lord: keep not silence: O Lord, be not far from me*" (35:17, 19, 22). His prayer is "*Stir up thyself, and awake to my judgment, even unto my cause, my God and my Lord*" (35:23). He is praying for justice because he feels to be the victim of injustice and knows that God is a just God.

This is the meaning of the New Testament exhortations to forgive those that trespass against us. Contrary to popular opinion, forgiveness is not a matter of forgetting that someone wronged you, for, short of some physiological disease that results in the loss of memory, forgetting an offense is not possible. A human being cannot simply erase his/her memory bank. But forgiveness is a matter of turning the adjudication of justice over to God and God alone. To forgive means to refuse to become judge and jury, executing punishment on the offender, taking matters into your own hands via some vigilante act, getting even. It means leaving vengeance to the Lord.

You see, the Lord knows the details of the case even better than you or I do. He knows if an injustice has, in fact, occurred. And He knows the dynamic that led to the offense. He is aware of which party is the true victim and which party is the perpetrator. Further, He knows if extenuating circumstances should be considered that may have led to the current situation.

It is for this reason that Paul advises us to "*Judge nothing before the time, until the Lord come, who both will bring to light the hidden things of darkness, and will make manifest the counsels of the hearts: and then shall every man have praise of God*" (1 Cor. 4:5). Our God is a righteous Judge. He does not, yea, He cannot err (Cf. Deut. 32:4). Moses learned by revelation that even though Jehovah is merciful, gracious, longsuffering and abundant in goodness and truth, yet "*He will by no means clear the guilty"* (Ex. 34:6-7). And the prophet Nahum reminds us that God *"will not at all acquit the wicked"* (Nah. 1:3). Every wrong will be made right, either in this world or at the resurrection of the just. No one will ever get away with wrongdoing.

Forgiveness means that you refuse to live in the future as a victim of the past. It means that you will no longer be controlled by yesterday's pain. It has to do with the *"be harmless as doves"* imperative in Jesus' wise counsel to His disciples (Mt. 10:16). Exacting justice on an alleged offender, getting even, or doing unto others what they did unto you, is not your business. That belongs to the Lord.

But there is also a place for the other side of our Lord's counsel, i.e. *"Be wise as serpents,"* in the lives of those who have been mistreated. Both harmlessness and wisdom are important. The Puritan Thomas Watson strikes the balance well:

> We must have the innocence of the dove—that we may not harm others; and we must have the wisdom of the serpent—that others may not harm us. We must have the innocence of the dove—that we may not betray the truth; and the wisdom of the serpent—that we may not betray ourselves. In short, innocence without wisdom is too weak to be safe. Wisdom without innocence is too subtle to be good. When wisdom and innocence appear together, they preview the soul's happiness.[2]

So, if you have, in fact, been victimized by someone else's mistreatment, take it to the Lord in prayer. Ask Him to defend you. Petition the High Court of Divine Justice for a remedy. Flee to your Rock of refuge and hide yourself, if you must. But leave the adjudication of justice to a God who knows all and does all things well. You can trust Him to take care of your case.

---

[2] http://www.gracegems.org/Watson/wise_as_serpents.htm

9
A Conscience Void of Offense
Forgiveness for the Guilty

"And herein do I exercise myself to have always a conscience void of offense toward God, and toward men" Acts 24:16

The conscience is God's watchman in the soul. Its function is to monitor and register behavior. Like Mr. Recorder in Bunyan's *Holy War*, whose voice shook the whole town of Mansoul with words like thunder-claps, the conscience passes judgment from within the heart of man according to what it believes to be right and true. In a vivid reference to the conscience, Solomon said, *"The spirit of man is the candle of the Lord, searching all the inward parts of the belly"* (Pro. 20:27).

Conscience is a God-given, internal control by which a man is distinguished from an animal as a creature made in God's image. The root of the word, *science*, speaks of "knowledge." The prefix *con* means "with." Conscience, then, is knowledge with oneself, or knowledge from within. Man is created, in other words, with an innate knowledge, a capacity from within to scrutinize and pass judgment on himself. The Puritan John Trapp expressed the function of conscience when he said, "Conscience is God's spy and man's overseer."

As the resident "judge" within the heart, conscience either *"accuses or excuses"* (Rom. 2:14). When it "excuses" or vindicates, the individual experiences joy: *"For our rejoicing is this, the testimony of our conscience, that in simplicity and godly sincerity...we have had our conversation in the world, and more abundantly to you-ward"* (2 Cor. 1:12). When it "accuses" or convicts (Jno. 8:9), the individual experiences bitter agony of heart: *"And Peter remembered the words of Jesus... 'Before the cock crow, thou shalt deny me thrice.' And he went out, and wept bitterly"* (Mt. 26:75).

Because the pain of a guilty conscience is so intense, Paul made it his ambition to conduct himself in such a way that his conscience would be clear. A clear conscience, *"toward God and toward man,"* is inexpressibly sweet. It makes the step nimble and the burden light. An offended conscience, however, is unspeakably bitter. It makes one's going "staid and slow" and complicates the ordinary cares of life by a preoccupation with guilt and regret. Everyone who has ever lived with a defiled conscience knows the reality of Solomon's words: *"Heaviness in the heart of man maketh it stoop"* (Pro. 12:25a).

Arguably, one of the best illustrations of a guilty conscience is Edgar Allan Poe's 1843 short-story entitled "The Tell-Tale Heart." The story is told by an anonymous narrator who labors to convince his hearers that he is not mad, or insane. He had murdered an old man living in his house and carefully hidden the corpse beneath the planks of the floor. Shortly thereafter, three police officers knocked at his door. A neighbor had heard a shriek of terror and called the police, who came to search the premises. They were calmly welcomed, admitted to the house, and informed that the sound heard by the neighbor was due to a bad dream. He explains:

> The old man, I mentioned, was absent in the country. I took my visitors all over the house. I bade them search—search well. I led them, at length, to his chamber. I showed them his treasures, secure, undisturbed. In the enthusiasm of my confidence, I brought chairs into the room, and desired them here to rest from their fatigues, while I myself, in the wild audacity of my perfect triumph, placed my own seat upon the very spot beneath which reposed the corpse of the victim.

His calm demeanor satisfied the officers. So, the matter was dropped and friendly conversation took its place. It wasn't long, however, until the pleasantries ended. The narrative continues:

> But, ere long, I felt myself getting pale and wished them gone. My head ached, and I fancied a ringing in my ears: but still they sat and still chatted. The ringing became more distinct: it continued and became more distinct: I talked more freely to get rid of the feeling:

but it continued and gained definiteness until, at length, I found that the noise was not within my ears.

No doubt I now grew very pale; but I talked more fluently, and with a heightened voice. Yet the sound increased, and what could I do? It was a low, dull, quick sound, much such a sound as a watch makes when enveloped in cotton. I gasped for breath, and yet the officers heard it not. I talked more quickly, more vehemently; but the noise steadily increased. I arose and argued about trifles, in a high key and with violent gesticulations; but the noise steadily increased. Why would they not be gone? I paced the floor to and fro with heavy strides, as if excited to fury by the observations of the men but the noise steadily increased. Oh God! what could I do? I foamed – I raved – I swore! I swung the chair upon which I had been sitting, and grated it upon the boards, but the noise arose over all and continually increased. It grew louder, *louder*, ***louder***! And still the men chatted pleasantly, and smiled. Was it possible they heard not? Almighty God! – no, no! They heard! They suspected! They knew! They were making a mockery of my horror! This I thought, and this I think. But anything was better than this agony! Anything was more tolerable than this derision! I could bear those hypocritical smiles no longer! I felt that I must scream or die! And now – again! –hark! louder! *louder*! ***louder***! ***Louder***!

"Villains!" I shrieked, "dissemble no more! I admit the deed! Tear up the planks! Here, here! It is the beating of his hideous heart!"

Was the victim's heart really beating beneath the floor? No. The sound the murderous man heard was his own guilty conscience. He could not escape the thunderous roaring of his own heart until, at last, he incriminated himself.

Though the typical person's struggle with guilt is not quite as dramatic as this, the sense of being hunted, inability to escape the haunting fear of being found out, and intense desire to escape shame is indigenous to the guilty conscience.

In *Whatever Became of Sin?*, the widely-acclaimed 1973 book by psychiatrist Dr. Karl Menninger, the author stresses that every person in every church congregation is "worried about something…health, finances, family relations…threats, rumors, bad news from afar, and especially guilt feelings." He writes,

> Mrs. A in the front pew is thinking about her sister who is better off than she but has cancer. There has been a queer twist in her envy. Mrs. B nearby has three children, two of whom have to be taken to the dentist this week, a great expense which is going to anger her husband and disarrange their summer plans. Besides which she is worried about some deceptions. Miss C has no children to worry about and no husband to be angered, but why doesn't she have them? She wonders what is wrong with her that she doesn't have a husband and children. Perhaps, she reasons, it is because of something she can't bear to recall. Mr. D is dreading tomorrow when the bank examiners come again; will they notice?…[1]

Is it any wonder Paul "exercised" (lit. trained, disciplined) himself to maintain a pure conscience? A conscience in which there is no cause for offense liberates for energetic labor and unimpaired usefulness in Christ's service: "*Beloved, if our heart condemn us not, then have we confidence toward God. And whatsoever we ask, we receive of him, because we keep his commandments, and do those things that are pleasing in his sight*" (1 Jno. 3:21-22). Nothing is more essential than that the believer live in such a way that he will have no cause for regret.

The best way to deal with sin in your life, in other words, is to prevent it (Ps. 119:11; 1 Jno. 2:1). But what may be said to the individual who has not exercised diligence to live with a clean conscience? Is there any hope for the person who lives every day with vain regret over past sins, or the person who continues to offend his/her conscience by ongoing surrender to temptation? Is there hope for people who feel guilty every day?

---

[1] Karl Menninger, M.D., *Whatever Became of Sin?*, p. 194.

Indeed, there is hope. Hope for those who struggle with subjective feelings of guilt is really a matter of understanding and embracing two important biblical concepts: *repentance* and *forgiveness*. Let's discuss repentance first.

Repentance: Path to Restoration

As the concept of "sin" has fallen on hard times, so has the biblical concept of repentance. The fallen nature of a person does not like to be told that he is wrong and doesn't see a need, consequently, for change. But repentance is not a hard doctrine. It is a soul-cheering, happy and hopeful theme. The fact that God gives His erring child space to turn around and to return to Him—that He doesn't operate on the principle "one strike and you're out"—is good news to sensible sinners.

The term "repentance" derives from the Greek word *metanoia* meaning "to change the mind." In military imagery, it involves performing an "about face." So repentance is a change of mind that issues in a change of direction. In particular terms, repentance is a process that involves four primary components: *conviction, confession, commitment,* and *consecration.* We will address them in order.

Conviction: Calling Sin "Sin"

In the title previously referenced,[2] Dr. Menninger laments the refusal of popular culture to call sin "sin." Menninger's main thesis is that morally wrong behavior (what the Bible calls "sin") is a matter of personal responsibility, not clinical classification. And he deplores the disappearance of the moral concept of sin from popular culture, particularly in the context of psychotherapy and other medical disciplines, and even from the pulpit. The reclassification of sin as sickness or criminality, he argues, robs the preacher in the pulpit of any voice of moral authority.

It may be that preachers are more blameworthy than the secular professionals for soft-peddling sin in modern culture. They certainly

---

[2] Menninger, *Whatever Became of Sin?*

possess greater potential for exercising a moral authority over people. Menninger writes:

> No psychiatrists or psychotherapists, even those with many patients, have the quantitative opportunity to cure souls and mend minds which the preacher enjoys. And the preacher also has a superb opportunity to do what few psychiatrists can, to prevent the development of chronic anxiety, depression, and other mental ills.[3]

Yet, in far too many cases, Menninger argues, the modern sermon fails to deal with sin, either generally or particularly. He writes about the preacher who faces a congregation of worried people—worried, that is, about "health, finances, family relations, impending decisions, threats, rumors, bad news from afar, and especially guilt feelings":

> What shall he say to these people? Scold them? Warn them? Tell them that he is worried, too? Bless them and urge them to pray? Promise them peace? Should he, like Moses, cover his face so as not to look too holy? God is good, he could remind them; God means well for all of us; He has promised us His grace; He has forgiven us already. It is darkest just before dawn. So the Lord bless you and keep you…make His face to shine…and please, will you all come back again next week?[4]

Menninger editorializes, "The clergyman cannot minimize sin and maintain his proper role in our culture…We need him as our umpire to direct us, to accuse us, to reproach us, to exhort us, to intercede for us, to shrive us. Failure to do so is *his* sin."[5]

Dr. Menninger makes a lot of sense. I agree with his basic argument and thank God that such a reputable secular professional dared to highlight this issue. I do wish he had defined "sin," however, in Biblical rather than secular terms.

---

[3] Karl Menninger, M.D., *Whatever Became of Sin?*, p. 201.
[4] Ibid. p. 195.
[5] Ibid. p. 198. (Italics original).

The entire book operates on the premise that sin is mere "human misbehavior toward people or the environment." On the contrary, God's word defines "sin" in terms of an offense against God via violation of His moral law. Menninger's definition, in other words, views "sin" on a strictly horizontal level. Scripture, however, describes it as a vertical problem.

Does it really make a difference, someone queries? Indeed, it does. It is the difference between a man-centered and a God-centered approach to life in this world. In fact, the irony of Dr. Menninger's book is that at the very moment he lobbies for the rediscovery of an emphasis on sin in modern society, he inadvertently encourages his readers to suppress it by means of his refusal to define it in God-centered terms.

Let me explain. Sin is essentially man's declaration of independence from God. By its very nature, sin is man-centered. Someone has said that the letter "I" is at the heart of the word "sin" for a reason—because sin is essentially selfishness. When Adam transgressed God's law in the Garden of Eden, he said, in effect, "I don't want to do what God said; I want to do what I want." So sin is basically man's effort to elevate self above God, to be his own god—the master of his own fate and the captain of his own soul.

By defining sin only in terms of the pain human behavior causes to other people or the damage human irresponsibility does to the environment—that is, by defining sin in purely man-centered terms without any consideration of man's responsibility to God and relationship with Him—Menninger unwittingly falls into the very trap he condemns in contemporary society.

Many folk make the same mistake as the learned doctor. If one's primary emphasis in addressing the problems with which people struggle is to maximize personal happiness or improve someone's self-concept, then no ultimate progress toward dealing with guilt will be made. Dr. Jay Adams writes:

Much change that is offered today in counseling—even in the name of Christ—is sub-Christian. Aimed at little more than making counselees happier, it neglects the basic reason why a believer must change: to please God. As if God's glory were of secondary importance, His Name's sake is omitted from the picture, out of deference to better health or a more smoothly running marriage. Such considerations, not wrong in themselves, are quite wrong when they are not subordinated to the greater purpose of pleasing and honoring God.[6]

All sin—both "Saturday night" and "Sunday morning" sins[7]—is ultimately against God, an act of cosmic treason against His right to govern our lives (Ps. 51:4). I cannot stress enough just how basic and essential it is for the guilty sinner to understand that his/her relationship with God takes priority over everything else. If God is not pleased with your behavior, attitudes and decisions, no attempt to deal with what Dr. Menninger calls "sin" will affect a positive or permanent change in personal peace or happiness. Nothing is more important than to recognize that sin separates a person from fellowship with God (Is. 59:2). Unless an individual starts here—at the source of a right relationship with Him—the result will be merely a superficial, external change in behavior that does not last, and feelings of guilt will resurface.

Generally speaking,[8] people feel guilty because they are guilty. Subjective guilt feelings, in other words, derive from objective or actual guilt before God.

---

[6] Jay E. Adams, *How to Help People Change*, p. 109.

[7] When most people think of sin, they think only in terms of the "Saturday night" sins of promiscuity, drunkenness, drug addiction, bank robbing, and murder. But "Sunday morning" sins—like pride, broken promises, self-righteousness, jealousy, envy, covetousness, bitterness, and malice—are just as abominable before God.

[8] I suspect that our post-modern culture talks so much about the problem of "false guilt" that it leaves the impression that all guilt is false. On the contrary, I argue here that most guilt is legitimate, but concede that there is such a thing as "false guilt." I suspect, however, that so-called "false guilt" generally stems from an overly-scrupulous conscience, i.e. an unbiblical framework of right/wrong developed, perhaps, in early experience. When people are taught to think something is morally wrong that the Bible does not label as such, then

The biblical term for these subjective feelings of guilt is *conviction*. Conviction of sin is the special work of the Holy Spirit through the word (Jno. 16:8-14). When the prophet Nathan came to David (after his theft of Uriah's wife) with the story of the rich man who took the poor man's one little ewe lamb and the accusation *"Thou art the man!"* (2 Sam. 12:7), the Lord awakened his slumbering conscience to see his monstrous sin in all of its ugliness and shame.

In one of the penitential Psalms, David describes the sensation of suppressed guilt, during the interim between the sinful act and Nathan's confrontation, in terms of inner turmoil: *"When I kept silence, my bones waxed old through my roaring all the day long. For day and night thy hand was heavy upon me: my moisture is turned into the drought of summer"* (Ps. 32:3-4). Notice the negative effect on both psychological and physical health produced by his attempt to silence a guilty conscience. Inward "roaring" and the inescapable sense of God's heavy hand of displeasure led to physical weakness ("...my bones waxed old") and the loss of energy and enthusiasm for life ("...my moisture [lit. strength and vitality] is turned into summer drought").

Unresolved guilt does, in fact, exert a heavy toll on sound health, both in body and mind. Even Sigmund Freud, the noted psychiatrist, lamented in his latter days that he had "underestimated the importance of the destructive (read 'sinful') element in man's psychological constitution—his hate, his envy, his aggressive drive turned outward and inward."[9]

Paul described contrition or conviction of sin in terms of "godly sorrow": *"Godly sorrow worketh repentance unto salvation, not to be repented of: but the sorrow of the world worketh death"* (2 Cor. 7:10). Notice the contrast between genuine conviction, *vis a vis* "godly sorrow," and carnal regret. The first is real remorse due to the dishonor done to God and the pain inflicted on others by the sin. The second is mere regret for the personal shame and inconvenience incurred as a result of the sin. Godly sorrow expresses itself in terms of "I'm sorry for

---

conscience sends a false signal of shame. How important it is that conscience be educated by God's word!

[9] Menninger, p. 202.

the sin"; the sorrow of the world expresses itself in terms of "I'm sorry for myself that I was discovered."

Now, back to King David... David's resolution to the inner turmoil of suppressed guilt began when God broke his heart and convicted him of his sin: He describes the painful experience of conviction in other penitential Psalms:

- Mine inquities are gone over mine head: as a heavy burden they are too heavy for me. My wounds stink and are corrupt because of my foolishness. I am troubled; I am bowed down greatly; I go mourning all the day long. For my loins are filled with a loathsome disease: and there is no soundness in my flesh. I am feeble and sore broken: I have roared by reason of the disquietness of my heart...For I am ready to halt, and my sorrow is continually before me. For I will declare mine iniquity; I will be sorry for my sin (Ps. 38:4-8, 17-18).
- The sacrifices of God are a broken spirit: a broken and a contrite heart, O God, thou wilt not despise (Ps. 51:17).
- My soul is full of troubles: and my life draweth nigh unto the grave...Thou hast laid me in the lowest pit, in darkness, in the deeps. Thy wrath lieth hard upon me, and thou hast afflicted me with all thy waves" (Ps. 88:3, 6-7).

I know of no heart trouble like conviction of sin. Nothing is right in the life of the person who is out of fellowship with God. And yet, the mourner's tear is a happy thing,[10] for it is evidence that the individual belongs to the Lord as one of His children: "*As many as I love, I rebuke and chasten*" (Rev. 3:19a; cf. Heb. 12:6; Ps. 94:12). Further, it is a blessing to mourn because it demonstrates that the Lord has granted repentance to His erring child. Conviction of sin, i.e. the awakening of the conscience to see one's sin in all of its heinousness (though an incredibly painful experience) is the first indication that a person is on the road to repentance and a restored relationship with

---

[10] Jesus said, "Blessed are they that mourn, for they shall be comforted" (Mt. 5:4).

God. There will be no rainbow of reassurance shining in the heavens until the sinner first feels the thunderstorm of conviction deeply in his soul.

Confession: Assuming Personal Responsibility

The next step in the process of biblical repentance is *confession*. After suppressing his guilt for several months, King David responded to the prophet's accusation by confessing his sin to the Lord: "*I acknowledged my sin unto thee, and mine iniquity have I not hid. I said, I will confess my transgressions unto the Lord; and thou forgavest the iniquity of my sin*" (Ps. 32:5). An offended conscience may only find peace when the sinner assumes personal responsibility for his/her sin and admits it, without qualification, to God.

Repentance, in other words, involves more than godly sorrow for sin. The experience of feeling conviction of conscience is not, in itself, the end of the matter, but the beginning. In fact, I suspect that it is precisely at this point that most of us feel a strong temptation to try to circumvent the process and take an illusory short-cut to peace. I call this natural impulse "the Great Cover-up."

Proverbs 28:13 reads, "*He that covereth his sins shall not prosper: but whoso confesseth and forsaketh them shall have mercy.*" The first half of this antithetical couplet warns the individual who attempts to hide his sins from God that his efforts will not be successful. One would think humanity would have learned this lesson by this late date in human history. The very first couple attempted to hide in shame from God after breaking His commandment, sewing themselves aprons of fig-leaves to hide their nakedness (cf. Gen. 3:7-8). The attempt did not work. The only covering for shame they found was in a sacrifice that God graciously provided for them (cf. Gen. 3:21), a powerful foreshadowing of the atonement (lit. "covering") God provided for His elect in the Lord Jesus Christ.

What form does the deceptive attempt to cover-up sin take? First, some people try to deny that the sin ever occurred. The problem with this tactic is that it is nigh impossible to escape the heart-beat of conscience buried beneath the floor planks. Others try to rationalize the sin by downplaying its importance. "I made a mistake," says one person, or "…an error in judgment" says another. Proverbs 16:2 (*"All the ways of a man are right in his own eyes…"*) suggests that people tend to be masters at self-justification. Thirdly, other people tend to shift blame to childhood experiences or some former mistreatment. Adam and Eve were, of course, the first blameshifters, with Adam blaming Eve and Eve blaming the devil. Still others attempt to explain the misdeed in the context of extenuating circumstances: "I was at a very low point in my life…" etc.

But none of these attempts to cover-up sin will be ultimately successful. *"He that covereth his sins shall not prosper."* Confession alone brings the prospect of mercy.

Through Jeremiah, God called the backslidden southern kingdom of Judah to return to Him, the merciful God, and thereby avoid Divine judgment: *"Return, thou backsliding Israel…and I will not cause mine anger to fall upon you: for I am merciful, saith the Lord, and I will not keep anger for ever"* (Jer. 3:12). But what would repentance involve in their case? What did God require of them? The Lord continues: *"Only acknowledge thine iniquity, that thou hast transgressed against the Lord thy God, and hast scattered thy ways to the strangers under every green tree, and ye have not obeyed my voice, saith the Lord"* (v. 13). Only acknowledge thine iniquity. The Lord called upon them to confess their sins, to assume personal responsibility, to be their own accusers.

It is significant that when the Prodigal son returned home, he did not say to his father, "Father, I've made a few mistakes in the past, but I'm home now. So, please don't bring up the past to me; I don't want to talk about it. I'd like my old room back. Let's just act as if this little glitch in our fellowship never happened. I hope everything will be the same as it always was. I mean, no one is perfect. I'm sure you probably made a few bad decisions yourself in the past. So, when is supper?" No, he returned home with no claims to make. He had no expectations of restoration to his former position, but was willing to think it a mercy if he might be permitted to occupy the meanest position of servitude. Humbly and penitently, the lost boy confessed, *"Father, I have sinned against heaven and in thy sight, and am no more worthy*

to be called thy son: make me as one of the hired servants" (Lk. 15:18-19).
That is confession.

Such an admission displays an attitude of humility; further, it
exhibits an understanding of the nature and seriousness of the
offense. If a person (or nation, as in the Jeremiah 3 example) is going
to affect positive change in his life, such an acknowledgment of sin is
crucial. The individual who does not grasp the seriousness of the sin
and the damage it does to others is likely to repeat the offense.

Commitment: Turning from Sin

Still, remorse for and admission of sin do not completely
constitute authentic repentance. Repentance involves a third step: a
resolve or *commitment to forsake the sin.*

Perhaps you noticed that the promise of mercy in Proverbs 28:13
is to the individual who both confesses and forsakes his sins: "...*but
whoso confesseth and forsaketh them shall obtain mercy.*" Admission of the
sin without a deliberate and decisive effort to abandon the practice of
sin will not satisfy the Divine criteria for clemency.

Genuine repentance manifests itself both in terms of intense
visceral sorrow for the pain caused to God and others by sin, and
intense visceral hatred toward the sin that caused such heartache. In 2
Corinthians 7, the apostle Paul catalogs the response of a truly
penitent soul in terms of a new wariness, watchfulness and hatred
toward sin:

> For behold this selfsame thing, that ye sorrowed after a godly sort,
> what *carefulness* it wrought in you, yea, what *clearing of yourselves*, yea,
> what *indignation*, yea, what *fear*, yea, what *vehement desire*, yea what *zeal*,
> yea, what *revenge!* In all these things ye have approved yourselves to
> be clear in this matter. (2 Cor. 7:11 – emphasis mine).

Notice the list of holy passions that attend true repentance.
Carefulness speaks of "eagerness and dedication." Paul encourages the
repentant church at Corinth by pointing to their eagerness to
rededicate themselves to pleasing God. *Clearing of yourselves* suggests

the thought of "giving a defense in terms of correcting the wrong." They wanted to make things right with God.

Indignation speaks of the righteous anger they now felt toward the sin that caused this situation. *Fear* refers to their renewed sense of reverence toward God. It is a healthy fear that takes God seriously and dreads the sin that would offend Him.

Vehement desire means "intense longing" and suggests the idea of an inward yearning to please God and enjoy His fellowship. *Zeal* speaks of enthusiasm to press forward in righteousness and *revenge*, to recover the ground lost because of sin.

This passage reads like a scientific analysis in which the writer explores every conceivable nuance of resolve to turn away from sin, from hatred of the sin to longing for righteousness and renewed enthusiasm for holiness. The individual who knows by experience these passions is wary of falling into the sin again and committed to making a clean break with it. This is the very sentiment expressed by the English poet William Cowper in the classic hymn "Oh, For a Closer Walk With God!" He laments his current backslidden state, comparing it to the spiritual fervor of his earliest love. And then he prays:

> Return, O holy Dove, return,
> Sweet Messenger of rest;
> I hate the sins that made Thee mourn
> And drove me from Thy breast.

Cowper's antipathy toward his sins, then, leads him to resolve to turn from sin:

> The dearest idol I have known,
> Whate'er that idol be,
> Help me to tear it from its throne
> And worship only Thee.

Can you hear his penitent passion in the plea? It reminds me of the renewed commitment to abandon sin expressed in Hosea 14:8: *"Ephraim shall say, What have I to do any more with idols?"* What a happy sickness it is when the little child of God becomes sick of sin and resolves to leave it behind!

Jesus' word to the woman caught in the act of adultery is also His word to you and me: *"Go and sin no more"* (Jno. 8:11). He doesn't say to phase-out sin a little at a time, or try to cutback by fifty-percent. He says, in the words of Isaiah 1:17, *"Cease to do evil; learn to do well."* Notice that the development of new, godly, biblical habits is a discipline. It is something that must be learned and developed over time. But there is no "learning curve" applied to the cessation of sin. The Lord simply says to "stop it."

Daniel similarly counseled King Nebuchadnezzar: *"...Break off thy sins by righteousness, and thine iniquities by showing mercy to the poor; it may be a lengthening of thy tranquility"* (Dan. 4:27). And Paul explained the general exhortation to *"put off the old man"* in the specific terms of *"putting away lying... [sinful] anger... stealing... corrupt communication... bitterness...wrath...and malice"* (Eph. 4:22-31). The idea of each of these various references is simply that God holds the individual responsible for making a clean break with the past. That very fact indicates both that the past life of a child of God does not (and must not be allowed to) predetermine his/her future, and that it is possible to stop sinning, for God does not hold a person accountable without also granting the ability to obey Him.

Consecration: Turning to God

Nature abhors a vacuum. The same is true in the spiritual realm. If an individual turns from wrong-doing without also, at the same time, turning to something better, the vacuum will be filled with even a worse, sinful habit. Moral reform, in other words, is not synonymous with biblical repentance.

This is precisely the point of our Lord's teaching in Matthew 12:43-45: *"When the unclean spirit is gone out of a man, he walketh through dry places, seeking rest, and findeth none. Then saith he, I will return into my house from whence I came out; and when he is come, he findeth it empty, swept, and garnished. Then goeth he, and taketh with himself seven other spirits more wicked than himself, and they enter in and dwell there: and the last state of that man is worse than the first...*" The description of the man's "house" as "empty, swept, and garnished" suggests the thought of mere moral reform, or a turning from sinful behavior without a turning to something better.

Repentance involves yet a further step beyond conviction, confession, and commitment. It involves *consecration*, or a giving of oneself entirely to God, in soul, mind, body, will, ability, relationships, and possessions. Consecration, or turning to the Lord, completes the process of repentance and shows it to be genuine.

The church at Thessalonica is an example of genuine repentance: "*For they themselves show of us what manner of entering in we had unto you, and how ye turned to God from idols to serve the living and true God*" (1 Ths. 1:9). This church turned "from idols," i.e. they made a break with the past, "to...God," i.e. they consecrated themselves to a new desire.

The energy once invested in the sinful behavior, in other words, must be rechanneled toward that which is godly. Revisiting an earlier example, Nebuchadnezzar would only "*break off [his] sins,*" according to Daniel, "*by righteousness,*" that is, by replacing them with something better, "*and [his] iniquities by showing mercy to the poor*" (Dan. 4:27). Paul's general exhortation to "*put off the old man*" must be balanced with the equally important effort to "*put on the new man*" (Eph. 4:22ff). Notice how he applies this "put off/put on" formula to specific areas of sinful habits. Each directive includes a negative "turning from" and a positive "turning to":

Wherefore putting away lying, speak every man truth with his neighbor...Let him that stole steal no more: but rather let him labor, working with his hands the thing which is good, that he may have to give to him that needeth. Let no corrupt communication proceed out of your mouth, but that which is good to the use of edifying, that it may minister grace unto the hearers...Let all bitterness, and wrath, and anger, and clamor, and evil speaking, be put away from you, with all malice: and be ye kind one to another, tenderhearted, forgiving one another, even as God for Christ's sake hath forgiven you (Eph. 4:25-32).

If a person, in other words, does not replace the old, sinful habit with a new, godly, biblical habit, no permanent progress toward positive change will be made. Further, the ultimate evidence that a person has forsaken sin and genuinely repented is the presence of spiritual fruit in place of the previous ungodly behavior. John the Baptist's instruction to the Pharisees to *"Bring forth fruits meet for repentance"* (Mt. 3:8) signals the importance of this particular matter of consecration to God.

Forgiveness: Cleansing the Guilty Conscience

Proverbs 28:13 indicates that authentic repentance will be met with pardoning mercy: *"He that covereth his sins shall not prosper: but whoso confesseth and forsaketh them shall have mercy."* First John 1:9, likewise, promises forgiveness and cleansing to the penitent soul: *"If we confess our sins, He is faithful and just to forgive us our sins, and to cleanse us from all unrighteousness."*

What precious promises! To the individual who refuses to conceal, blameshift, or justify his sins, God pledges to wipe the slate clean, to bypass His wrath and issue a judicial pardon for Jesus' sake. There is no note on the gospel scale quite so melodious to the burdened sinner as the promise of forgiveness:

Who is a God like unto thee, that pardoneth iniquity, and passeth by the transgression of the remnant of his heritage? He retaineth not his anger for ever, because he delighteth in mercy. (Micah 7:18)

Granted, God never extends grace at the expense of His justice. The acknowledgment of sin itself is not adequate to satisfy the demands of His law. But a confession of sin that includes a petition to the Father for clemency by virtue of the substitutionary merits of

Christ, your Elder Brother who has already atoned for that sin, will be met with forgiving mercy.

Unlike the blood of animal sacrifices which could only cleanse a worshipper externally so as to make him ceremonially compliant, the blood of Christ is effective to reach within the heart to resolve the tension of a condemned conscience: *"For if the blood of bulls and goats, and the ashes of a heifer sprinkling the unclean, sanctifieth to the purifying of the flesh: how much more shall the blood of Christ, who through the eternal Spirit offered himself without spot to God, purge your conscience from dead works to serve the living God?"* (Heb. 9:13-14).

No doubt the penitent Publican experienced this experiential peace of conscience when he left the temple that day after praying, *"God be merciful to me a sinner"* (Lk. 18:13). The Lord Jesus editorializes, *"I tell you, this man went down to his house justified rather than the other"* (Lk. 18:14a). He came to the temple that day a burdened sinner, but returned home with blessed assurance in his soul, justified by faith in the blood of the Lamb, that God had forgiven him.

Such an experience of quiet peace replacing the roarings and rumblings of a condemned conscience is promised to every penitent child of God. Paul describes it like this: *"Therefore, being justified by faith, we have peace with God through our Lord Jesus Christ: by whom also we have access by faith into this grace wherein we stand, and rejoice in hope of the glory of God"* (Rom. 5:1-2). Notice that the individual under consideration in this passage is already a child of God, for he is described positionally as "standing in grace." Notice further that this individual who is standing in grace has present access into that grace by means of the Lord Jesus Christ through faith.

This raises the question, "Why would someone who is already positionally right with God need further access into His grace?" The answer, of course, is because sin separates God's children from fellowship with Him.

Thankfully, our sins do not negate the redemptive work of Christ on behalf of His elect, nor alter the legal status of a right relationship with God. Neither is spiritual life, imparted to the soul in regeneration, lost due to practical sins committed in daily life. There are no punitive consequences at all to the sins that a child of God commits since Jesus has already been judged for those sins (cf. Rom. 8:1, 32-34).

There are, however, parental consequences to the sins of God's children. Though we may not deal with the punitive wrath of God the Judge since Jesus has already been judged in our place (cf. Rom. 8:34; Heb. 9:27-28), we must deal with the displeasure of God the Father for violating the Family code spelled out in His word.

Consider the case of the Prodigal Son (Lk. 15). This rebellious son turned his back on every kindness shown him in the father's house to pursue his own dreams in the world. I'm sure it broke his dad's heart when the boy left home.

The young rebel soon found himself broke, bereft of food and shelter, and alone in a hog pen. I daresay that the Prodigal was just as much his father's son in the pigsty as he had been for those previous years in the father's house. The relationship was never broken. But the fellowship he once enjoyed with his father and the rest of the family had been lost.

Likewise, our sins separate us from fellowship with God the Father in daily experience, hiding His face from us (cf. Is. 59:2). Restored fellowship with God requires confession and repentance. Romans 5:1-2 describes how the gospel gives the penitent sinner incentive to pursue a restoration of fellowship with God.

It works like this. When we believe the gospel and its message that Christ has already justified us freely by redeeming grace (cf. Rom. 3:24), it brings peace to the guilty conscience (just as it did in the case of the Publican previously cited). Such peace gives us confidence to apply to God, by faith in Christ, for the grace of forgiveness in daily experience, which, in turn, restores joy to the soul. Hence, "*Being justified by faith, we have peace with God through our Lord Jesus Christ: by whom also we have access by faith into this grace wherein we stand, and rejoice in hope of the glory of God.*"

This is the only remedy for the convicted soul whose conscience is guilt-ridden because of sinful indulgence. The only way to get rid of your guilt feelings is to admit your guilt, determine through the strength of the Holy Spirit to forsake it, consecrate your life anew to God, and believe that He is faithful and just to forgive your sin, and to wash you fresh and clean from all unrighteousness.

It is regrettable that there is so much talk today about "self-forgiveness." I think I understand what people are saying when they argue for the necessity of "forgiving oneself," but the Bible does not once mention such a concept. It does urge a person, however, to believe that God has forgiven him/her. And it is important that the guilt-ridden soul actually embrace the fact that God will do what He said He will do in response to genuine repentance.

Instead of "forgiving yourself," then, I urge you to appropriate the truth that God is "faithful and just to forgive…and cleanse." If you believe that wonderful fact, guilt will give way to peace and vain regret to a new resolve to avoid repetition of the sin that brought you, others, and (most especially) the Holy Spirit such grief and pain.

Summary

Let's review and offer a few further thoughts on the importance of maintaining a good conscience. In order to keep "a conscience void of offense," it is important to understand four basic principles concerning the conscience.

Conscience doesn't have the last word. It is a lower court, not "Supreme Court." The judgment it passes is not final. First John 3:20 says, "*For if our heart condemn us, God is greater than our heart, and knoweth all things.*" The judgments of conscience, in other words, are not infallible.

In 1 Corinthians 4, Paul asserted, "*But with me it is a very small thing that I should be judged of you, or of man's judgment: yea, I judge not mine own self. For I know nothing by myself; yet am I not hereby justified: but he that judgeth me is the Lord*" (vs. 3-4). Though Paul knew of nothing in his life at the moment that was necessarily wrong or sinful, yet the potential for self-deception was present; therefore, he said, "yet am I not hereby justified." In other words, Paul recognized that the Lord may know of some area in his life where repentance was necessary.

Even though his conscience was clear, ultimate judgment of his case rested with the Lord.

Does this fact, however, preclude the judgments of conscience? Does the fact that conscience may be misinformed mean that one should disregard the judgments of conscience? No. It means, first, that one should not sink in total despair if conscience offends, for God has the last word regarding eternal destiny: *"Who is he that condemneth? It is Christ that died, yea rather, that is risen again, who is even at the right hand of God, who also maketh intercession for us"* (Rom. 8:34).

Secondly, it means that one should not retire in self-satisfaction if conscience is silent, for God may know something about me of which I am unaware. People who are serious about maintaining a good conscience, therefore, should regularly pray, *"Search me, O God, and know my heart: try me, and know my thoughts: And see if there be any wicked way in me, and lead me in the way everlasting"* (Ps. 139:23-24). That leads us to the second principle.

Conscience should never be violated. Martin Luther said, "...to go against conscience is neither right nor safe...." The general rule is that people feel guilty because they are guilty. Of course, there are some exceptions to that rule. Conscience, again, is not infallible. But as a rule, it is not safe to disregard the mechanism God created in the soul called "conscience."

When David cut a swath from Saul's garment, *"his heart smote him"* (1 Sam. 24:5). Conscience screamed, "That was wrong!" Was this a malfunction of conscience? Was this "false guilt"? Pop-psychology would probably answer "yes," for he did no personal harm to this man who was trying to kill him, but rather, stood up for himself. But David lifted his hand against one who occupied a Divinely-ordained role. He took matters into his own hands, usurping, in an act of vigilante justice, the role of God who said, "Vengeance is mine; I will repay." His conscience did not, in fact, short-circuit. He had every reason to feel guilty. To deny the pangs of conscience would be to sacrifice the soul for the sake of his ego.

Romans 1:18 speaks of those who *"hold* [lit. suppress or hold down] *the truth in unrighteousness."* By nature, man attempts to silence and suppress "that which may be known of God" through general or natural revelation (v. 19). The sin that evokes God's wrath in Romans 1 is not a lack of knowledge, but a refusal to acknowledge God and his law. It is not, in other words, an intellectual problem but a moral problem. One of the manifestations of this natural aversion to God is the popular tendency to suppress and silence the conscience.

When a person trains himself to disregard the warnings of conscience, he inevitably loses his sensitivity to sin. The conscience can become so seared that it loses its sensibility, like nerve endings that have been damaged lose their capacity to warn of danger. Just as pain, in the natural realm, is meant to protect a person from a greater threat or danger, so the conscience serves as a warning to the soul of the long-term consequences of sin and disobedience. Even if the conscience is overly scrupulous or misguided, Romans 14:14, 20 makes it clear that to disregard the warnings of conscience tends to develop a pattern of thinking called "rationalization" in which the conscience is bypassed and eventually totally ignored. Sin, then, becomes a downward spiral, a habit that seems so common to a person's thought patterns that he becomes convinced that the behavior cannot be helped. In time, conscience ceases to properly function and there is no longer remorse.

Many people today have trained their minds to silence the pain of a wounded conscience through diversions like recreation, music, alcohol, drugs, and other distractions. When the conscience is systematically circumvented, however, it becomes *"past feeling"* (Eph. 4:19) and *"seared* [lit. cauterized] *with a hot iron"* (1 Tim. 4:2). Like damaged nerves, the mind no longer senses the pain of remorse, but sin continues to do untold damage to the soul (cf. 2 Pet. 2:7-8; 1 Pet. 2:11).

How then, should one deal with an offended conscience? If the tendency to silence, ignore, suppress, and disregard the warnings of conscience is so destructive, what should a person do when his heart smites him?

The offended conscience may be cleansed by the blood of Christ. Hebrews 9:14 says that the blood of Christ *"purges the conscience* *from dead works to serve the living God.*" The blood of animal sacrifices could never remove the conviction of sin in the heart. It could not give a sense of pardon and assurance of sins forgiven (Heb. 9:9). But the sacrificial death of Jesus Christ is effectual not only to blot out the legal guilt of sin before God, but also to wash and purge the guilt feelings of sin in the conscience (Ps. 51:1-2). The blood of the Lamb, in other words, has both an eternal or objective benefit before the bar of God's justice and a temporal or subjective efficacy in the courtroom of the individual's conscience. "*The blood of Jesus Christ,*" says John, "*cleanseth* [on an ongoing basis] *us from all sin*" (1 Jno. 1:7).

How may a believer, then, keep a pure conscience? By keeping short accounts with God, confessing and forsaking all known and unknown sins every day (Ps. 32:5-6; Pro. 28:13). The once for all "washing of regeneration" will never need to be repeated (Titus 3:5), but the partial washings of the feet which have accrued dust from the journey are a daily necessity (Jno. 13:10). To maintain a conscience void of offense, the Christian must regularly and humbly admit his sins before God in the confidence that "*If we confess our sins, he is faithful and just to forgive us our sins, and to cleanse us from all unrighteousness*" (1 Jno. 1:9). When a penitent sinner applies to Jesus for pardon and cleansing, he will go away like the publican of Luke 18, "justified" by faith, with peace and blessed assurance in his own conscience. To live with a conscience free from the stain of sin, one more thing is essential.

Conscience needs to be enlightened and instructed by the word of God. As stated, some people have a conscience that is overly scrupulous. Others have a conscience that is not scrupulous enough. One person thinks it is a sin to play cards or to wash clothes on Sunday. Another thinks it is perfectly appropriate to forego public worship for a trip to the lake. Which one is correct? Probably neither. Both have, what Paul calls, a "weak conscience," a conscience in need of education (Rom. 14; 1 Cor. 8).

Because conscience functions on the basis of conviction, and because a person's convictions are determined by various influences (e. g. the influence of parents, peers, society, church, etc.), people feel strongly about different issues. In the church, it is imperative that we exercise grace toward those whose opinions on certain non-essential issues are different from our own. Though we would like for everything to be "cut and dried" or "black and white," life is not always that simple. Granted, there are certain non-negotiables that are essential. There is an irreducible minimum, without which a person has no right to call himself a believer; therefore, we must be cautious of the creeping influence of "relativism" in our thought patterns. But I think it is apparent that the greatest problem we face today is not excessive strictness but extreme complacency toward the things of God.

On the other hand, there are issues that fall into that "gray" category of uncertainty—issues about which Scripture is non-specific and about which valid arguments can be produced on both sides. The solution to these kinds of dilemmas is the exercise of "Christian liberty," in which each believer leaves the judgment of his brother to the Lord, trusting a sovereign God's capacity to keep his own children in check (1 Cor. 8; Rom. 14).

When I leave my brother and his conscience to the Lord's discretion, and he mine, we are then freed to channel our respective energies into the further education and instruction of our own consciences by exposing them to God's word. As my brother brings his thinking into harmony with Holy Scripture, and as I am trained to think more and more Biblically, disagreements on peripheral matters will be increasingly rare and unity of mind will increasingly prevail.

None of us has totally the mind of Christ. Our thinking is not always Biblical. My conscience has been influenced, I'm sure, by sources other than Scripture. For that reason, I may be overly scrupulous in some areas and too soft in others. Spiritual growth, however, involves the ongoing conformity of my ideas to the mind of Christ as it is revealed in Holy Scripture. When, as Luther said, the conscience is "held captive by the word of God," the believer has taken a bold stride forward in his quest to have always a conscience void of offense, toward God and toward man.

How, then, did Paul strive to maintain a good conscience? First, by applying his mind to the ongoing study of the word of God so that his conscience might be educated by Scripture. Secondly, by committing himself to be true to his own convictions, not to violate or disregard the warnings of conscience. Thirdly, by maintaining an attitude of vulnerable willingness to have his sin exposed so he may deal with it Biblically. Finally, by applying to the Lord for cleansing in repentance when he felt convicted of sin.

In this way, too, it is possible for each believer to enjoy the blessing and peace of an unoffended heart. Make it your ambition and priority today to keep your conscience pure and clean. Aim to live in such a way that you may have no cause for regret. And if you fall in sin, repent, applying to the precious blood of Jesus Christ as your righteousness: *"My little children, these things write I unto you that ye sin not; and if any man sin, we have an advocate with the Father, Jesus Christ the Righteous"* (1 Jno. 2:1-2). Then rise again, believing that you are forgiven, and determine, with the help of the Holy Spirit, not to sin again. So, God's people may keep their hearts from the trouble of guilt.

10
Man of Sorrows: What a Name!
God's Grace in Your Grief

"Jesus wept." John 11:35

Grief is universal human experience. If you have not previously had occasion to be acquainted with it at any significant level, you will before the journey of life is complete. It is impossible to journey through a world that is under the curse of sin—a world that old writers sometimes called "a vale of tears"—without experiencing the painful, albeit very human, emotion of grief at some point.

Some realist (or pessimist, depending on one's perspective) quipped that life is comprised of smiles, sighs and sobs, with sighs predominating. Grief refers to those sad episodes on the journey of life that make us sob.

What exactly is it? Grief may be defined as a response of inward desolation arising from a love lost, whether the loss has to do with a person dear to the heart or a long-time family pet, an event such as the breakup of a relationship or some thing that is integrally related to the affections, like the loss of family heirlooms and precious memories in a house-fire. Theologian J. I. Packer writes,

> *Loved* is the key word here. We lavish care and affection on what we love and those whom we love, and when we lose the beloved, the shock, the hurt, the sense of being hollowed out and crushed, the haunting, taunting memory of better days, the feeling of unreality and weakness and hopelessness, and the lack of power to think and plan for the new situation can be devastating.[1]

Of course, to escape the pain of grief, one need merely resist the magnetic pull to love. But who is able to live such a relationally detached life? Further, who would want to live without love? Loving

---

[1] J. I. Packer, *A Grief Sanctified: Passing Through Grief to Peace and Joy*, p. 11.

and being loved is part of our humanness, created in the image of the God who is Himself love. The comfort of love, then, supersedes the misery of grief, making the potential of heartache a risk worth taking, the very perspective that prompted the thoroughly human Tennyson to observe, "Tis better to have loved and lost than never to have loved at all."[2]

It was precisely this element of love and affection that led to our Lord's grief at the grave of Lazarus. "*Jesus wept*" (Jno. 11:35) is the shortest verse in the bible, but don't be misled by its brevity. It expresses a sublime and profound truth.

It suggests for us a view of our Lord's very real *humanity*, a "*man of sorrows and acquainted with grief*" (Is. 53:3). Jesus did not assume the form of an angel when He came to this earth, but took upon Himself "bone of our bone and flesh of our flesh," sin excepted (cf. Heb. 2:14-18). He experienced every aspect of human experience, with the exception (again) of personal failure through sin; therefore, the Lord Jesus is able to empathize with those who grieve: "*Wherefore in all things it behoved Him to be made like unto His brethren that He might be a merciful and faithful High Priest...for in that He Himself hath suffered being tempted, He is able to succour them that are tempted*" (Heb. 2:17-18; cf. Heb. 4:15-16).

This short statement also suggests for us a view of our Lord's compassionate *heart*. The tender sympathy of Christ to suffering humanity is on display here. What comfort to know that Jesus knows and cares for you in your deep sorrow! Man of sorrows: what a name!

I've drawn sweet consolation from Frank Graeff's (1860-1919) song "Does Jesus Care?" The chorus answers this deep, heart-cry,

> Oh yes, He cares; I know He cares;
> His heart is touched with my grief;
> When the days are weary,
> The long nights dreary,
> I know my Savior cares.

---

[2] Alfred Lord Tennyson, "Memoriam: 27", 1850.

"Jesus wept" reminds us that the heart of Christ, our Great High Priest, resonates with the broken-hearted believer, marking and remembering the mourner's every tear (cf. Ps. 56:8):

> Jesus wept! Those tears are over,
> But His love is still the same;
> Kinsman, Friend, and Elder Brother
> Is His everlasting name.
>
> Jesus wept! And still in glory,
> He must mark the mourner's tear;
> Loving still to trace the story
> Of the hearts He strengthened here.
>
> Jesus wept! That tear of sorrow
> Is a legacy of love;
> Yesterday, today, tomorrow,
> He the same doth ever prove.[3]

Our grief is, likewise, a mark of our thorough humanness. The Bible never once forbids us to grieve, any more than it prohibits us to love. To maintain the stoical pretense of a "stiff, upper lip" as if grief does not exist is as unhealthy and dehumanizing as the opposite extreme of grieving forever and allowing grief to morph into despair. But finding that balance between stifling grief on the one hand and sliding into despair on the other is not always as simple as it may appear.

And here is the rub. If escape from the experience of grief (by detaching oneself from relational love) is not an option, how may a person manage grief in a God-honoring way, not to mention survive it so that it doesn't determine the rest of life? Perhaps the best way to answer this question is to address the most common expression of grief with which we are familiar, the grief of bereavement, an

---

[3] J. Calvin Bushey, "Weeping One of Bethany," No. 133, Old School Hymnal (12th Edition).

experience arising through the death of a loved one. "Bereavement..." writes Packer, "brings grief in its most acute and most disabling form..."[4]

The Grief of Bereavement

The etymology of the word *bereave* reveals just how life-shattering is the grief of loss. Originally, the Old English verb *reave* meant "to break or tear." By 1594, it came to mean "to rob, to spoil, or to plunder" and had to do with something painfully torn away from someone's possession.[5] Today, the verb *reave* is seldom used, having been replaced by the noun *rift* and the verb *bereft*.

The pain of grief does, in fact, make a person feel that the heart has been broken in half. Some precious object of affection has been forcibly torn away, leaving the victim broken and alone. Packer writes:

> Grief is more draining and harrowing that we thought [or, expected it to be]... All our attempts to put it into words are inadequate. At the very time when grief and our verbalizing of it brings us to tears, we find ourselves feeling that it is really too deep for tears and too agonizing for words. As we struggle with the ache of loss, the grip of our grief imposes a kind of relational paralysis—the sense that no one, however sympathetic and supportive in intention, can share what we are feeling and it would be a betrayal of our love for the lost one to pretend otherwise. So we grieve alone, and the agony is unbelievable...The loneliness of grief is one of the worst and most draining things about it—and, be it said, one of the most dangerous too...The capacity for initiative and enterprise melts—dissolves—away, and so does the power of empathy with and response to others. A half-numb apathy, frequently alternating with bouts of tears, sets in. The first paragraph of C. S. Lewis' *Grief Observed* written within a month of bereavement describes grief as feeling like fear ("the same fluttering in the stomach, the same restlessness, the

---

[4] Packer, p. 12.
[5] *The Oxford Universal Dictionary*, p. 1668.

yawning. I keep on swallowing.") The next paragraph begins "At other times it feels like being mildly drunk, or concussed. There is a sort of invisible blanket between the world and me. I find it hard to take in what anyone says." Then a bit later: "And no one ever told me about the laziness of grief. Except at my job—where the machine seems to run on much as usual—I loathe the slightest effort...even shaving."[6]

Such is the brokenness felt in grief. And if the loved one was torn away suddenly and unexpectedly (say, in some tragic accident, homicide or suicide) so that there was no occasion for a final "goodbye" or "I love you," the sorrow of loss is complicated by other emotions such as anger, guilt and fear, tearing the heart and, indeed, whole life in two so that the bereaved person wonders if life will ever return to any semblance of normalcy.

What can be done for the person reeling beneath the paralyzing obsession of bereavement? Secular solutions to grief, whether through "grief therapy"[7] or alchemy, really offer no solution at all. One popular, secular theory, for instance, suggests that it is normal (and even healthy) for a person to feel angry at God for allowing the loss to occur. Expressing one's rage toward God is deemed an appropriate and helpful step toward recovery.

Holy Scripture disagrees. Not once does the Bible ever suggest that it is appropriate, much less normative, for the bereaved (or anyone else in whatever trying circumstance, for that matter) to lash out at God in anger. Such convoluted ideas show just how little

---

[6] Packer, pp.159-162.

[7] Much modern "grief therapy" is based on the Kubler-Ross model of five stages of grief, i.e. denial, anger, bargaining, depression and acceptance. Elizabeth Kubler-Ross (1926-2004) was a Swiss-born psychiatrist whose 1969 book *On Death and Dying* became a national bestseller. The book, however, sprang from interviews with patients at a Chicago hospital who were themselves in the process of dying. The fact that her research failed to target the grieving parties left behind after the patient died makes its scientific value for dealing with grief intrinsically suspect.

unbelievers (and immature believers) understand about faith and authentic Christian discipleship.

In contrast to the secular theory of "grief work" popularized by Freud, Eric Lindemann and Elizabeth Kubler-Ross, God's word offers real help to the bereaved. The Christian has resources at his/her disposal enabling him to live through and recover from bereavement in a way that will glorify God. These spiritual resources, or more accurately, God's grace to His suffering children, chart a course for successful navigation through the valley of the shadow of death. Let's consider three of these "graces," or gifts from God, for grieving souls.

The Grace of Truth

Unlike the unbeliever who fears death as a dark mystery, we know what happens at death. God's word affirms that at the very moment the eyes of the body close in death, the eyes of the soul awake to behold the Lord Jesus Christ in His immediate presence: *"We are confident, I say, and willing rather to be absent from the body and to be present with the Lord"* (2 Cor. 5:8). Notice that, for the child of God, the spirit's absence from the body is presence with the Lord. There is no intermediate state.

Scripture affirms that the soul (or spirit), i.e. the immaterial part of a human being, does not die with the physical body. Consider the following references concerning the immortality of the soul:

- And he stretched himself upon the child three times, and cried unto the Lord, and said, O Lord my God, I pray thee, let this child's soul come into him again. And the Lord heard the voice of Elijah; and the soul of the child came into him again, and he revived. (1 Kings 17:21-22)
- Fear not them which kill the body, but are not able to kill the soul... (Mt. 10:28a)
- I saw the souls of them that were beheaded for the witness of Jesus, and for the word of God...and they lived and reigned with Christ a thousand years. (Rev. 20:4b)

Perhaps the clearest reference is in this very chapter, 2 Corinthians 5: "*For we know that if our earthly house of this tabernacle were dissolved, we have a building of God, an house not made with hands, eternal in the heavens*" (v. 1). Like a disintegrating building, Paul says, our bodies are systematically breaking down; however, God has prepared a heavenly home for the soul at death. What rich reassurance this truth provides!

It is this understanding of the truth of God that led Paul to offer his readers this autobiographical view into his attitude toward death: "*For to me to live is Christ, and to die is gain*" (Phi. 1:21). Such a confession sounds preposterous to the unbeliever. He cannot understand, in a million years, why anyone would speak of death as a positive, rather than a negative. But to the Christian, death is no longer the "king of terrors" (Job 18:14). The King of kings has already conquered it on behalf of His people.

The individual who looks at life in the same way that Paul viewed it will understand his affirmation that death is gain. If Christ is your life here, then death is merely the gateway to more intimate fellowship with and more complete knowledge of Christ in heaven. Understanding that death is not the end of the story, but, as C. S. Lewis termed it, "the beginning of the real story...which goes on forever and in which every chapter is better than the one before,"[8] gives us reason to affirm with the Psalmist, "*Precious in the sight of the Lord is the death of his saints*" (Ps. 116:15). We share the perspective of Revelation 14:13: "*Blessed are the dead which die in the Lord from henceforth: Yea, saith the Spirit, that they may rest from their labors, and their works do follow them.*"

Death, you see, is simply a "home-going" for the child of God. That's the thought in 2 Corinthians 5 (notice the references to houses and homes in verses 1, 2 and 6). Jesus termed heaven "*the Father's house*" in John 14:1. That means heaven is home. Ecclesiastes 12:5 further employs the metaphor of a home-going at death: "*...Man goeth to his long home, and the mourners go about the streets.*" And, we might

---

[8] C. S. Lewis, *The Last Battle* (Chronicles of Narnia Series, Book 7), closing lines.

ask, who is afraid to go home? Picking up on this imagery of a royal home, the influential British preacher John Henry Jowett (1864-1923) said,

> Death is not the end; it is only a new beginning. Death is not the master of the house: he is only the porter at the King's lodge, appointed to open the gate and let the King's guests into the realm of endless day.[9]

Another term used in Scripture to speak of what happens at death is "departure": "*For I am now ready to be offered and the time of my departure is at hand*" (2 Tim. 4:6). Now, everyone knows that a departure is not the cessation of existence. The departure of an airplane from its point of origin does not imply that the fuselage, cockpit, flight crew and passengers ceased to exist. It simply means that it left one place to arrive at another. So, every heaven-born soul departs from this world at death for a heavenly destination. And that soul is just as conscious (in fact, more so) in its heavenly existence as it was in its earthly pilgrimage.

To understand the truth of what happens at death, namely that the soul of God's loved one lives on in conscious existence in heaven and that by grace, we shall soon join them in that happy, sinless clime, affords real help to those whose hearts are broken by the grief of bereavement. That brings us to the next grace God has given to help us in our grief.

The Grace of Hope

Not only does God's word inform us with truth, it encourages us with hope. The body, which is just as much a part of the deceased individual as the soul, will be raised again at the Redeemer's return.

The Bible employs the metaphor of sleep to describe death. Jesus informed his disciples concerning Lazarus' death saying, "*Our friend Lazarus sleepeth; but I go, that I may awake him out of sleep*" (Jno. 11:11; cf.

---

[9] George Sweeting, *Who Said That?*, p. 138.

Lk. 8:52). Taking his cue from the Lord Jesus, the apostle Paul likewise used this image to speak of the death of God's people (cf. Acts 13:36; 1 Cor. 15:51; 1 Ths. 4:14). I especially love the prepositional phrase he adds to the metaphor in 1 Thessalonians 4:14, where he speaks of those who "sleep in Jesus."

In what sense is death compared to sleep? Not in terms of the soul, as we have already noted. The soul never dies. Instead, the metaphor of sleep is used to speak of the state of the body in death.

The metaphor of sleep indicates that the Lord is not finished with the individual when he/she dies, but intends to awaken the body in resurrection and reunion with the soul. At the moment of physical death, the soul is immediately transported into the presence of the Lord in heavenly paradise. The body, however, returns to the dust, i.e. it begins the process of decomposition, from whence it came (cf. Ecc. 12:7). As far as the Lord is concerned, though, the body is asleep, until resurrection morning when it will be awakened, reunited with its disembodied soul, and glorified. When the saints awake on that happy morning, whether they've deceased ten minutes or ten thousand years ago, their absence will seem as brief as a good night's sleep.

The Christian response to grief is spelled out in 1 Thessalonians 4:13-18:

> But I would not have you to be ignorant, brethren, concerning them which are asleep, that ye sorrow not, even as others who have no hope. For if we believe that Jesus died and rose again, even so them also which sleep in Jesus will God bring with him. For this we say unto you by the word of the Lord, that we which are alive and remain shall not prevent them which are asleep. For the Lord himself shall descend from heaven with a shout, with the voice of the archangel, and with the trump of God: and the dead in Christ shall rise first: then we which are alive and remain shall be caught up together with them in the clouds, to meet the Lord in the air: and so shall we ever be with the Lord. Wherefore comfort one another with these words.

Notice several salient points from this passage. First, *the Christian's hope serves to prevent grief from turning into despair.* "*...that ye sorrow not, even as other which have no hope.*" God's word does not forbid sorrow, but prescribes that sorrow should be mitigated by hope, lest it turn to despair.

Discussing this distinction in 1 Thessalonians 4:13 between grief and despair, notable Christian pastor Jay Adams writes,

> "Grief, on the one hand, is proper and good according to the Scriptures; despair, on the other hand, is quite wrong...[Paul] is interested in steering the course between an unbiblical stoicism that stifles emotion and the despair that comes from lack of hope. Christian grief lies in between. This grief is a painful sorrow that issues in an honest expression of one's feelings; yet even in the midst of these intense feelings, the Christian may look with confidence beyond the tragedy to its solution in Christ...It is just this element of hope or anticipation that is lacking in despair. Indeed, faith and hope may grow tall in the rich soil of grief."[10]

Hope tempers grief both in terms of its degree and its duration. In degree, grief must never be allowed to reach the magnitude of hysteria. The Christian who looks to the future in heavenly bliss with biblical optimism, i.e. hope, possesses the necessary resources to mitigate the magnitude of his sorrow. The disconsolate Christian who "refuses to be comforted" (cf. Gen. 37:35; Jer. 31:15) by factoring hope into the equation of grief effectively forsakes his own mercy.

In terms of duration, hope should also mitigate the length of time someone mourns. Now, how long is too long? There is no definitive answer to that question. I suspect the duration of grief will vary from person to person and situation to situation. I would never discourage the bereaved soul from taking his/her time to mourn love lost, for one day it will be me in that place and taking directives from outsiders regarding the appropriate duration of grief from people

---

[10] Jay E. Adams, *Shepherding God's Flock*, pp. 138-139.

who do not stand in my shoes will seem awfully intrusive. How long is too long must be an individual decision.

But decide we must. One thing is sure: the Christian must not grieve forever. If we believe that Jesus died and lives again, then life must proceed for the bereaved individual at some point as well. Indeed, your life may never be quite the same, but God will not be pleased if you freeze your life at a single point in time and refuse to be comforted. The God who has been your help in ages past is also your hope for years to come.

On December 13, 2011, the 150th Anniversary of Prince Albert's passing, numerous news outlets told the story of Queen Victoria's inconsolable grief.[11] Albert died at age 42, twenty-one years after marrying Victoria. For the next three years, Victoria abandoned all public duties as the British Queen. But even after resuming her role, she never really recovered from his passing, even laying out the dead man's clothes every evening for dinner. In fact, for the next forty years, her grief came to define her entire reign, so that the public and politicians alike began to ask whether the Queen's period of mourning would ever end:

> The Blue Room in which Prince Albert died remained unaltered for the rest of Victoria's life, a snapshot of the time when her life changed forever. The glass from which he had taken his last sip was kept on his bedside table, his blottingbook and pen forever opened at its last entry, fresh flowers delivered every day…She wore black for the rest of her life.[12]

What leads to such chronic and obsessive grief? Perhaps the individual who is fixated on his/her grief has the unhealthy idea that he owes it to his loved one to mourn for the rest of his life. Under the guise of respect for the deceased, this kind of obsession may very well be an attempt to keep the loved one around rather than letting

[11] http://www.dailymail.co.uk/news/article-2073792/Queen-Victorias-unbearable-grief-death-Prince-Albert.html
[12] http://www.historyinanhour.com/2011/12/14/death-of-prince-albert/

them go, and it effectively serves to "pick the scab" and keep the wound of bereavement from healing.

Let me caution again, however, against forming judgments about the duration of someone else's grief. People have to work their own way through this experience and the best help that outsiders can be is to offer loving, quiet friendship, fervent prayers, and regular biblical reminders about God's promises and grace.

I need to say to the bereaved themselves, however, that you are not to sorrow like an unbeliever, who has no hope in Christ, might sorrow. That necessarily means that you need to think about the loss you've suffered in light of the glorious future God has prepared, both for your love lost and for you. Such hope will necessarily temper the duration of your grief. God's message to you is His message to the grieving, faithful remnant of true worshipers at the destruction of Jerusalem:

> A voice was heard in Ramah, lamentation, and bitter weeping; Rachel weeping for her children refused to be comforted for her children, because they were not. Thus saith the Lord; Refrain thy voice from weeping, and thine eyes from tears: for thy work shall be rewarded, saith the Lord; and they shall come again from the land of the enemy. And there is hope in thine end, saith the Lord, that thy children shall come again to their own border. (Jer. 31:15-17)

Secondly, **the ground of the Christian's hope is the resurrection of the Lord Jesus Christ.** "*...For if we believe that Jesus died and rose again, even so them also which sleep in Jesus will God bring with him.*" Because He lives, there is no such thing as a hopeless situation. Even death is not hopeless, for nothing is impossible if Jesus walked away from the grave.

"*Because I live,*" the Savior promises, "*ye shall live also*" (Jno. 14:19b). God's acceptance of the offering of firstfruits under Moses' Law guaranteed the rest of the harvest. Even so, Christ is called "the firstfruits of them that slept" (1 Cor. 15:20) and his resurrection guarantees ours also (1 Cor. 15:21-26).

The fact of the empty tomb and subsequent post-resurrection appearances of Christ to His disciples energized the early church. Though Peter's hopes dissolved when Jesus was crucified and buried (for he and the other disciples, as yet, did not remember or understand Jesus' prophecy concerning the resurrection), his hope was revived by the Savior's rising: "*Blessed be the God and Father of our Lord Jesus Christ, which according to his abundant mercy hath begotten us again unto a lively hope by the resurrection of Jesus Christ from the dead*" (1 Pet. 1:3). Because He lives, dear friend, you can face tomorrow with a bright outlook of Christian optimism.

Thirdly, the 1 Thessalonians 4 passage teaches that *the Christian's hope consists of the glorious prospect of reunion with the whole family of God and with the Lord Jesus Himself at the second coming*. "*...then we which are alive and remain shall be caught up together with them, and so shall we ever be with the Lord*." Note the repetition of the preposition "with." We will be caught up "with" the rest of the glorified saints to be "with" the glorified Christ forevermore. It is not wrong to take comfort from the prospect of reunion with departed loved ones. Even David found solace in the hope that he would see his deceased child again in glory (cf. 2 Sam. 12:23). Indeed, the chief glory of heaven will be the joy of uninterrupted communion with the Christ who saved us in His immediate presence. But the enjoyment of that happy exercise in the company of those we have "loved long since, and lost awhile" runs a close second.

Packer writes, "Grieving was never meant to be a permanent state; it is a natural process which, if not inhibited, will run its course and from which we may hope in due time to recover."[13] It is hope that will be your compass on this challenging journey through the winding valley of grief. With a view of the happy prospect awaiting you, the various bends in the road of sorrow may be navigated safely until you emerge into the sunlight once again.

---

[13] Packer, p. 166.

The Grace of Joy

God has provided yet a further gift of grace for grieving souls, the grace of joy. According to Nehemiah 8:10, rejoicing in the Lord is the antidote for sorrow: "*...neither be ye sorry, for the joy of the Lord is your strength.*"

Nehemiah chapter eight describes the first worship service observed in Jerusalem in almost a century and one-half. In 586 B.C., Nebuchadnezzar, king of Babylon, made the final of three trips to Jerusalem,[14] leveling the city and Solomon's magnificent temple to the ground. Fifty years later, in 536 B.C., Cyrus and the Medo-Persians overthrew Babylon and granted the Jews freedom to return home. Very few, however, wanted to leave Babylon. Those few, brave souls who did return to Jerusalem found Judea occupied by foreigners. Circumstances dictated that they live once again as virtual nomads, with little solidarity among themselves and no religious routine.

In 445 B.C., Nehemiah occupied a position of significant responsibility in the court of Artaxerxes, the Persian king. It had been 140 years since Jerusalem was destroyed, and 90 years since Cyrus had liberated the Jews. When Nehemiah encountered some Jewish travelers from Jerusalem who came to the palace in Shushan, he inquired about the welfare of the brethren and condition of the city of God. Their report broke his heart:

And they said unto me, The remnant that are left of the captivity there in the province are in great affliction and reproach: the wall of Jerusalem also is broken down, and the gates thereof are burned with fire. (Neh. 1:3)

Nothing had changed, in other words, since the deportation some 140 years ago. Nehemiah began to fast and pray in deep concern over the situation and, somewhere along the line, became convinced that he might be part of the solution.

---

[14] The first deportation of captives to Babylon was in 605 B.C. The 70 year period of Babylonian captivity is counted from this date.

The next few chapters record how God providentially opened the way for him to take a leave of absence, return to Jerusalem, and superintend the project of reconstructing the walls of the city. Under the blessing of God, Nehemiah and the builders completed the project, rebuilding two miles of wall surrounding Jerusalem in a mere fifty-two days.

Chapter eight records the first worship service observed in Jerusalem in almost 150 years. As Ezra and the Levites read and interpreted God's holy law, the people began to weep (8:9b). No doubt they grieved at the realization of the nation's apostasy and because of the great interval of time that had passed since God had been glorified in worship by His covenant people. It is probable that they also mourned because of the glory that had been lost. Solomon's magnificent temple had been destroyed. The former grandeur of the city of God enjoyed by their ancestors was now a pile of rubble and ruin.

But Ezra and the priests checked the congregation's sorrow: "*Mourn not, nor weep...Go your way, eat the fat, and drink the sweet, and send portions unto them for whom nothing is prepared: for this day is holy unto our Lord: neither be ye sorry; for the joy of the Lord is your strength*" (Neh. 8:9b-10). This was a day to rejoice in God, not mourn the past in regret. Significant progress had been made and such joy in the Lord would empower them for further tasks to come in the near future.

The celebrated coach Vince Lombardi once commented, "Fatigue makes cowards of us all." Weary souls have little courage or strength to move forward. When a person is happy in the Lord (cf. Ps. 144:15), however, the step is light and swift. When the prophet Habakkuk resolved to rejoice in the God of his salvation in spite of the dismal circumstances around him, God gave him strength and vigor:

Although the fig tree shall not blossom, neither shall fruit be in the vines; the labor of the olive shall fail, and the fields shall yield no meat; the flock shall be cut off from the fold, and there shall be no herd in the stalls: yet I will rejoice in the Lord, I will joy in the God of my salvation. The Lord God is my strength, and he will make my feet like hinds' feet, and he will make me to walk upon mine high places (Hab. 3:17-19).

He will do the same for you. The joy of the Lord will give you strength to bear your burdens, to persevere in spite of disappointments, to stand fast in the face of suffering, to resist the pull of temptation, and to move forward in the wake of deep grief.

But, someone wonders, how may I find such joy? Joy comes during the process of rejoicing in the Lord. In a word, you will find joy when you practice doxology.

Job is the epitome of what it means to worship in the face of bereavement. I cannot begin to fathom the tremendous grief he felt in the aftermath of losing all of his financial holdings to marauders, children to tragic death, and physical health to disease. And then, on top of it all, he lost his reputation, his friends, and even the respect of his wife. Beside the Lord Jesus on the cross, no human being has ever suffered an occasion of grief comparable to Job's case.

Yet through it all, Job bowed before the Lord and worshiped: *"Naked came I out of my mother's womb, and naked shall I return thither: the Lord gave, and the Lord hath taken away; blessed be the name of the Lord"* (Job 1:20-21). Such humble submission before God's sovereignty and willingness to say "blessed be His name" is exemplary. Every grieving soul should follow Job's lead at precisely this point.

David, also, practiced doxology in the wake of his sorrow. When his little baby died, he *"arose from the earth, and washed, and anointed himself, and changed his apparel, and came into the house of the Lord, and worshipped"* (2 Sam. 12:20). Nothing is more helpful to the grief-stricken soul than to refocus the eye of faith on God's glorious character, immutable promises, wonderful works, and sovereign grace in such an hour. I suspect that vigorous praise and worship in the company of God's people in the church, in spite of how you may feel at the outset of the service, will prove to be a real help to the sinking spirit.

I've witnessed this dynamic at funeral services. How many times have I watched a grieving family march into the service to the cadence of a funeral dirge, only to march out, though still heavy-hearted, with a new spring in the step. As the Lord blessed the minister to refocus their collective gaze on God's redeeming love to His people in Christ, promises of His sufficient grace and the abiding presence of His Holy Spirit, the happy prospect of the resurrection at the Savior's second coming, and the glorious hope of blissful reunion with the deceased in a tearless, deathless, painless and sinless realm, new courage and new hope was infused into their grieving hearts. Despair turned to hope as the family found renewed strength to carry on.

The joy of the Lord was their strength, and it will be yours as well when you practice doxology in the wake of earthly bereavement. The Great Physician's prescription to every grieving soul is "Go to church and engage in public worship with the saints. Sing the hymns; pour out your complaints before the Lord; apply to Him for help; listen to His word as His personal message to you; refocus your gaze on the greatness of His grace; remember the great things that He has done; claim His promises as your own; and rejoice in Him." Worship is soul exercise and there is nothing better for the spiritual atrophy of grief than the practice of stretching your soul and exerting your heart in praise to the God who loved you and gave Himself for you.

Final Thoughts

Grief, especially the grief of death, tends to paralyze life and labor. But there are certain rehab therapies for those who feel debilitated and crippled by grief. As the bereaved individual practices these exercises, progress may be made, slowly but surely, toward recovery and, in fact, toward growth in grace as grief is sanctified to your spiritual benefit.

First is *the exercise of thanksgiving*. Spend time in your sorrow thinking about all that you valued in the person lost, as well as the happiness he/she now enjoys in the presence of the Lord, and thank God for it all. What a blessing the Lord bestowed on your life to know and enjoy fellowship with this special person! How rich was your experience! And what a wonderful impact this individual, under the blessing of God, made upon your life! Be thankful.

Second is *the exercise of submission to the Lord*. It is salutary to the soul to humbly bow before God and resign your all into His sovereign, very capable hands. You and I have no claims upon the lives of others. They belong to the Lord, not to us, just as we belong to the Lord. And He is perfect and all wise; He does all things well. He knows what is best for us and the only posture that is appropriate before Him is to say, *"It is the Lord; let him do what seemeth Him good"* (1 Sam. 3:18). To humble ourselves before the living God, entrusting our loved ones and ourselves to Him, is to find great peace and comfort in times of distress.

Finally, we recommend *the exercise of patience*. God is not usually in as much of a hurry as we are. With the passage of time and the application of the principles discussed in this chapter, the intensity of grief will be reduced. Please do not allow yourself to feel that you have let your loved one down as grief subsides. This is precisely what God intends to happen.

Be advised, however, that grief may subside slowly, a step at a time, a day at a time. Each day, then, commit yourself to biblical thinking, prayer for strength and help, and faithful service to the Lord and others. The just shall live by faith, so keep on keeping on. And the days will turn to weeks and the weeks to months and the months to years. With patience, deliberate effort to implement godly counsel, and an attitude of ongoing dependence on the God who loves you, you will make it through this valley. So, let not your heart be troubled by grief. *"Weeping may endure for a night, but joy cometh in the morning"* (Ps. 30:5).

11
Think on What is True
Overcoming Fear & Anxiety

"What time I am afraid, I will trust in thee." Psalm 56:3

A dear sister in Christ and member of the church I served gave me a handwritten note some time ago when I was passing through a season of great heartache and change in my life. It contained two Bible verses, Isaiah 41:13 and Psalm 17:7, as well as the following quote from Francis de Sales (1567-1622). The words had been originally written to a dear friend who was also facing radical changes in his circumstances. I read the note (literally) every day for months, taking great comfort from it. De Sales wrote:

> Do not look forward in fear to the changes in life;
> Rather, look to them with full hope that as they arise,
> God, whose very own you are,
> Will deliver you out of them;
> He has kept you hitherto, - and
> He will lead you safely through all things;
> And when you cannot stand,
> God will bear you in His arms.

> Do not fear what may happen tomorrow;
> The same Everlasting Father who cares for you today
> Will take care of you tomorrow and every day.

> Either He will shield you from suffering or
> He will give you unfailing strength to bear it.
> Be at peace, then, and
> Put aside all anxious thoughts and imaginations.

That is relevant, biblical advice. And at some point in the path of life, most every Christian will need it.

The Pervasiveness of Fear

I know of no experience more universally pervasive and thoroughly debilitating than fear. In childhood, fear presents itself earlier than many other emotions, and it seems that each stage of development is marked by a struggle to learn to face and overcome various fears.

Every new experience, whether visiting the pediatrician for immunizations, a first haircut, a thunderstorm, riding a bike without training wheels, the first day of Kindergarten, or encountering bully tactics for the first time from the big kid down the street, is an occasion to either give in to or to conquer fear. A fear of the dark, of things that go 'creak' in the night, is an almost universal experience in early child development. And it doesn't stop there.

Adolescence is replete with experiences that feed and exacerbate fear. The fear of rejection, popularly termed "peer pressure," is one of the most common adolescent fears. This can be a brutal period in a young person's life as he/she deals with complexion issues, yesterday's clothing styles, an awakened interest in the opposite sex, and a host of other reasons to feel self-conscious. Throw a bully, intent on making the teen's life a living nightmare, into the mix and you have a situation tailor-made for feelings of personal insecurity.

Growing up is challenging enough when the home is a safe place. But when the family atmosphere lacks love, encouragement, structure, discipline and godly conviction, adolescence and its culture of fear tends to feed what would otherwise be a natural struggle with insecurity until it becomes a very unhealthy habit of mind. A child that grows up in a family characterized by physical or emotional abuse, or a home in which one or both parents is passive, self-centered, addicted, deceptive, irresponsible, lazy, angry, promiscuous, undisciplined or given to any number of other vices as a lifestyle tends to enter the wider world of society without an awareness of personal identity that is so critical to his/her sense of safety. It doesn't take much ridicule or many failing grades then to drive that young person deep within himself behind layers of self-protection.

Add to these early struggles the breakup of a relationship, the loss of a job, an automobile accident, the unexpected death of a friend or relative, an experience in which you embarrassed yourself in public, the discovery of a painful secret, and the snide attitude of a coworker and one can understand how easy it would be to simply succumb to the temptation to lock oneself away from every potential experience of hurt and disappointment. Fear can be a debilitating and paralyzing master, keeping the individual in bondage.

Most people struggle, to one degree or another, to overcome the paralyzing influence of fear in life. Fear may present itself in many shapes and sizes. The *fear of death* imprisons multitudes (cf. Heb. 2:15). "The *fear of man*," that is, an excessive concern for the opinion of others, "is a snare," says Solomon (Pro. 29:25a). So called "peer pressure" is nothing more than what the Bible terms "the fear of man." The *fear of the unknown, of rejection, of change, of public speaking*, and *of failure* are emotions that most of us know all too well.

A website named "The Phobia List"[1] catalogs 533 different kinds of fear, among the more unique are *atomosophobia* (fear of atomic explosions; I understand that one), *consecotaleophobia* (fear of chopsticks), *ecclesiophobia* (fear of church; a bunch of professing Christians are apparently troubled by this one), *ergophobia* (fear of work; many Americans seem to have been stricken with this fear), *hippopotomonstrosesquipedaliophobia* (fear of long words), *triskaidekaphobia* (fear of the number 13), *phobophobia* (fear of fear), and *panophobia* (fear of everything). Of course, some of these fears may appear to many of us as exaggerated and embellished, but to those who struggle with them, they present a monumental challenge to overcome.

Five hundred thirty-three different phobias! If you feel somewhat "normal" before reading the list, you are sure to feel differently afterward. In popular teenage vernacular, we might say that people are really "messed up." Indeed, we are. In fact, such has been the case since Adam and Eve first took flight from God to hide in the Garden of Eden. When God inquired for the motive behind the

---

[1] http://phobialist.com/

action, Adam explained, *"I heard thy voice in the garden, and I was afraid, because I was naked; and I hid myself"* (Gen. 3:10). Such self-conscious fear has been the struggle of humanity since that first sin. In fact, it may be said that a large portion of life in this sinful world is taken up with the effort to overcome the many fears that tend to dominate the heart and mind.

Life Involves Risk

I heard about a woman who, in order to protect herself from further pain, decided to never leave the house. She felt she could protect herself from accidents, mistreatment, and conflict by staying inside all the time. So, in order to preserve life, she shut herself away from the outside world. Fear made her a prisoner in her own home.

Do you see the paradox in the story? In order to preserve her life, she shut herself away from life. Life involves risk. Everyone who gives a speech risks the controversy of disagreement. The individual who takes a test risks failure. The person who visits the doctor risks discovery of some dread disease. The individual who reaches out to another risks rejection. Does it make sense then to never speak up, or sit for the test, or visit the doctor when necessary, or interact with others? What kind of life would that be? It would be no life at all. Fear deceives the individual into thinking that eliminating risk will preserve life. Instead, eliminating risk eliminates life, for life involves risk. Fear makes prisoners of us all, leaving us to waste away in the dark little dungeon of "what if?"

It is common for someone who has suffered some form of pain to avoid in the future and attempt to escape from new situations that might produce a repetition of the former misery. A person, for instance, who has suffered the pain of a rejection and a broken heart tends to surround himself/herself with layers of protection, or emotional walls, to safeguard the heart from being hurt again. The fear is sometimes so strong and the protective psychological fortress so impregnable that a relationship with any semblance of intimacy with such a person is impossible. Only superficial, cursory, clinical interaction is allowed.

The walls are intended to protect life. The paradox, however, is that life is essentially relational. It is not job performance or intellectual achievement or athletic prowess or social prestige that makes a life. Life is a matter of relationships. It is the people in my life that have the capacity, more than anything else, to bring me the greatest joy and, yes, to produce the greatest challenges to my character. When I come to the end of my pilgrim journey, I will not reflect on the trophies or medals I won in athletic competition, or the I.Q. score I attained. I will think about my wife, my children, my grandchildren, my parents, my siblings, my brothers and sisters in Christ, and my friends. Relationships are what life is all about. As risky and frightening as it is to invest in those relationships, life is worth the risk of a personal slight or disappointment from time to time.

God is not the Source of Fear

Though fear, as a human experience, is pervasive, God calls upon His people to live in this frightening world with fearless courage. "Fear not" is one of the most common exhortations in Scripture. Approximately one hundred fifteen times, the Bible employs the imperative to "fear not" or "be not afraid."

The first occurrence of this imperative is Genesis 15:1: "*Fear not, Abram: I am thy shield, and thy exceeding great reward.*" Abraham had just returned from a military victory in which he rescued his nephew Lot. When the king of Sodom offered to divide the spoils with him, Abraham refused to take anything, not even a thread or shoe-lace, lest the king take credit for making Abraham wealthy. I'm sure the fear of poverty and the daily pressure to keep a family fed was considerable for a Bedouin in the desert, but God says, "Fear not, I am thy exceeding great reward."

Further, I feel certain that Abraham, like any of us, might have felt the need to look over his shoulder lest the folks he had defeated in battle gather reinforcements to launch a retaliatory attack and revenge their losses. But God said, "Fear not, I am thy shield."

The message was very appropriate for the moment: "Abraham, don't be afraid, but trust in me. I'll be your Protector. I'll be your Provider." Any fear he might have felt did not come from the Lord. God was not the source of his fear; God was the solution.

This truth is also taught in the New Testament. It was a dangerous thing to be a Christian in the first century A.D. A few believers in Jesus Christ had been martyred and others imprisoned. Paul, who was himself a prisoner at the time, knew that Timothy, his colleague in ministry, was struggling with feelings of intimidation because of the pressure of persecution.

Wouldn't it be easier, Timothy must have thought, to sort of lay low, to fly under the radar, and to hope that the climate of unpopularity will soon change? In what would prove to be his final epistle before his own martyrdom, Paul wrote to inform Timothy that the climate of persecution would not change—that persecution is every Christian's lot (cf. 2 Tim. 3:12). He encourages Timothy not to be *"ashamed of the gospel of our Lord Jesus Christ, nor of me His prisoner,"* but to be *"a partaker of the afflictions of the gospel according to the power of God"* (2 Tim. 1:8). And he does so on the basis that *"God has not given us the spirit of fear, but of love and of power and of a sound mind"* (2 Tim. 1:7).

It helps me when feeling afraid to remember that God is not the source of fear: *"God has not given us the spirit of fear."* Fear doesn't originate with Him.

If fear doesn't come from God, then what is its source? The answer may surprise you. The preponderance of biblical evidence suggests that fear rises in the heart when a person loses sight of the Lord.

Consider a couple of biblical examples.

1. In 1 Samuel 17, both King Saul and all Israel were "greatly afraid" when they heard Goliath's proposed solution to the standoff (v. 11). Each time the giant of Gath emerged from his tent to repeat the challenge, the mere sight of this imposing figure struck fear into their hearts: *"And all the men of Israel, when they saw the man, fled from him, and were sore afraid"* (v. 24). But David did not flee in fear. He retorted, *"Who is*

this uncircumcised Philistine, that he should defy the armies of the living God?" (1 Sam. 17:26). It is noteworthy that this is the first time in the entire narrative of 1 Samuel 17 that the name of God is mentioned. The Israelite soldiers were afraid because they had forgotten God. They viewed the situation only in secular terms of human might and human ability. David, however, saw the entire scene as an affront to the glory of the God of Israel.

2.   In Matthew 14, Jesus approaches the disciples in the midst of a storm on the Sea of Galilee. They are startled by the amazing sight of this figure walking on the water, but the Lord assuages their fears by identifying himself: *"Be of good cheer; it is I; be not afraid"* (v. 27). Then Peter, in an act of tremendous faith says, *"Lord, if it be thou, bid me come unto thee on the water,"* and Jesus said *"Come"* (vs. 28, 29a). While his eyes were on the Lord Jesus, Peter did the impossible. He *"walked on the water, to go to Jesus"* (v. 29b). Then, he took his eyes off the Lord and faith turned to fear: *"But when he saw the wind boisterous, he was afraid; and beginning to sink, he cried, saying, Lord, save me."* (v. 30). Fear filled the vacuum left by his flagging faith.

The Fear of God Remedies Every Other Fear

No, God not the source of fear, but He is the remedy of it. In fact, the clearer is a person's sight of God, the less room there is for fear to invade the heart. *"What time I am afraid,"* resolved David, *"I will trust in thee"* (Ps. 56:3). According to the caption, Psalm 56 was composed during the apprehensive time in David's fugitive years "when the Philistines took him in Gath." I'm sure that, surrounded by Israel's perennial enemy in the hometown of the giant he had slain, David had ample reason to be afraid; nevertheless, on each occasion fear began to raise its head, he deliberately turned his thoughts to the Lord in believing trust.

No doubt, he also prayed, for prayer is an expression of faith in God. The very man who wrote the salient words of the previous Psalm, *"Cast thy burden upon the Lord, and he shall sustain thee"* (Ps. 55:22), most certainly put his own counsel into practice during this tenuous experience. We may be sure that he acknowledged his fears to the Lord and asked for God's protecting providence, resting in the knowledge both of God's ability and willingness to answer his prayer.

Not only did David find that faith in God was the antidote to the paralyzing poison of fear in the heart, but Nehemiah did as well. When tattling to the Persian officials and ridiculing the builders—the initial efforts of Sanballat and Tobiah to halt Nehemiah's rebuilding project—failed, they hatched a sinister plot with the help of the Arabians, Ammonites and Ashdodites to attack the workers while they worked (Neh. 4:7-8). The threat together with the monumental challenges involved in the reconstruction project was enough to discourage the builders: *"And Judah said, The strength of the bearers of burdens is decayed, and there is much rubbish; so that we are not able to build the wall. And our adversaries said, They shall not know, neither see, till we come in the midst among them, and slay them, and cause the work to cease"* (vs. 10-11).

Fatigue and fear make for a disastrous combination; and Nehemiah had a real problem on his hands. What should he do? The wise leader first took physical steps to protect the people, positioning the builders according to their families on the wall and arming them for self-defense (v. 13). Then he verbally encouraged the builders saying, *"Be not afraid of them: remember the Lord, which is great and terrible, and fight for your brethren, your sons, your daughters, your wives, and your houses"* (Neh. 4:14).

Be not afraid: remember the Lord! In particular he reminded them that the Lord is "great and terrible," or if you please, awesome and terrifying. Whatever terror Sanballat and Tobiah may be able to strike in the hearts of the Jews, God was more terrifying still.

This verse, together with several others, reveals an important principle. Simply stated, it is the truth that the fear of the Lord is the remedy for every other fear. When the believer possesses an accurate understanding and abiding perception of God's reality in his heart, in other words, there is literally no room for any other fear to invade the mind. This is precisely the point made in Isaiah 8:12b-13: "...*neither fear ye their fear, nor be afraid. Sanctify the Lord of hosts himself; and let him be your fear, and let him be your dread.*"

In this passage, God warns Isaiah not to adopt the conventional wisdom of his day. It was common then, as it is now, for nations under threat from an enemy to seek alliances with other nations. God counsels Isaiah not to allow fear to tempt him to make a confederacy with other nations, but to find refuge and security in God alone (cf. v. 14). Fear the Lord alone and seek asylum in Him, and there will be no need either to fear an approaching army or to pay the price of compromise necessary to ally yourself to a pagan nation.

Indeed, fear frequently leads a person to compromise conviction for the sake of security. The adolescent who silences conscience to take a drink or smoke a joint lest he be rejected by the group is a classic example of the power of fear. If that young man had just remembered that his God was near and able to protect him from whatever recrimination his refusal to participate might bring, and in fact ready to bless him for his steadfast commitment to biblical values, he would have both the necessary motivation and strength to resist the temptation.

The fact is that people are more real to us than God is; consequently, we fear man and forget God. How preferable it is to forget man and fear the Lord! Make it your aim to live every moment with such a prevailing sense of His presence and power that no circumstance with which you may meet in daily life may sway your heart.

Jesus teaches his disciples to face potential persecution by remembering the reality of God's providential involvement: "*Fear not them which kill the body, but are not able to kill the soul: but rather fear him which is able to destroy both soul and body in hell*" (Mt. 10:28). The worst that man may do to another person is to inflict temporary, physical harm. Other people are incapable of doing harm to your relationship with God or who you are on the inside. Live your life, says Jesus, with an eye to pleasing God, not trying to make other people happy.

Contrary to most other fears, the fear of the Lord is a healthy fear. Just as there is a righteous anger and a godly jealousy, there is such a thing as a healthy fear. We train children not to rush willy-nilly into the road, or to keep a safe distance from a fire, or to stay relatively close to shore when swimming, because of the attendant dangers of these various phenomena. Such respect for the power of nature is a healthy fear.

Likewise, a reverential respect for the power of God and a cognitive awareness of his presence every moment of the day is a healthy fear. The more attuned a person is to God's reality, the less intimidated he/she will be by other people or daily circumstances, for who or what could be greater than Him?

Love, the Best Medicine for Fear

The gospel teaches us a truth, even more sublime. It teaches that the individual who is sensible of God's love to poor sinners has even better reason to bid farewell to fear: *"There is no fear in love; but perfect love casteth out fear: because fear hath torment. He that feareth is not made perfect in love"* (1 Jno. 4:18). The reality of God's power and presence is sufficient to allay our fears, but nothing puts fear to flight like a sense of His wondrous love.

Nothing infuses courage and confidence in the heart of a child quite like the awareness that he/she is loved by father and mother. The safe environment of a loving home equips a young person to face a cruel world without intimidation, for he knows that, come what may, he is not alone in this world. He will always have a place, an identity, a purpose, a helper, and a safe haven from the storms of life. He can stand up for a persecuted classmate against the schoolyard bully; she can resist the pressure of her peers to conform to the crowd; he can compete for the championship without fear of failure; she can endure the possibility of a broken heart or unrequited love, for filial love more than compensates for every other setback.

Even so, a sense of the perfect love of God as demonstrated at the cross, expels fear. If God loved you enough to give His only begotten Son—the Darling of heaven, the Best of the best—to die in your place, then what does it really matter if people reject, ridicule, or ignore you? Indeed, it may smart for a moment, but an abiding sense that your Heavenly Father knows, accepts and highly values you—that you are an object of His wondrous love—is better than life (Ps. 63:3), sweeter than wine (S.S. 1:2), and stronger than death (S. S. 8:6).

What place is there for fear where one possesses a knowledge that *"the Father himself loveth"* him (Jno. 16:27a)? Have you ever observed a little infant embraced in the arms of a loving mother, or seated on the lap of a gentle father? Do you notice any trepidation in the child's countenance? Does he tremble with anxiety? Is she troubled with doubts or fears? No. There is not the slightest hint of careful thought. No thought of potential threat or danger even dares to enter that little one's mind. Love has produced in the child a sense of total confidence and trust.

Love dispels fear because love cultivates trust, and faith and fear cannot coexist. If that is true in terms of a parent/child relationship, it is certainly so in redemptive terms. Assurance of my personal interest in the merits of the Lord Jesus Christ gives me confidence that it shall be well with me in the end.

> "His love in times past forbids me to think
> He'll leave me at last in trouble to sink;
> Each sweet Ebenezer I have in review
> Confirms His good pleasure to see me right through."

Faith reasons from the premise of God's love as follows: If God loved me enough to spare not His own Son, then He loves me enough to supply my every present need (cf. Rom. 8:32). If God loved me enough to forgive my many sins, then He loves me enough to sustain me in present trials.

The best remedy for addressing the malady of your gripping and paralyzing fears, therefore, is to pitch camp close to the cross of Calvary. Meditate frequently on God's great love to your unworthy soul. Acquiesce your troubled soul on the downy bed of redeeming love. Bathe away the grime of fear in meditation on the cleansing efficacy of the blood of the Lamb. Fix your gaze firmly on the Christ of the cross, and rest in the shade of His smiling favor. The God of heaven accepts you because of His beloved Son (cf. Eph. 1:6). Come what may in this life, nothing will ever change that fact.

Winning the Battle for Your Mind

The thrust of my counsel to you in terms of overcoming fear and anxiety is simply this: Take control of your thought life. In a very real sense, the battle to overcome fear and worry is won or lost in the mind.

The importance of thinking biblically, as an essential discipline of daily discipleship, is the primary theme of Philippians 4. Paul concludes this "thank you" epistle to the church at Philippi by saying, "*Finally, brethren, whatsoever things are true, whatsoever things are honest, whatsoever things are just, whatsoever things are pure, whatsoever things are lovely, whatsoever things are of good report; if there be any virtue, and if there be any praise, think on these things*" (Phi. 4:8). What will be the result of such a targeted mental focus? Two priceless benefits, one inward and one outward, will result: 1. Inwardly, the peace of God will guard your heart and mind from anxiety (v. 7); 2. Outwardly, the God of peace will be with you (v. 9).

"Yes," you ask, "but how?" How may I direct my thoughts to focus more on things that are virtuous, true, pure and lovely? By what means may I break the habit of rolling my fears over and over again in my mind? As it is true with any bad habit, you must work at it. It is hard; it takes deliberate effort, but it is not impossible to break the cycle.

Paul counseled, "*Exercise thyself unto godliness*" (1 Tim. 4:7). *Gumnasio*, the Greek word translated "exercise" gives us our English word "gymnasium." The point is unmistakable: Godliness doesn't happen by magic. It takes decisive, disciplined, diligent effort, just like an athlete training for competition.

What would you think of an athlete training for the Olympic games who slept until 10 a.m. every day, ate marshmallows for breakfast, and decided after a bit of muscle stretching that he needed to take a break for his favorite television show? Everyone knows that progress toward a goal will not be made without a detailed plan and a commitment to follow it over the long-term.

No, that athlete must rise early, take in plenty of carbohydrates, train stridently, and continue to do so day after day until the competition event. Progress may be slow at first, but over time, muscles will be trained for peak performance.

Likewise, the spiritual disciplines of Bible reading and daily meditation are the hard work necessary to break free from the ruts of fear. When a believer in the Lord Jesus Christ is tired of living as a slave to habits of thinking such as fear and anxiety, disciplined Scripture intake may provide slow, initial progress, but perseverance in this new biblical habit will bring incredible results. I know it is true. I've proven it to be so in my own life.

It works like this. Just as the human body will not operate properly without the proper and regular intake of its appropriate fuel, your heart and mind will not function spiritually without daily input from the word of God. What happens to your body when it is not adequately hydrated or starved of protein? It shuts down, doesn't it? Similarly, spiritual vitality in the inward man depends on a regular, balanced, spiritual diet from God's word.

The Bible is the tangible resource God has provided to nourish the soul. Show me someone who reads regularly in God's word, listens to recorded sermons throughout the day, and regularly interacts with fellow believers, and I'll show you someone whose mind is disciplined for peak performance in daily life. Such a biblical perspective on other people, current events, and the world in which he lives gives him a context for interpreting every circumstance and encounter during the day. It's hard to frighten or worry someone with news of a coming economic collapse or the growth of a terrorist group who believingly read Psalm 46 that morning:

God is our refuge and strength, a very present help in trouble.

Therefore will not we fear, though the earth be removed, and though the mountains be carried into the midst of the sea; though the waters roar and be troubled, though the mountains shake with the swelling thereof.

There is a river, the streams whereof make glad the city of God, the holy place of the tabernacles of the most High.

God is in the midst of her; she shall not be moved: God shall help her, and that right early.

It's nigh impossible to intimidate the man who spent time in meditation on Psalm 27 at the break of the day:

The Lord is my light and my salvation; whom shall I fear? The Lord is the strength of my life; of whom shall I be afraid?

When the wicked, even mine enemies and my foes, came upon me to eat up my flesh, they stumbled and fell.

Though an host should encamp against me, my heart shall not fear; though war should rise against me, in this will I be confident.

Isaiah 26:3 is a good illustration of the role of the mind in terms of the quest to overcome fear and anxiety: *"Thou wilt keep him in perfect peace whose mind is stayed upon Thee, because he trusteth in Thee."* You may keep your mind "stayed" or focused on God by means of filling your mind with God's word, i.e. daily biblical input. But it must be read *believingly* ("...because he trusteth in Thee"), or existentially, if you will.

What does it mean to read the Bible existentially? It means that you read it as if you are having a personal worship service between you and the Lord. It means that you use your Bible as a springboard to think thoughts like, "This is my God; this is His promise to me; this is what He has done for His people in former days and what He is still able to do for me; this is what He requires of me in this situation; this is how one of His children reacted when they went through a similar circumstance as I now face, and by His help, I can respond in the same way; etc." It means reflecting on who God is and what He has done for His frail and fallible children in days past and gone, praising Him for His wondrous grace, and applying the truths you consider to your own case even now. It means using your Bible reading as a springboard to prayer, and pouring out your complaints of fear and anxiety to a Father who truly loves you, and petitioning Him to engage His heavenly resources to meet you at the point of your need, and doing it with total confidence that He hears the cries of His little ones and has pledged Himself in covenant commitment to do what is in your best interest, then leaving your cares in His very capable hands.

God's word to every fearful heart today is as contemporary as His word to Joshua many years ago: "*Only be thou strong and very courageous, that thou mayest observe to do according to all the law...turn not from it to the right hand or to the left, that thou mayest prosper whithersoever thou goest. This book of the law shall not depart out of thy mouth; but thou shalt meditate therein day and night, that thou mayest observe to do according to all that is written therein: for then shalt thou make thy way prosperous, and then thou shalt have good success. Have not I commanded thee? Be strong and of a good courage; be not afraid, neither be thou dismayed: for the Lord thy God is with thee whithersoever thou goest*" (Jos. 1:7-9). Stay close to the word of God, friend, and the God of the word will stay close to you.

Part III

General Comfort

12
Songs in the Night

"Where is God my Maker, who giveth songs in the night." (Job 35:10)

One of my earliest religious impressions concerned the case of a widow woman in the church of my childhood. I distinctly recall the story of her fright.

It seems that on Monday evening of the previous week, a motorcycle gang parked in her front yard just outside of her bedroom window. She lay in bed, paralyzed with fear, listening to them laugh and talk. She slept not a wink all night. The next morning she found empty beer cans under the tree on her front lawn.

On Tuesday night, they returned. Again, she lay as still as she could, afraid of what they might do. After an hour or so in fear for these strangers just beyond her window pane, she began to sing. In a soft soprano voice, she sang,

> Amazing Grace! How sweet the sound!
> That saved a wretch like me;
> I once was lost but now am found;
> Was blind, but now I see.

When she reached verse three, an increase in volume marked her growing confidence:

> Thro' many dangers, toils and snares
> I have already come;
> 'Tis grace has brought me safe thus far,
> And grace will lead me home.

By the time she finished the hymn, the unwelcome visitors had left, never to return again. Her fellow church members repeated the story among themselves that Sunday, thankful for the Lord's protection of His dear child, encouraged by her genuine faith in God.

Our gracious and benevolent God gives many rich gifts to His children. Eternal life is a gift of His sovereign grace (Rom. 6:23; Eph. 2:8). He gives grace now and glory later (Ps. 86:11). He gives gifts of spiritual capacity for Christian ministry and service (Eph. 4:11ff). But one of our Lord's best gifts to his people is the gift of song in the midst of affliction. God gives "songs in the night."

The text that heads this chapter contains the words of Elihu, one of Job's friends. Perhaps there is no more classic example of suffering affliction (that is, beside the Lord Jesus Christ on the cross) than the narrative of Job. The inspired biography of Job's great losses and attending anguish of soul and mental perplexity it spawned is the epitome of an experience old writers sometimes referred to as "the dark night of the soul."

Elihu makes the point in this particular speech that in his efforts to clear himself of any wrong-doing, Job had not even bothered to pray and come to God during the entire ordeal. He says, in effect, "Job, not once have you even applied to the Lord to give you a song to sing in your night of sorrow."

"God...who giveth songs in the night..." It is, admittedly, a unique and intriguing way to describe our God. Though He may dispel the darkness of circumstance, it is not generally His way to do so. Instead, the Lord typically provides resources to assist the believer to endure the long night of heartache and affliction. One such grace is the gift of a song in the night.

Prisoners in the Philippian jail heard such a midnight melody echo one night about two thousand years ago: *"And at midnight, Paul and Silas prayed, and sang praises unto God: and the prisoners heard them"* (Acts 16:25). How strange it must have sounded to them to hear two fellow prisoners sing praises to God in a jail cell! They had heard many a fellow scream and curse and blaspheme God and king, but never before had they be privy to such a concert of jubilant praise. Here it is that we may see the triumph of a living faith over the dark circumstances of life. Though feet and hands were shackled fast, their unchained hearts soared far above circumstance in communion with Christ. Only God can give such a freedom of soul.

Has the Lord ever given you a "song in the night"? As I think back on the various seasons of perplexity and distress through which I've passed, I can pinpoint certain hymns that proved to be a source of great comfort and strength to my soul until the night had passed.

Early in my personal experience, I felt deep conviction of sin. The old hymn by Isaac Watts, "Show Pity, Lord, O Lord forgive" became my theme song during those few months. The lyrics spoke to my heart with profound relevance, as if they had been penned just for me. I especially felt the weight of the third verse:

> Should sudden vengeance seize my breath,
> I must pronounce Thee just in death;
> And if my soul were sent to hell,
> Thy righteous law approves it well.

Through the tears of repentance, however, I found unique comfort in the plea for mercy from a gracious God:

> My crimes are great but don't surpass
> The power and glory of Thy grace;
> Great God, Thy nature hath no bound,
> So let Thy pard'ning love be found.

> Yet save a trembling sinner, Lord,
> Whose hope still hov'ring round Thy word,
> Would light on some sweet promise there,
> Some sure support against despair.

Although my night of initial conviction has long since passed, yet my heart is still tender toward this particular hymn. Whenever it is selected by some unwitting worshipper, it takes me back to that bittersweet season of soul travail I experienced those many years ago and gives me cause to rejoice in the Lord for sweet relief in the gospel of free grace.

Christian people have been given a tremendous resource in the hymns of the faith. Of course, the word of God and prayer should always be the believer's mainstay when he/she seeks help in affliction, but wise is the person who also keeps his hymnal close to his side. If you are like me, you may find your own experience described in detail in one or more of these hymns or spiritual songs, whatever the particular trial you currently face may be. The following are some of the "songs in the night" that have seemed especially contemporary to my case through the years—hymns that the Lord has used to encourage and strengthen me in my time of need.

"How Firm a Foundation!"
A Song for the Night of Trial

I do not know of a Christian hymn more suited to every sufferer's case than the stately, faith-building hymn titled "How Firm a Foundation!" Whatever the particular circumstances of trouble you may face, the precious promises of this hymn will speak poignantly to your need.

This beloved hymn is peculiarly helpful because it is so thoroughly biblical. In fact, the first verse defines the song's theme in terms of the sufficiency of Scripture to buttress the believer in times of trial. Each succeeding verse builds on a particular biblical promise.

In verse two of this hymn, the writer draws from the promise in Deuteronomy 33:25b: "*As thy days, so shall thy strength be.*" Here is a comprehensive, biblical promise, applicable to every circumstance and eventuality of life:

> In every condition, in sickness, in health,
> In poverty's vale, or abounding in wealth,
> At home, or abroad, on the land, on the sea,
> "As thy days shall demand, shall thy strength ever be."

Verse three highlights Isaiah 41:10: "*Fear thou not; for I am with thee: be not dismayed; for I am thy God: I will strengthen thee; yea, I will help thee; yea, I will uphold thee with the right hand of my righteousness.*" The repetition of the affirmation "yea" in the text emphasizes the certainty of God's intention to keep His promise. Note the poet's take on this great promise:

> Fear not, I am with thee, O be not dismayed,
> For I am thy God and will still give thee aid;
> I'll strengthen thee, help thee, and cause thee to stand,
> Upheld by my righteous, omnipotent hand.

Verse four is taken from the precious promise in Isaiah 43:2: "*When thou passest through the waters, I will be with thee; and through the rivers, they shall not overflow thee: when thou walkest through the fire, thou shalt not be burnt; neither shall the flame kindle upon thee.*" The hymn-writer expresses the sentiment of this text as follows:

> When through the deep waters I call thee to go,
> The rivers of woe shall not thee overflow;
> For I will be with thee thy troubles to bless,
> And sanctify to thee thy deepest distress.

How precious is the repetition of this Divine pledge to accompany His loved one through the deep waters of affliction and the raging rivers of sorrow! And, may I add, don't miss the significance of that preposition "through" in the text. *Through the waters…through the rivers…through the fire…* The Lord does not intend to take His child into the midst of suffering and to leave him there. His abiding presence will be with them all the way through until they emerge on the other side.

In verse five, the poet couples the last half of Isaiah 43:2 with the Father's reply to Paul's request for removal of his thorn in the flesh ("*My grace is sufficient for thee…*" – 2 Cor. 12:9):

> When through fiery trials thy pathway shall lie,
> My grace, all sufficient, shall be thy supply;
> The flame shall not hurt thee—I only design

Thy dross to consume and thy gold to refine.

Like Paul (and the three Hebrews – Dan. 3), we too pass through the furnace of affliction from time to time in our pilgrimage here. The purpose of the flame is not, however, to consume the believer but to purge out the residual impurities that we may emerge as a sanctified vessel that is "meet for the Master's use" (cf. 2 Tim. 2:21). How reassuring to know that the fire will not harm any part of personal character except that which needs to be removed! Though the lump will not be as big when it comes through the furnace as it was when it went in, it will be more pure. And while the heat is put to the metal, His grace will be sufficient (lit. enough; adequate) to see you through to the end.

Verse six draws from Isaiah 46:4: "*And even to your old age I am he; and even to hoar hairs will I carry you: I have made, and I will bear; even I will carry, and will deliver you.*" Taking his cue from this cheering Divine pledge to attend the needs of His loved ones all the way to the end of life's journey, the poet writes:

> E'en down to old age, all my people shall prove
> My sovereign, eternal, unchangeable love;
> And when hoary hairs shall their temples adorn,
> Like lambs they shall still in my bosom be borne.

What unspeakable comfort to those who struggle with "age and feebleness extreme"! The God who loved His own before time began has pledged Himself in covenant commitment to carry them to the very end.

The final verse of this wonderful hymn builds on the promise of Hebrews 13:5b: "*For He hath said, I will never leave thee, nor forsake thee.*" Interestingly, the Greek term translated "never" in this verse suggests a double-negative. It means, literally, "never, no never." The hymn-writer picks up that unique feature twice in this final stanza:

> The soul that on Jesus still leans for repose,
> I will not, I will not desert to his foes;
> That soul, though all hell should endeavor to shake,
> I'll never, no never, no never forsake.

This stalwart old hymn first appeared in Dr. John Rippon's 1787 production titled *Selection of Hymns*. It made its first appearance in America in William Caldwell's 1837 publication *Union Harmony*. It was a favorite among Civil War soldiers (one may readily understand the comfort and strength they derived from its biblical sentiment). Andrew "Stonewall" Jackson requested it to be sung at his bedside shortly before he died at the Hermitage. Robert E. Lee also selected it for his funeral hymn "as an expression of his full trust in the ways of the Heavenly Father."[1] Perhaps you may also find heavenly comfort in meditation on this time-tested "song in the night."

"Lead, Kindly Light"
A Song for the Night of Uncertainty

John Newman's (1801-1890) hymn, "Lead, Kindly Light," is a prayer for guidance. All who feel to have lost their way and cry out for direction may find language in this old hymn to resonate with their need. The tune *Lux Benigna* by John B. Dykes (1823-1876) was composed peculiarly for this hymn poem.

The first verse is the *petitionary* portion of the prayer—a prayer breathed from the darkness of uncertainty, addressed to God as the hymn-writer's "kindly [*sympathetic; considerate*] Light":

> Lead, kindly Light, amid the encircling gloom,
> Lead Thou me on!
> The night is dark and I am far from home;
> Lead Thou me on!
> Keep Thou my feet;
> I do not ask to see the distant scene;

---

[1] Kenneth W. Osbeck, *101 Hymn Stories*, p. 97.

One step enough for me.

Verse two is the *confessional* portion of the prayer. The poet admits that this request to be led by the Lord was not always his desire. Instead, he previously wanted to live life as he saw fit and as he deemed best. It is evident that God has wrought a great change in the hymn-writer's life, for he now seeks the Lord's will and begs forgiveness for his stubborn self-will:

> I was not ever thus, nor prayed that Thou
> Should'st lead me on;
> I loved to choose and see my path, but now,
> Lead Thou me on!
> I loved the garish day,
> And, spite of fears,
> Pride ruled my will;
> Remember not past years!

The final verse contains the *praise* portion of the prayer. It breathes the spirit of resolved faith and steady confidence in the Lord. The writer knows that God, through His mighty power, had faithfully led him thus far, and his confidence for the future, whatever the circumstantial terrain through which he must travel, is in this same almighty God, until his journey culminates in happy reunion with loved ones gone before:

> So long Thy power hath blest me, sure it still
> Will lead me on
> O'er moor and fen, o'er crag and torrent, 'til
> The night is gone;
> And with the morn
> Those angel faces smile,
> Which I have loved long since,
> And lost awhile.

"Abide With Me"
A Song for the Night of Change

Henry Lyte (1793-1847) was an obscure pastor in Lower Brixham, Devonshire, England, a poor fishing village. For twenty-three years, Lyte loved and served the humble congregation. During the week, residents of Brixham regularly saw the devout minister walking by the seashore, meditating and talking to the Lord.

But though Lyte was strong in faith and spirit, he was also a man of frail health. He had recurring bouts of tuberculosis and chronic asthma throughout his lifetime. In the latter years of his pastorate at Brixham, his health grew progressively worse until his doctor advised him to move to Italy for the sake of his health. Lyte replied, "I know no other personal sacrifice I would more regret than to be forced to leave the ocean. From childhood it has been my friend and playmate and I have never been weary gazing on its glorious face."[2]

On Sunday, September 4, 1847, Lyte was so weak that he almost had to crawl into the pulpit to deliver his final sermon, a message in which he expressed his desire for his congregants "to prepare for the solemn hour which must come to all by a timely appreciation and dependence on the death of Christ."[3]

That afternoon, somewhat revived in body, Lyte took a final stroll along the seacoast, thinking of the friends with whom he had shared the joys and sorrows of life for the past quarter-century. As twilight approached, the dramatic changes facing him prompted him to pray and meditate on the urgent solicitation made by two disciples to the risen Christ: *"Abide with us, for it is toward evening and the day is far spent"* (Lk. 24:29). He penned the words of his twilight prayer to God:

Abide with me; fast falls the eventide;

---

[2] J. C. Yoakum, "Hymn Time," unpublished manuscript.
[3] Osbeck, p. 17

The darkness deepens; Lord with me abide;
When other helpers fail and comforts flee,
Help of the helpless, O abide with me!

Swift to its close ebbs out life's little day;
Earth's joys grow dim, its glories pass away;
Change and decay in all around I see;
O Thou who changest not, abide with me!

Thus on my head in early youth didst smile;
And though rebellious and perverse meanwhile,
Thou hast not left me, oft as I left Thee;
On to the close, O Lord, abide with me.

I need Thy presence every passing hour;
What but Thy grace can foil the tempter's power?
Who like Thyself my guide and stay can be?
Through cloud and sunshine, O abide with me!

I fear no foe, with Thee at hand to bless;
Ills have no weight, and tears no bitterness.
Where is death's sting? Where, grave, thy victory?
I triumph still, if Thou abide with me.

Hold Thou Thy cross before my closing eyes;
Shine through the gloom and point me to the skies;
Heaven's morning breaks and earth's vain shadows flee;
In life, in death, O Lord, abide with me![4]

Mr. Lyte never reached Italy. He died November 20, 1847 in Nice, France, two months after preaching his final message to his beloved people. His twilight prayer by the sea at the close of what had been the happiest chapter of his life, however, has since resonated in the

---

[4] The original hymn actually includes two more stanzas. See *Primitive Baptist Hymnal*, Second Edition, No. 373.

hearts of numerous Christians who, like Henry Lyte, cried out to the God who changes not for His abiding presence.

"What a Friend We Have in Jesus"
A Song for the Night of Sorrow

Joseph Scriven (1819-1886) knew sorrow. In his early twenties, the young Irishman had just graduated from Trinity College in Dublin and was engaged to be married to his childhood sweetheart. The day before their wedding, Scriven's fiancé rode out to meet him at the River Bonn. Her horse was startled and threw her into the water, knocking her unconscious. She was accidentally drowned just moments before he arrived. As he looked into the lifeless face of the girl he was to marry the next day, the bottom dropped out of his world. The shock of grief he felt would remain with him for the rest of his life.

In 1845, Scriven migrated to Canada. Most historians agree that his motives for leaving Ireland included an attempt to escape the memory of that terrible tragedy. For the next forty-odd years in Port Hope, Ontario, Joseph Scriven lived a life of indefatigable service and ministry to the poor and earned the nickname "the Good Samaritan of Port Hope." He shared his meager possessions with those in need, at times even donating the clothes on his body to the needy. He sought out orphans and did patch-carpentry *free gratis* for widows while refusing to labor for those who could pay him. The story is told of the man who, seeing Scriven on the street with his sawbuck and saw, asked "Who is that man? I want him to work for me." A local resident replied, "You cannot get that man; he saws wood only for poor widows and sick people who cannot pay."[5]

In 1850, Scriven was hired as tutor to the ten year old son of Robert Pengelley near Bailieboro, Ontario. He lived with the Pengelleys for the next five years. There he met Eliza Roche, Mrs. Pengelley's niece. In 1859, Joseph and Eliza were engaged. He was 39 and she 22.

---

[5] Ibid., p. 276.

Then tragedy struck a second time. The Plymouth Brethren to whom Scriven belonged required that Eliza be baptized by immersion. The service was performed in the frozen waters of Lake Rice in April, 1860. Eliza, who was already ill with consumption, developed pneumonia from the experience and, despite Joseph's diligent care for her, died four months later on August 6, 1860. The incredible heartbreak of losing another woman he loved drove him, once more, to draw nigh to the Lord in humble prayer.

It was about that time that Joseph Scriven received news from Dublin of his mother's serious illness and depression. In the letter he sent to comfort her, he included a poem he had written, entitled by him "Pray Without Ceasing." The profoundly simple (yet simply profound) lyrics display the kind of solace he himself had found in his dark night of sorrow:

> What a Friend we have in Jesus, all our sins and griefs to bear!
> What a privilege to carry everything to God in prayer!
> O what peace we often forfeit; O what needless pain we bear,
> All because we do not carry everything to God in prayer.
>
> Have we trials and temptations? Is there trouble anywhere?
> We should never be discouraged: take it to the Lord in prayer.
> Can we find a Friend so faithful who will all our sorrows share?
> Jesus knows our every weakness: take it to the Lord in prayer.
>
> Are we weak and heavy laden, cumbered with a load of care?
> Precious Savior, still our refuge: take it to the Lord in prayer.
> Do thy friends despise, forsake thee?[6] Take it to the Lord in prayer;
> In His arms He'll take and shield thee; thou wilt find a solace there.

The friendship of Jesus Christ was a reality in Scriven's life. Some years later when an acquaintance called on him, he saw the poem

[6] The original may have read, "Has thy brother, sister grieved thee?" (www.porthopehistory.com/jmscriven/josephscriven.htm; from *The Guide*, Dec. 14, 1900.)

scribbled on a scratch piece of paper near Joseph's sick bed. He asked Joseph if he had written the poem and the humble man replied, "The Lord and I did it together."

Scriven's "song in the night" of his sorrow highlights the incredible privilege of going to the Lord in prayer and finding refuge in Jesus our Helper and Friend. Indeed, the child of God may find his prayer closet to be a quiet refuge in the time of need. There you may unburden your soul in the confidence that your Heavenly Father knows and He cares. There you may gain an audience with the only One who can remedy your situation, and One who has promised to provide grace sufficient for your every trial. There you will find your soul's true Friend, who is also the Father's dear Son, to take your case as your own heavenly Advocate before the throne of God. When you do not know which way to turn, never forget you have a true Friend in Jesus who shares the very feeling of your infirmities:

> When all things seem against us to drive us to despair,
> We know one gate is open; one ear will hear our prayer.

The person who knows the Lord Jesus to be the "Friend that sticketh closer than a brother" (Pro. 18:24b) has all, though he appears to have lost all from a mere human perspective. Joseph Scriven was a wealthy man, not because he had money or lived in a mansion, but because he knew the reality of daily fellowship with Jesus Christ.

"O Love That Will Not Let Me Go"
A Song for the Night of Despair

Few hymns in Christian hymnals contain poetry more sublime than George Matheson's hymn, "O Love That Will Not Let Me Go." The composition of the hymn, however, was not a mere literary exercise. "O Love" was Matheson's very own "song in the night." The blind hymnwriter describes the writing of it as "the fruit of much mental suffering."

Even as a young Scottish lad, George Matheson (1842-1906) had very limited vision. With each passing year, his eyesight grew worse. During his studies at Glasgow University, the news that he would soon be totally blind was too much for his fiancé. She broke off the engagement.

By the age of eighteen, Matheson was totally blind; nevertheless, with the help of his sister taking dictation for him, he completed his studies with high honors. He took the pastorate of St. Bernard's Parish Church in Edinburgh, Scotland, aided by the same devoted sister, who assisted him in his various pastoral duties, even studying Greek, Latin and Hebrew to help him in his theological studies.

In 1882 during his fortieth year, Matheson's sister, his faithful companion for the previous two decades, prepared for marriage. On the day of her wedding, he suffered what many have conjectured to be a profound sense that he was all alone in this world. Unrequited love from his own fiancé years before, coupled with the departure of his sister to pursue her own marital love evidently occasioned what he termed "the most severe mental suffering." His own account of that evening, though devoid of any details of his sadness, includes a clue in terms of a single, seemingly innocuous sentence: "I was at that time alone." Further, images from and references in the hymn itself, such as the "flickering torch" in verse two, the reference to "pain" together with the image of "tracing the rainbow through the rain" in verse three, and the bowed "head" in verse four, suggest the kind of sadness and dejection he then felt.

But God gave him a "song in the night." He writes of the experience: *"It was the quickest bit of work I ever did in my life. I had the impression rather of having it dictated to me by some inward voice than of working it out myself. I am quite sure that the whole work was completed in five minutes, and equally sure it never received at my hands any retouching or correction…All the other verses I have ever written are manufactured articles; this came like a dayspring from on high."*[7]

---

[7] Ibid., p. 190.

The first stanza highlights a "love that would never let him go," unlike the love of romance or even of filial affection. Is it not highly probable that the forlorn man found great comfort in the wake of personal disappointment in the unfailing love of God? That nothing can separate God's children from his sovereign, saving love (cf. Rom. 8:35-39) means that He will never relax His mighty grip on them. He will never let go of them. That reassurance prompted the hymnwriter to recommit himself that day to even more devoted service:

> O Love, that will not let me go,
> I rest my weary soul in Thee;
> I give Thee back the life I owe,
> That in Thine ocean depths its flow
> May richer, fuller be.

The key word of stanza two is "Light." Just as God's love comforts the broken heart, so God's light rekindles the flickering flame of the weary heart. Spiritual renewal, personal restoration, or as the old writers sometimes called it "the revival of religion in the soul" is the theme of this verse.

> O Light that followest all my way,
> I yield my flickering torch to Thee;
> My heart restores its borrowed ray,
> That in Thy sunshine's blaze its day
> May brighter, fairer be.

Verse three focuses on the key word "Joy:"

> O Joy that seekest me through pain,
> I cannot close my heart to Thee;
> I trace the rainbow through the rain,
> And feel the promise is not vain
> That morn shall tearless be.

Notice the poet's references to his heartache. He employs the metaphor of a devastating storm bringing in its aftermath the pain of loss and despair. I think of some natural catastrophe such as a tornado, hurricane, or earthquake, leaving in its wake a chaotic pile of rubble. The survivor, buried beneath the ruins, has almost lost hope. His life appears to be over. The will to survive another day is gone. He is ready to give up.

Yet, in his abject hopelessness and grief, a search and rescue effort led by "Joy" finds him, and almost irresistibly reawakens hope ("I cannot close my heart to Thee"). All at once, he spies a rainbow on the other side of the rain and dares to hope again for a brighter, happier day.

Has this not been your experience in sorrow? This is, indeed, my story. In my night of dark despair, Jesus has heard and answered prayer. Inevitably, the sun has pierced through the threatening skies, bringing strength for the day and bright hope for tomorrow. Perhaps "Joy" found me during Bible reading when a single phrase from God's word broke forth with light in my heart. At times, it came by means of an unexpected phone call, letter, or visit from a tender friend. Or, then again, "Joy" has sought me out while listening to a sermon or recordings of congregational singing, when a particular line or word was used by the Holy Spirit to speak to my case precisely at the point of my need. Mr. Matheson must have experienced this very joy on that day when his heart was so saddened, when he despaired of strength to go forward; but suddenly, "Joy" discovered him beneath the rubble of despair, reminding him that God's love would never let him go.

The final stanza highlights the "Cross" as its key word:

> O Cross that liftest up my head,
> I dare not ask to hide from Thee;
> I lay in dust life's glory dead,
> And from the ground there blossoms red
> Life that shall endless be.

It is here that the explanation is given for the experience described in the previous stanzas. How do we explain the sudden change in the poet's mindset? Where is his evidence that God's love will never let him go? What ray of sunshine might possibly renew his enthusiasm for life and ministry after such a disappointment as he had suffered? How may we account for his expression of renewed hope for the future? The answer is the "Cross" of the Lord Jesus Christ.

It is at the "Cross" that we perceive God's everlasting love for His people (cf. 1 Jno. 4:10). And it is that same redeeming love that energizes zeal for service, just as the sunshine energizes creation (cf. 2 Cor. 5:14). Further, hope springs eternal in the love of Jesus (cf. Rom. 5:5).

Stanza four of this great hymn is what makes this a thoroughly Christian hymn and not some mere psychological exercise. A view of the Christ of the cross and His finished work of redemption is the remedy for every spiritual malady. Even when we have suffered great loss, as Mr. Matheson had evidently suffered, we may "lay in dust life's glory" with hope that there will be a glorious resurrection—a happy rising day—because of our crucified and risen Savior and Lord, Jesus Christ.

Numerous other hymns which the Lord has employed as "songs in the night" to my soul, as well as countless other believers through the centuries, might be cited beside these. William Cowper's "God Moves in a Mysterious Way" has frequently been the instrument of heavenly consolation to my heart, as has the precious old hymn "Be Still My Soul." Luther's hymn "A Mighty Fortress is Our God" has been employed to infuse courage into the hearts of numerous Christians during the dark night of persecution, and Horatio Spafford's "It Is Well With My Soul" written at the very spot where his daughters perished in the chilly waters of the Atlantic has helped many a person who faced his own dark night of bereavement.

What a treasure God has given His church by means of these doctrinally sound, experientially rich, and spiritually substantive hymns of the faith! Christian hymnody is a precious resource to the suffering saint. I encourage you to make good use of it to draw you closer to the God who delights to give "songs in the night" to His struggling children.

13
Never Beyond Hope

"Now the God of hope fill you with all joy and peace in believing, that ye may
abound in hope, through the power of the Holy Ghost." Romans 15:13

In what is arguably the most celebrated song of Disney lore,
Cinderella sings:

A dream is a wish your heart makes,
When you're fast asleep;
In dreams you will lose your heartache,
Whatever you wish for, you keep.

But biblical hope is not a mere flight of fancy, whimsical wish, or
imaginary dream. Hope is built on something solid—something
substantive (cf. Heb. 11:1). Unlike the abstract yearning of a dream,
Biblical hope is described by the metaphor of an anchor, something
firm, real, and concrete (Heb. 6:19). It is sure. It is steadfast. Hope
deals with reality, not fantasy.

In what way does the biblical concept of hope differ from the
secular concept of dreams? Hope is different because, unlike a dream,
it is connected to an object: "*Hope thou in God,*" the Psalmist
reminded himself (Ps. 42:5b). Hope is an anchor, not swinging adrift
in suspended animation, but fastening itself firmly to the Lord Jesus
Christ, the Rock of ages (Heb. 6:19-20). The believer's hope is in the
Lord—who He is, what He has done, what He has promised;
therefore, the person who hopes in God will never have occasion to
be embarrassed or to feel that his hopes were misplaced. "*Hope
maketh not ashamed, because the love of God is shed abroad in our hearts by the
Holy Ghost which is given unto us*" (Rom. 5:5).

Because it is anchored in Christ, biblical hope is closely akin to
assurance. In fact, the writer to the Hebrews couples the two terms
together in Hebrews 6:11: "*And we desire that every one of you do show the
same diligence to the full assurance of hope unto the end.*" Like assurance,

there is a kind of certainty and conviction to hope, both in terms of the facts of the gospel and of one's personal interest in those facts.

Hope, one of the triad of Christian virtues (cf. 1 Cor. 13:13), has to do with the future. Someone defined it as a "desire accompanied with expectation." If I ever write a dictionary, I will define hope as "a bright outlook on the future; a kind of Christian optimism." Because of the character of our God, the finished work of the Lord Jesus Christ, the reliability of His promise and inerrancy of His word, the believer can afford to be optimistic about the future.

In fact, he must be optimistic about the future. That is especially true for those who suffer. To the sufferer, hope is indispensible. It is a life-line that keeps the tempest-tossed soul from being overwhelmed in a sea of problems. It is a firm foundation on which to place his feet when the undertow of burdens is strong. It is a rock on which to cling when the winds of affliction threaten to change the landscape of life.

The nihilist Friedrich Nietzsche once allegedly told a colleague, "Stop hoping; it hurts too much." He wrote, "In reality, hope is the worst of all evils because it prolongs man's torments."[1] But if hope is anchored in the Lord as its object, then it is not a mere pipedream or wish, as Nietzsche conceived of it. Biblical hope is not the worst of all evils, but the best of all cordials. It is a vitamin to the weary heart, an essential mineral for spiritual health. Orison Swett Marden put it well: "There is no medicine like hope, no incentive so great, and no tonic so powerful as expectation of something tomorrow." For the Christian, such "expectation" is firmly rooted, not in self or another human being, but in the character of a faithful God.

In fact, a hopeless Christian is an oxymoron. "Take away hope," says contemporary theologian J. I. Packer, "and life, with all its fascinating variety of opportunities and experience, reduces to mere existence—uninteresting, ungratifying, bleak, drab and repellent, a burden and a pain…Hope generates energy, enthusiasm, excitement;

---

[1]Nietzsche, *Human, All Too Human*, 1878

lack of hope breeds only apathy and inertia...Hopelessness is thus at the root of many of today's psychological disorders... ."[2]

Hopeful is my favorite character in Bunyan's inimitable allegory Pilgrim's Progress. And my favorite scene is when *Christian* and *Hopeful* strayed from the King's Highway into By-Path Meadow and were taken captive by Giant Despair. He took the two hapless pilgrims to the dungeon of Doubting Castle and made their feet fast in the stocks. As the time passed, the cold and hungry prisoners began to despair of life. The Giant made periodic visits, encouraging them at each opportunity to put an end to their misery. He showed them the bones of pilgrims who, passing that way before, had perished by their own hand in lieu of a desperate existence in the dungeon. When his temptation to make an end of themselves was unsuccessful, the angry Giant informed them of his intention to fall on them himself the next morning if they lived until daybreak.

Christian and *Hopeful* stayed awake all night praying for deliverance. Then, as day began to dawn, *Hopeful* suddenly sprang to his feet as a man half-amazed and declared, "Ah! How foolish I've been!" *Christian* replied, "What is it, brother?" *Hopeful* said, "All of this while, I've had in my bosom a key called 'Promise' which is able to unlock every door in Doubting Castle." *Christian* responded, "That's good news, brother. Let's try it." *Hopeful* took the key of promise from his breast pocket and unlocked one door, then another, and finally another, until they found themselves clean escaped from Doubting Castle and Giant Despair, on course back to the King's Highway.

Thank God for the *Hopefuls* in this world. I've had a few of them along my pilgrimage in this world. I want to be such a person to others. I want to be the man who has, in his heart, the Key of Promise, unlocking doors for those who feel to be sinking in the mire of despair and despondency.

Hope is the first and most basic thing needed when trouble comes. The individual in crisis typically possesses a strong and

---

2 Packer, *Never Beyond Hope*, pp. 9-11.

inescapable feeling of hopelessness. Nothing is more crucial at this point than to refocus perspective on the God of hope.

A Reason to Hope

"The God of hope." What a thrilling title! Among the several Divine prepositional phrases of the New Testament,[3] each of which is designed to demonstrate that God is the fount of every Christian virtue, this one is rich in pastoral significance. It means that as long as God is, there is no such thing as a hopeless situation. He is "the God of hope."

The character and being of God is the very reason that Abraham, an aged man with a barren wife, continued to hope for the promised child: "*Who against hope*," that is, when everything within him and around him argued that the situation was hopeless, "*believed in hope, that he might become the father of many nations, according to that which was spoken, So shall thy seed be*" (Rom. 4:18). He trusted a God with whom nothing was impossible.

You too, friend, may trust the Lord and hope in Him regarding your case: "*Blessed is the man that trusteth in the Lord, and whose hope the Lord is*" (Jer. 17:7). You may trust Him because of His *power.* There is nothing too hard for the Lord (cf. Gen. 18:14; Jer. 32:17). If God can make the universe out of nothing by a mere verbal command, He possesses the ability to solve your current dilemma. You may trust Him because of His *wisdom.* He knows every detail of your peculiar circumstance in life (cf. Ps. 139:1-6), as well as what is needed to remedy your malady: "*The Lord knoweth how to deliver the godly out of temptations, and to reserve the unjust unto the day of judgment to be punished*" (2 Pet. 2:9). He knows, though you and I may not. That is enough for me.

And then, you may trust Him because of His marvelous *love.* If God loved His children enough to send His only begotten Son to die in their stead, then He loves them enough to care for them in the

---

[3] e. g. "the God of all grace' (1 Pet. 5:10); "the God of peace" (Phi. 4:9); "the God of patience and consolation" (Rom. 15:5); "the Father of mercies and God of all comfort" (2 Cor. 1:3); etc.

day-to-day tribulations they encounter in this life. *"He that spared not His own Son, but delivered Him up for us all, how shall He not with Him also freely give us all things?"* (Rom. 8:32).

"But," someone objects, "I don't see any evidence of God's love in my current circumstances. If God loves me, why is my way so hard?" The ultimate evidence of the love of God, my friend, is not your current circumstances in life (though if you look carefully, I'm sure you will see a golden thread of mercy weaving its way through the tapestry of your pain), but the cross of Christ: *"Hereby perceive we the love of God, because He laid down His life for us: and we ought to lay down our lives for the brethren"* (1 Jno. 3:16).

Look to the cross and discover anew His amazing love for sinners. Consider the great sum your salvation cost the Lord Jesus Christ. Yet, He patiently bore the pain and suffering and paid the ultimate price for you because of the great love wherewith He loved you. Hope springs eternal in the light of such amazing love.

Hope Saves

The apostle Paul knew how crucial it was for Christians to maintain an attitude of hope in the midst of the sufferings of life. To the Romans, he wrote of the saving benefit of hope in the believer's present life:

> "For I reckon that the sufferings of this present time are not worthy to be compared with the glory which shall be revealed in us. For the earnest expectation of the creature waiteth for the manifestation of the sons of God. For the creature was made subject to vanity, not willingly, but by reason of him who hath subjected the same, in hope, because the creature itself also shall be delivered from the bondage of corruption into the glorious liberty of the children of God. For we know that the whole creation groaneth and travaileth in pain together until now. And not only they, but we ourselves also, which have the firstfruits of the Spirit, even we ourselves groan within ourselves, waiting for the adoption, to wit, the redemption of our body. For we are saved by hope: but hope that is seen is not hope: for what a man seeth, why doth he yet hope for? But if we

hope for that we see not, then do we with patience wait for it" (Rom. 8:18-25).

Several thoughts are noteworthy in this extremely comforting passage. First, notice how he defines hope. He defines it as an "earnest expectation" for some future, unseen and glorious deliverance into a state of liberty, or freedom.

Second, notice his description of our present state in this world. Man was made, he says "subject to vanity," that is, to a transient or transitory existence. In other words, our lives now have been exposed to a kind of bondage. Limitations have been imposed. Mankind is no longer free, but under the control of stronger and more dominant powers.

"Made," here, does not mean "created," but "subjugated." The reference is not to God's initial act of creation, for He made Adam to live for ever and he would have lived forever had he not disobeyed God's command. Yet as a result of his sin, God, who is the implied agent of the act of subjugation, imposed sentence upon mankind, limiting his life span and subjecting him to a world that was no longer under his control. God, as a result of Adam's transgression, imposed futility upon creation. The world in which we exist now is a world under the curse of sin.

Notice, in the third place, how life in a world under the curse of sin affects us. We "groan and travail." God's children are not exempt from the experience of suffering, for "*not only they, but we ourselves also who have the firstfruits of the Spirit, even we ourselves groan within ourselves...*" That is to say, the diseases that strike others also strike us. Believers are not exempt from experiences of victimization, exploitation, and abuse to which other people in this world are subjected. We also feel the pain of theft, slander, infidelity, addiction and violence. God's people are also victims of murder, child abuse, heart attacks, unemployment, and other tragedies. We also have handicapped children, dysfunctional families, grandchildren born with birth defects, broken hearts, and financial setbacks. These things control us. They dominate our lives. We are unable to liberate ourselves from the painful experience of living in a world under the curse of sin.

Fourthly, notice the one thing that distinguishes the suffering of the believer from the suffering of the unbeliever. It is *hope*. Though we suffer the same as a worldling suffers in this sin-cursed existence, yet, unlike them, we are saved by hope.

How does hope save the believer? The answer to that question may be discovered by noticing how Paul uses the metaphor of "travail." Travail speaks of the birth pangs of childbirth, or what we call "labor and delivery." The pain of birth labor, I am told, is tremendous. In fact, it is almost unbearable.

Yet if you speak afterward to a mother who has given birth and ask her if the pain was insufferable, it is not uncommon to hear a retort such as, "Ah, it wasn't that bad." What could possibly account for the change in tune? Jesus words in John 16:21 offer an explanation: "*A woman when she is in travail hath sorrow, because her hour is come: but as soon as she is delivered of the child, she remembereth no more the anguish, for joy that a man is born into the world.*" Doubtless, that explains why she would do it again in just a matter of time.

It is hope that saves the mother from despair during labor—the hope of holding that precious little bundle of joy in her arms. She endures the pain, perseveres in the face of exhaustion, and pushes through the pressure because she has a special blessing awaiting her on the other side of the agony.

Periodically, however, we hear the heartbreaking story of an expectant mother whose child has died *in utero*. Psychologists say that trying to comfort such a mother is one of the most impossible cases they encounter in therapy. The mother must still go through the pain of childbirth, but she does so without hope. Her labor is unrequited. The pain has no remedy.

This is precisely Paul's point in Romans 8:18-25. The difference between the unbeliever and the believer is not that one suffers pain in this world while the other does not. The difference is that the one labors under the pain of a sin-cursed world without anything to which he may look forward, while the other is able to endure the pain of life in this world because of his hope in Christ. We are saved from despair by hope.

Consider an Old Testament example of how hope saves the believer from despair. Jeremiah reached the point of hopeless despair as he walked in the smoldering ruins of Jerusalem. He cried, *"My strength and my hope is perished from the Lord"* (Lam. 3:18). Suddenly, like Hopeful, he was startled by an epiphany. As a man half amazed, he remembered something else: *"This I recall to my mind, therefore have I hope. It is of the Lord's mercies that we are not consumed, because His compassions fail not"* (Lam. 3:21-22). Hope replaced hopelessness when he realized that though the destruction around him was significant, yet life remained. He was still alive, as well as many, many others. The nation had not been annihilated. Indeed, the temple was gone, but the people themselves had not been wiped out. Life remained, and the mercy of God remained in fresh supply at the beginning of each new day. This salutary reminder gave him hope to face the unknown tomorrow.

It will give you hope to face the unknown tomorrow as well when you focus your mind on the things that remain, not the things you have lost. Life remains. Today remains. His mercy for today remains. His compassion for you in your misery remains. His promise remains. His love remains the same, whether in sunshine or in shadow.

Because all of this remains, you can move forward today. Then when tomorrow arrives, His mercies will again be in fresh supply for the demands of that day. And the next. And the next. And, yes again, the next day after that as well.

Bright Hope for Tomorrow

What about when you reach the end of the journey and the doctor tells you that you have only a few weeks or months to live? Is there hope for your case then? Indeed, there is hope. There is hope that the God with whom nothing is impossible may miraculously intervene to spare your life, as He did King Hezekiah's of old (cf. 2 Kings 20; Is. 38). He is certainly able to do what man deems impossible. But whether He will or not, we do not know. We do know, however, that He knows what is best for us. We further know that life in this world, with all of its losses and crosses, was never intended to be permanent. There is a better world, where all is peace and love, awaiting every blood-bought and heaven-born soul.

Hope, in other words, if it concerns only the betterment of life in the present existence of this earthly pilgrimage, makes us the most miserable of men (cf. 1 Cor. 15:19). How thrilling to hope in Christ for revival in the church now! How wonderful to hope in Him regarding an improvement in your family relationships, or in terms of positive developments in your job search, or financial stability, or the political climate in the nation! But none of these more immediate concerns seem to matter much when someone comes face to face with the last enemy, death. Does the Christian hope exercise any bearing on that most formidable of trials?

Indeed it does! Our hope in Christ extends beyond the veil of death, reaching into the eternal state of heavenly peace and bliss. Though death hurts like a blow in the solar plexus, yet even in the face of death, we *"sorrow not as others who have no hope"* (1 Ths. 4:13). So today, we stand, like Paul, *"in hope of eternal life which God that cannot lie promised before the world began"* (Titus 1:2). The anchor of our hope defies the natural laws of gravity, reaching upward to fasten itself in the Lord Jesus Christ, our Forerunner, who has entered into the veil of the Holiest of all. If He is there, we are sure to follow.

The believer's ultimate hope is the second coming of the Lord Jesus Christ. The Redeemer's return is the brightest star on the horizon of redemptive history: *"Looking for that blessed hope and the glorious appearing of the great God and our Savior, Jesus Christ"* (Titus 2:13). When that eternal day dawns, faith will give way to sight and hope to fruition. Then all our conflicts will end in everlasting rest.

So, don't listen to the Nietzsche's of this world who tell you to stop hoping. Don't listen to the Tempter who whispers in your ear that God must not love you or He would not allow you to face such a staggering set of circumstances. Instead, follow the steps of Abraham, who "against hope believed in hope." Remember with

Jeremiah that you have reason to be hopeful, because God in His mercy has not suffered you to be completely annihilated. Discover in your breast pocket, like *Hopeful*, the "key of promise" which is able to unlock every door in Doubting Castle and to free you from the clutches of Giant Despair. Remember that your God is named "the God of hope" because as long as He is on the throne of the universe, there is not such a thing as a hopeless situation.

Keep hoping, my friend. Keep hoping in the Lord who loved you and gave Himself for you. One day soon, your faith and hope will turn to sight and fruition. Then, when you see His glorified face, tell him, if you will, that I long to see Him too.

14
Heaviness Now, but Heaven is Coming

"Wherein ye greatly rejoice, though now for a season, if need be, ye are in heaviness through manifold temptations…" (1 Pet. 1:6)

One of the most popular criticisms hurled at the Christian faith is that, with its emphasis on the "sweet by and by," it is supremely unrealistic and out of touch. "I'm interested," someone says, "in the challenging now-and-now, not the sweet by-and-by."

But the believer in Jesus Christ is not an ostrich with his head in the sand of denial, refusing to acknowledge the problems of living in this world. Neither does he live with his head in the clouds of illusory dreams. In fact, the Christian has a very healthy perspective on life in this world, admitting that the burdens of this present life are heavy, but assured that the bliss of heaven will more than compensate for present trials and troubles.

This heavenly perspective not only enables the Christian to survive, but holds out the prospect of an abundance of joy and peace that surpasses mere survival (cf. Rom. 8:37; Jno. 10:10). Many folks think that the only way to cope or survive life in the real world with all of its harsh realities and heavy burdens is to adopt the attitude of the cynic. The Christian, on the contrary, believes that he can live in the real world and face reality without becoming hard, calloused, or cynical, but cheerful and optimistic. His understanding of the glory awaiting him in heaven is no small reason for his incentive and strength to endure now.

The Practice of Heavenly Meditation

This volume has focused on how to keep one's heart out of trouble when trouble touches life as a whole. In each case, whether depression, loneliness, mistreatment, guilt, grief or fear, we've seen that the key to keeping a trouble-free heart is essentially a matter of maintaining a perspective of faith in God and the Lord Jesus Christ. When a child of God lives daily life in this world with such a heavenly perspective, the troubles of life assume their proper size and shape and the believer is equipped for faithfulness to Christ, come what may.

But faith is not a magical potion. We're not talking about "a little bit of pixie dust" or even an "I-think-I-can-I-think-I-can" kind of positive thinking that is so popular today. No, faith in God is something very substantive. It is based on truth—God's revelation in scripture—and involves the process of thinking through the present situation in the light of that truth, and deciding to do what God has said in spite of feelings within you, circumstances around you, and consequences ahead of you, trusting Him for the outcome.

One of the most harmful things ever done to the Christian virtue of faith is to define it as the antithesis of reason, for it suggests that faith is something purely mystical. I think I understand what people mean when they juxtapose faith and reason. They are saying that sometimes it is impossible to figure everything out and it is preferable at those times to just trust God even though you do not understand. That is certainly a legitimate point. But, at the same time, faith is essentially a matter of deductive reasoning. It involves the thinking mind and the application of Biblical truth to real-life situations.

Second Corinthians 4:16-18, one of the several autobiographical passages in the Pauline epistles, is our model here:

> For which cause we faint not; but though our outward man perish, yet the inward man is renewed day by day. For our light affliction, which is but for a moment, worketh for us a far more exceeding and eternal weight of glory; while we look not at the things which are seen, but at the things which are not seen: for the things which are seen are temporal; but the things which are not seen are eternal.

The key to the entire passage is the adverbial clause *while we look*. It is as a person maintains focus on the Lord in the midst of the more immediate pressures and concerns of daily life that he/she experiences the kind of daily, spiritual renewal necessary to prevent fainting, i.e. giving up in despair.

Note the contrasts in the passage. It is *while we look* at the invisible and eternal—as opposed to the visible and temporal—or, in other words, as we maintain a heavenly perspective, that *afflictions* appear *light*, *momentary*, and beneficial, i.e. *worketh for us*, and glory appears *weighty* and *eternal*. Without the perspective of faith, afflictions seem heavy, permanent and harmful.

So, I guess the question to be asked is, "Where is your focus?" Are you looking unto Jesus in the course of your daily affairs (cf. Heb. 12:2) or have you lost sight of Him in the face of the pressures and storms around you? It is not an easy thing to stay focused on the Lord, is it? To assist us in this matter of living by faith, God has given us His precious word. And one of the best helps to maintaining focus on the Lord is to practice what some have called the discipline of heavenly meditation.

What is it? Heavenly meditation is the practice of taking our cue from God's word to consider the glory that awaits us in His immediate presence in heaven. It involves reflection on the pilgrim character of our lives here and the heavenly citizenship that is ours by grace. It is essentially a matter of recalibrating focus on the eternal realm in order to faithfully persevere—without giving up, giving out or giving in—through the challenges and demands of this temporal existence.

Such a regular habit of reflection on the world to come may prove to be a real help to your inward peace and strength as you bear the heavy load of daily burdens. Let's consider a couple of examples of the pastoral value of heavenly meditation. First, we will look at an extra-biblical example, then a biblical one.

The Saint's Everlasting Rest

During the winter of 1646, a non-conformist[1] minister named Richard Baxter (1615-1691) thought he was dying. Suffering from daily physical pain, Baxter retired from public employment for a few months in a private house. It was during this period that he began a

---

[1] Theologically, Baxter subscribed to Amyraldism which, like Arminianism, rejects limited atonement in favor of a general offer of salvation to all mankind.

practice of daily meditation on the glory of heaven. The practice was such a benefit to his frame of mind that Baxter later looked back with gratitude on the suffering that led to the task.

Even after resuming regular duties, Baxter continued the practice of what he called "heavenly meditation." For one-half hour each evening, usually just before dinner, Baxter would focus his thoughts on the beauty, splendor and joy of the world to come, usually writing his thoughts on paper. The notes he took became the basis of his first and arguably most popular work entitled *The Saint's Everlasting Rest* (1650).

During one of his daily, half-hour sessions, for instance, Baxter recorded this acrostic using the New "Jerusalem" as his basis for meditation:

J   Jesus will be there.

> We will see Him face to face.

E   End of sorrow and suffering

> Both in our lives, and in the lives of fellow Christians.

R   Renewed creation

> We will live in the new heavens and new earth, in all its splendor.

U   Undeserved

> We will know that we deserve condemnation and are only there by Christ's blood.

S   Sinless

> We will no longer sin, offending God and hurting others

A   Adoring God perfectly

> We will finally love God as we should & spend eternity praising Him.

L   Love

> We will finally understand and experience just how much God loves us.

E   Everlasting

> There will be no prospect of ever losing glory – we'll be there in perfection forever.

M   Multitude

> There will be people from all nations, a new society, joyfully serving God together.

Elsewhere in the book, Baxter employs the delights of this world to help him think of the greater delights of heaven: "What delight hath the taste in some pleasant fruits! Oh, what delight, then, must my soul needs have in feeding upon Christ, the living bread, and in eating with him at his table in his kingdom."[2]

To help his readers to meditate on heaven, Baxter encourages us to consider all that will be left behind: "Farewell sin and suffering, forever…and now welcome, most holy, heavenly nature which, as it must be employed in beholding the face of God, so it is full of God alone, and delighteth in nothing else but Him."[3] Then he urges us to consider that we will have eternity to study all of Christ's personal excellencies, to behold the King in His beauty.

Further, Baxter breaks into periodic heavenly raptures as he anticipates the breathtaking glory of heaven and the "pleasures that are at his right hand forevermore:"

> Oh the incomprehensible, astonishing glory! Oh the rare, transcendent beauty! O blessed souls that now enjoy it; that see a thousand times more clearly what I have seen but darkly at this distance, and scarce discerned through the interposing clouds! What a difference is there betwixt my state and theirs! I am sighing, and they are singing: I am sinning, and they are pleasing God: I have an ulcerated, cancerous soul, like the loathsome bodies of Job or Lazarus, a spectacle of pity to those that behold me; but they are perfect and without blemish: I am here entangled in the love of the world, when they are taken up with the love of God…They have none of my cares and fears; they weep not in secret; they languish not in sorrows; these tears are wiped away from their eyes. O happy, a thousand times happy souls![4]

Baxter even employs the beauty and variety of nature as a springboard for heavenly meditation:

---

[2] Richard Baxter, *The Saint's Everlasting Rest*, p. 601.
[3] Ibid. p. 624.
[4] Ibid. pp. 583-584.

What a beautiful fabric is this great house which here we dwell in! The floor so dressed with various herbs, and flowers, and trees, and watered with springs, and rivers, and seas! The roof so wide expanded, so admirably adorned, such astonishing workmanship in every part! The studies of a hundred ages more, if the world should last so long, would not discover the mysteries of divine skill, which are to be found in the narrow compass of our bodies. What anatomist is not amazed in his search and observations! What wonders, then, do sun, and moon, and stars, and orbs, and seas, and winds, and fire, and air, and earth, etc afford us! And hath God prepared such a house for our silly, sinful, corruptible flesh, and for a soul imprisoned? ...Oh, then, what a dwelling must that needs be, which he prepareth for pure, refined, spiritual, glorified ones; and which he will bestow only upon his dearly beloved children, whom he hath chosen out, to make his mercy on them glorified and admired.[5]

In a day like ours when so many people are obsessed with this world, believing that physical health and financial wealth are the supreme good, Baxter's example of taking time each day to delight in heaven may seem out-of-touch. On the contrary, heaven is the ultimate reality for the people of God. It is the "Father's house" (cf. Jno. 14:2), our eternal home, and regular meditation on the prospect of reaching that home at length and the sublimity of that place will prove especially useful in bearing present trials with patience. I know of nothing so beneficial to counteract the disappointments with which we meet in this present evil world as the discipline of preoccupation with that heavenly home.

Paul exhorted the Colossians to "*Set your affection on things above, not on things on the earth. For ye are dead, and your life is hid with Christ in God. When Christ, who is our life, shall appear, then shall ye also appear with him in glory*" (Col. 3:1-3). Such heavenly-mindedness will make a person of great earthly good, for who can minister better to his fellow, suffering

---

[5] Ibid. p. 637.

brethren than one who has recently spent time with the Father and heard from home?

A Biblical Example of Anticipating Heaven

Revelation, the final book in the biblical canon, falls into the genre category of bible prophecy, but it is written with a pastoral aim. That the goal of the book is to comfort and encourage God's people is supported by the fact that the first three chapters are addressed to local churches, each with a pastor. This local context sets the pace for the pastoral intent of the rest of the book.

In fact, it seems that the entire New Testament treats eschatology, or the doctrine of future things, with a pastoral, rather than a mere academic, aim. The blessed hope of the second coming and resurrection of the dead is intended to comfort God's people (1 Ths. 4:13-16) and to motivate them to godliness (1 Ths. 5:4-6; 1 Jno. 3:3; 2 Pet. 3:13-14). The book of *Revelation* is the supreme illustration of the pastoral value of Bible prophecy.

John wrote the book while exiled on Patmos Island, a penal colony off the mainland of Asia Minor used for prisoners deemed subversive to the public peace. John was there *"for the word of God and the testimony of Jesus Christ"* (Rev. 1:9). He was suffering persecution for the sake of the gospel under Diocletian, one of the most anti-Christian of the Roman emperors.

The apostle identifies himself with the audience of the letter by the expression *"your brother and companion in tribulation, and in the kingdom and patience of Jesus Christ"* (1:9). The word translated "companion" is the familiar Greek word *koinonia* which means "to share in common." In the New Testament, *koinonia* is translated by the English words "fellowship, common, communion, communication, companion, and company" and refers to a kind of Christian reciprocity, or mutual giving and taking, within the local church community.

John, who was himself at the moment of writing the victim of persecution, writes to first century believers who comprised seven local churches in Asia Minor, people who were also presently suffering the pressure of persecution from the surrounding pagan culture in which they sought to live out their faith in Christ. He writes the revelation (Gr. *apokolupsis*, meaning "unveiling") given to Him by the Holy Spirit one Lord's Day on Patmos Island (1:10), a revelation specially aimed to comfort and encourage these battle-worn and weary Christians.

And in what form, specifically, does this message of pastoral encouragement to the persecuted church come? It comes in the form of a series of heavenly visions in which the Lord draws back the curtains of heaven, as it were, and permits John to see and write the vivid details that he sees.

Nothing is more salutary for beleaguered soldiers who are caught up in the fray of battle than to see their Captain standing high atop the mountain with the colors under which they labor unfurled. And nothing infuses such courage and spirit into the militant Church of Jesus, presently engaged against the enemy of sin and Satan, than to see the Church triumphant safely and victoriously gathered around the throne of God singing anthems of praise to the Lamb that was slain.

Such a heavenly focus promotes the strength and resolve necessary to persevere, i.e. to keep on keeping on, in the current crisis, knowing that the cause of Christ's kingdom will prevail at last. This is the meaning of the phrase *"your companion…in the kingdom and patience of Jesus Christ"* (1:9). "Patience," translated from the Greek word *hupomone*, means "endurance, perseverance," and is a regular word in the book of *Revelation*. Consider these references:

- 1:9 – "…the kingdom and patience of Jesus Christ…"
- 2:2-3 – "I know…thy patience…and hast borne, and hast patience, and for my name's sake hast labored, and hast not fainted…"
- 3:10 – "Because thou hast kept the word of my patience…"
- 13:10 – "Here is the patience and the faith of the saints."
- 14:12 – "Here is the patience of the saints…"

Note that the term is connected to Christ's *kingdom*, His *name's sake*, His *word*, and *faith*. The idea is that it is hard to keep going when we encounter tribulation and persecution, but in the interest of the kingdom of God and the glory of Christ's worthy name, Christian's must be steadfastly committed to God's word by faith in the Lord Jesus Christ. In other words, the saints have resources enabling them to persevere the current crisis and be faithful to their Lord.

Where are those resources of strength and courage to be found? They may be found by taking the uplook into heaven and finding assurance in the knowledge that victory is already ours in the risen and glorified Christ. We must live by faith, not by sight, and faith equips the believer to be patient until the coming of the Lord. He has already overcome the Great Dragon, and we too may overcome him by faith in the blood of the Lamb and commitment to the gospel of grace. The Church's living Lord will help her against the devil's various assaults, whether those assaults assume the form of an external assault of persecution or an internal assault of false doctrine, strife, or immorality. By following His inerrant word with faith in His unfailing promises, we may persevere through the current crisis.

That is the essentially pastoral message of the book of *Revelation*. The book teaches those of us who are in the midst of the current fray that Jesus Christ will win in the end. He will have the last word; every one He intended to have with Him in glory will at last be saved; every enemy will be finally vanquished beneath the feet of King Jesus.

With such a heavenly focus, you and I may be faithful to Christ, come what may. So, let not your heart be troubled, my friend. Ye believe in God; believe also in the Lord Jesus Christ. By faith in the One who has already won the war on your behalf, you may gain victory against the enemy of your soul in every side-skirmish and local battle within, until you finally reach your heavenly home at last.

May the Lord, then, "*direct your hearts into the love of God, and into the patient waiting for Christ*" (2 Ths. 2:5). May "*the grace of our Lord Jesus Christ be with your spirit*" (Gal. 6:18). May "*the peace of God that passeth all understanding keep your hearts and minds through Christ Jesus*" (Phi. 4:7). May "*our Lord Jesus Christ himself, and God, even our Father, which hath loved us, and hath given us everlasting consolation and good hope through grace,* *comfort your hearts, and stablish you in every good word and work*" (2 Ths. 2:16-17). Amen.

Epilogue
The Ministry of Helping[1]

"Bear ye one another's burdens and so fulfill the law of Christ." Galatians 5:2

Real people who live in a real world have real problems. My heart breaks to witness the great trouble that sin has brought into the world. Some of God's children are called upon to endure some truly nightmarish circumstances.

Here is a family whose beautiful teenage daughter was tragically killed just months before her high school graduation. Here is a loving mother called by God to spend her days ministering to the needs of a severely handicapped child. Here are the parents of a daughter whose husband has abused and betrayed her and escaped without apparent consequence. Here is the couple who cannot seem to communicate with civility or the spouse who has just been told the other no longer wants to be married. And here is the individual who discovers that the individual they thought they knew has been addicted to drugs or alcohol for many years.

Regardless of the particular circumstances, every problem touches many of the same spiritual issues. Whether a person has suffered the tragic loss of a loved one, the pain of personal failure and sin, the trauma of marital discord, the fear and anxiety associated with persecution or mistreatment, or the paralysis of depression and discouragement, the pastoral ministry is one of God's gifts to His children to aid in sorting through the rubble of problematic circumstances in order to address the spiritual issues and work toward a Biblical solution by applying the eternal principles of God's holy word.

But ordained ministers are not the only people charged with the responsibility of helping those who hurt. Everyone whose heart has been tendered by Divine grace and whose mind has been educated by

---

[1] This chapter was written some years ago, but due to the relevance of its content to some of the basic issues discussed in this volume, we include it here as an epilogue.

the word of God are both called and qualified to "admonish" (the word *noutheteo* means "to put in mind") others (Rom. 15:14). The need for this kind of ministry is great, but, currently, the laborers are few.

Basic Principles

Whenever someone approaches me and says "Pastor, I'm depressed," I understand that, generally speaking, the sad and hopeless emotions described are merely symptoms of a deeper cause. Depression is simply the surface issue. Of course, my friend just wants to feel better – to be happy again. But I am concerned to address the root of the problem.

Now, as a Christian friend, I can do one of three things for him: (1) I can flatter him and say, "Ah, you're a good person. Don't be so hard on yourself. Things will get better in time..." Such an approach, if my conscience allowed it, might make him "feel better" momentarily, but would merely palliate symptoms—soon the misery would return, for the cause of the depressed feelings has not been explored and exposed. Indeed, there is a place for giving hope, but hope is rooted in the God of hope (Rom. 15:13), not flattery or positive thinking.

(2) I can recommend this person to someone who might lawfully prescribe medication. Indeed, there is a connection between soul (*psyche*) and body (*soma*) – *vis a vis* "psychosomatic problems." For example, it is a fact that stress, anxiety, depression, fear, anger, etc.— essentially spiritual issues, in other words—can cause stomach ulcers, high blood pressure, colitis, headaches, heart disease, stroke, and other physiological or organic problems. The brain does indeed send messages to the ductless (or endocrine) glands to release chemicals into the body under different circumstances.

For instance, the emotion of fear or anger generates the release of adrenaline that affects the physical body in very distinct ways. A person who regularly experiences fear, or depression, or anxiety, or deep-seated anger, therefore, will inevitably have physical symptoms of these essentially spiritual problems. Medicine may indeed help to alleviate the symptoms, helping the depressed person "feel better" and to cope with daily life. But medicating a person for problems that are essentially spiritual (as opposed to physical) can only be a form of therapy at best, addressing the presentation problem or surface issue, not the root cause of the anger, or the depression, or anxiety, etc.

The pharmaceutical solution to psychological problems, therefore, is ultimately partial and short-term, with very little, if any, progress made toward a cure. I want to be very cautious here, lest I give the impression, first of all, that I know more than I know, and secondly, that I would dare to sit in judgment of the decision to employ the legitimate help of medical science to minimize suffering, for that is the very use of God's gift of true science. I cannot in good conscience speak definitively on the subject simply because by so doing I would need to assume an expert posture on the subject of psychosomatic relationships and, in all candor, I'm not sure that anyone has the credentials or insight necessary to perfectly decipher *cause and effect* in terms of psychosomatic connections.

I do feel comfortable, however, affirming that the danger in using chemicals as the ultimate solution to spiritual problems is that it plays to the natural tendency to be slothful, to look for the quick fix and to neglect a deeper issue. Alchemy, as a solution to the problems of life, may actually produce its own form of codependence. I would think that wisdom dictates that the individual using medication for psychological problems at least consider that there is a spiritual component in his/her case—if not an essentially spiritual cause—and tailor the approach to resolving his/her tensions with that in mind. The application of biblical principles to your case, in other words, is crucial, even if it may be proved that the cause of distress is essentially physiological or even biological.

(3) The Biblical method of helping a person who presents a problem such as depressed feelings or uncontrolled anger is to attempt to diagnose the root of these unpleasant emotions by tracing these symptoms to the underlying causes, then to attempt to sort through each respective area, addressing each one specifically with the appropriate Scripture passages and practical directions concerning

implementation of these Biblical principles in real life situations. As a person sorts through the rubble and identifies patterns of thinking and behavior that need to be changed, he can make amazing progress toward restructuring his life. Such a specific approach builds real hope. It gives the sense that one is actually working on the cause of his/her problems. Further, accountability to another believer provides the context necessary to produce real change.

The goal of such a context is not to make one person perpetually dependant on others, but to provide the setting necessary to restore order, both externally and internally, to the complex and seemingly formidable problems that currently exist. In time, the believer will become stronger, growing in holiness, until he/she is eventually self-controlled and able to "*keep [himself] in the love of God*" (Jude 21) by using the resources that God has given for a disciplined life, i.e. public preaching, Christian fellowship, personal prayer and Bible reading. Such an experience, further, equips the believer to minister to and help others, to "*comfort them which are in any trouble with the comfort that we ourselves have received from the Lord*" (2 Cor. 1:3-5).

It is important to note that there is nothing magic about such a setting. No one has a magic wand or a particular incantation they can utter to make problems disappear. But education in Biblical principles with its corresponding practical application is important. As an individual learns to think Biblically about problems and about life in general, he grows in his ability to sort through the issues and move toward the appropriate godly solution.

Understanding the Role of Divine Sovereignty

Without exception, the first order of business in the ministry of helping is to sharpen focus on the sovereignty of God. A high view of God is the ultimate solution to every complexity of life. Faith falters and flesh prevails when people lose a Biblical perspective on the character of God. To be reminded that He is "in His holy temple," ruling and reigning in sovereign majesty, ordering and superintending the affairs of His world with actual hands-on management so that a sparrow falls not to the ground without His notice, is the food that strengthens faith. How salutary is the reassurance that "*my times are in His hand*" (Ps. 31:15)! My good times and my bad times; my happy times and my sad times; my times of employment and times of unemployment; times of popularity and times of persecution; times of health and times of sickness; times of wealth and times of want; times of companionship and times of loneliness—all are "in His hands."

How vital it is for suffering souls to think clearly about the God they trust! He is a righteous God who will not suffer an injustice to continue forever. He is a faithful God who always keeps His promise. He is a merciful God whose compassions fail not. He is an omnipotent God and nothing is too hard for Him. Through His overruling providence, He is able to overrule even the wicked actions of men for the good of His children and the glory of His name (Ps. 76:10; Gen. 50:20). Indeed, helping hurting souls starts here.

Understanding the Principle of Human Nature

Another basic principle for Biblical problem solving is the ability to think Biblically about human nature. People are complex beings. They are comprised of both a physical and a spiritual dimension-a body and a soul.

The "inner man," or the soul, is not the same as the internal organs, i.e. liver, heart, gall bladder, lungs. The physical brain is not the same as what the Bible calls "the mind." If a surgeon were to open your body, he would see a muscle called the heart and an organ called the brain, but he would not see the intangible, yet very real, part of you that the Bible calls "the inward man." Jesus talked about this dual composition of human nature in Mt. 10:28: "*Fear not them that can kill the body...but rather fear Him which after he hath killed is able to cast both soul and body into hell.*" He also said, "*man shall not live by bread alone, but by every work that proceeds out of the mouth of God*" (Mt. 4:4).

What does he mean? He means that man's needs are not only physical, but also spiritual. He needs food for his soul, just like he needs food for his body. Most people are only concerned with the physical dimension of life. Like the "Rich Fool" in Luke 12:13-21, they think only in terms of the body, and forget the soul. But, people are not mere animals, bodies without souls; nor angels, souls without bodies. They are body and soul—composite beings.

Grasping this basic truth lays the foundation for understanding human nature and behavior. Why are people as they are? At least four different components affect human behavior.

First, *people are temperamentally and constitutionally different.* Some people are more introverted, timid, and reserved by the sheer nature of their personality, and some are more assertive and confident by nature. Some people are physically stronger and more resilient than others, e.g. "Jack Sprat could eat no fat; his wife could eat no lean". Most parents would agree that no two children in the family are exactly alike. Each has his/her own particular strengths and weaknesses, temperamentally speaking.

Add to this natural bent of personality the fact that *everyone has a fallen nature.* The Biblical story of man is a story of "good gone wrong." The sin nature is predisposed to wrong—bent toward evil. It tends to minimize, or perhaps I should say distort, one's natural personality strengths, turning them into monstrous substitutions for what God intended for man (e.g. think of how Adam's natural headship and leadership of the woman in God's created order tends to tyranny and despotism - Gen. 3:16), and to maximize one's natural areas of weakness. Because of sin, man naturally chooses "the path of least resistance" when it comes to life choices.

Add to this natural personality bent and sin nature, *the experiences that a person has had in life.* Every person met, movie watched, book read, sermon heard, etc., exercised an influence on the person you are today, either positively or negatively. Early home life, parental attitudes toward life, methods of solving problems and reacting to life, etc.—each are factors in the equation of an individual's current thought patterns. Every person is trained by example in this way. The purpose of highlighting this particular feature is not to justify "pinning blame" but to help a person to understand his/her own tendencies and proclivities. It doesn't help anyone to pin blame; we must look for solutions! Teachers in school, interaction with classmates, relationships with siblings—each of these inputs affect the way a person perceives his/her world. We learn to think of life and react to it by what we witness in others.

Finally, a person who has been born again has a further component in his/her composition that affects the way he lives, thinks, and behaves. *The new nature* that God implants within the soul loves God and godliness, wants to please God and glorify God, and desires to grow in its knowledge of and relationship with Him.

Understanding the Principle of Warfare

These principles explain why people are as they are. Based on their natural tendencies, coupled with the sinful nature and the experiential inputs and examples in life, people develop habits of reacting to life.

What is the "knee-jerk" reaction to an insult, for example? Early on, people habituate themselves to react to an insult in one of two ways: (1) They learn to "clam up," internalizing their anger; or (2) They learn to "blow up," ventilating their frustration. They may either try to protect themselves by sinking into a despondent frame of mind or by defending their sense of personal honor. Hebrews 12 speaks of both kinds of sinful reactions to Divine chastening: *"Despise not the chastening of the Lord nor faint when thou art rebuked of Him"* (v. 5). Both habits, i.e. despite and discouragement, are attempts to manipulate the situation so as to minimize future occasion for personal pain and unhappiness. The Christian must recognize that the dynamic behind these natural reactions is his own sinful nature.

Romans 7 depicts this dynamic as a warfare between the "flesh" (that is, the old person) and the "spirit" (the new person). It is a continual and irreconcilable war played out in the theater of the inner man (i.e. the mind and emotions).

Each of God's people is in a battle. It is the fight of our lives. It will never cease to be a fight as long as we are in this world. Satan wins the war when he can get a person to sink in despair so that they give up the daily fight. His ultimate lie is "What's the use; it's too hard; you're not making any progress; it's not going to work; you can't control the power of the flesh; just give in; quit; do what comes naturally." Many, many people have become casualties on the landscape of history simply because they listened to him instead of listening to God and living by faith. Proverbs says that the secret to success is getting up each time you've been knocked down and trying again: "*The just man falleth seven times, but riseth again.*" Defeat is defined in terms of desertion, and in a very subtle way, giving up the fight may very well be an act of rebellion against God.

Though it is painful to hear, the Christian life will always be a battle. It's hard to live a godly life in an ungodly world. It's hard to resist what comes naturally and to follow Jesus Christ. The Christian intellectual G. K. Chesterton once said, "Christianity has not been tried and found wanting, but has been found difficult and left untried."

The most frequent metaphor NT writers employ to describe the nature of the Christian life is the image of warfare: "*Fight the good fight of faith...Endure hardness as a good soldier of Jesus Christ...Put on the whole armor of God that you maybe able to stand against the wiles of the devil*" etc.

Every day, I have to fight—against my attitudes, moods, natural tendencies, ego, passions, etc. The world makes it more difficult to be faithful on the battlefield of life, for it bombards us with ideas, icons, and opportunities for indiscretion that feed the old nature. Like the elderly gentleman, the believer's attitude toward sin must be tenacious. "I'll bite the devil 'til my teeth fall out; then I'll gum him to death for the rest of my life." When the Bible says "Be strong in the Lord," we must hear that as an imperative to, again, toughen up.

Now, granted, most people don't feel very tough. But we're in a battle, whether we like it or not. That's the nature of living in a sin-cursed earth. The hope before us is heaven, a world that knows no sin—ah, blessed thought! The challenge we face now is to be faithful soldiers of the One who is the "Captain of our salvation". Learning to view our struggles in terms of a spiritual warfare is essential to gaining victory over them.

How does one resist the natural tendency to do what comes naturally and to follow Jesus Christ. Paul says, "*Walk in the Spirit and you shall not fulfill the lusts of the flesh"* (Gal. 5:17). The secret to living in the Spirit is to learn to live proactively instead of reactively. In other words, plan ahead for each day by feeding the mind and heart with good inputs; prepare in advance for each day so that you may respond to life instead of merely reacting to it.

Understanding the Role of Thought Patterns

We are living in a "feeling-oriented" society, but it is essential to remember that feelings are not reliable. Emotions are untrustworthy. They are like the ebb and flow of the tides. They change with the circumstances. When pressure is great, or you awaken with a headache, or if you happen to encounter one of those difficult people that God has strategically placed throughout the world, or if the skies have been overcast and dreary for four days running with no glimpse of the sun—each of these kinds of circumstances affect a person emotionally.

How should a Christian respond to adverse circumstances like these? Well, if he/she lives by feeling, that is to say, if a person allows circumstances to control his mood and makes no deliberate effort to gain control and master his mood, then there will be no spiritual stability and consistency in that person's life. A quaint poem illustrates the principle:

> *Three men went up on top the wall—Feeling, Faith, and Fact;*
> *Feeling had an awful fall, and Faith was taken back.*
> *Faith was so close to Feeling that when he stumbled, Faith stumbled and fell too.*
> *But Fact remained and held Faith up and that helped Feeling too.*

The Christian is a person who is governed not by his circumstances but by the truth that he knows. He does not look within himself to monitor his emotional state. He does not ask himself, "Am I happy? Do I really have pleasant feelings for my marriage partner? Am I enjoying life?"

This is precisely the error that most people make in life. They are so introspective and turned in upon themselves that they become preoccupied with themselves. They are constantly analyzing their own attitudes and problems and relationships and circumstances, asking themselves questions like "Am I really happy in this relationship? Do I or do I not really love the Lord? Have I really forgiven this person or not?"

What these people really need to do is to forget about themselves and quit thinking about themselves and redirect their focus to their God: "*Whatsoever things are true...just...pure...honest...of good report, if there be any praise and if there be any virtue, think on these things and the God of peace will be with you*" (Phi. 4:8-9).

The late Dr. Martyn Lloyd-Jones said, "We are so subjective, and we live in this unhealthy 'psychological' generation that starts with man and ends with man. Most of our troubles are due to that." He believed that the Christian who is in a constant state of defeat is there because he is being controlled by his subjective feelings instead of by an understanding of the truth. Deliverance from this condition depends on a total change in approach: Christians are to look not at themselves and their problems but at what God has done for them.

The following example, cited in Iain Murray's biography of his life entitled *The Fight of Faith*, illustrates Dr. Lloyd-Jones' approach:

> "Joan Hougham...gives this statement of the counsel she received from ML-J: 'His five-word prescription was unbelievably simple, though he well knew it was the hardest thing for me to do. Refuse to think about yourself. I felt like Naaman shattered by his instructions from Elisha, but like him, as I obeyed, I found release...I saw the Doctor several times; his humility was such that on one occasion he told me that my experience and struggles had helped him in his preaching. He encouraged me to write to him, each letter was answered personally, written in his own hand, and enclosed a repeat prescription. Never shall I forget his kindness and encouragement."

The fundamental need is to see the relevance of Christian doctrine to the practical problems of daily life. People need to learn to take the great "facts" of the word of God (e. g. The Sovereignty of God, the

Priestly Intercession of Christ, the Promise of His presence, the Hope of Eternal Glory, etc.) and to then preach the gospel to themselves by reminding themselves that these things are true. This art of learning to reason from the facts of Scripture to the circumstances of life will strengthen Faith, and that will help Feeling too.

Therefore, in order to control the thought life, we must regularly feed our minds with the word of God. Reading and meditating on Scripture is a spiritual necessity, not a luxury! "Commit thy ways unto the Lord, so shall thy thoughts be established" (Pro. 16:3).

A person's thought life is the single most crucial area of life. How vitally important it is to think God's thoughts after Him, to adopt His perspective on life and the world! "*God hath not given us the spirit of fear, but of power, and of love, and of a sound mind.*"

Let's get more specific. How should a believer think about the issue of changing circumstances? How does a Christian respond when health changes, or when he suffers the loss of a job, or when a relationship breaks up, or when he must relocate, leaving old friends and familiar surroundings, or when kids grow up and leave the nest, or when he stands at the graveside of someone who is dear to his heart? What does it mean to think Biblically about change?

It means that instead of dwelling on the pain of change, and giving in to the temptation to roll these thoughts over and over in your mind, the believer deliberately alters his perspective by reminding himself that life in this world was never intended to be permanent. A pain-free and trouble-free existence is an optical illusion: it is not realistic. Like the ancient Hebrews, we are like nomads or bedouins in the desert. We should not put our tent pegs down too deeply, but be ready to move when God in His providence determines to lead us to the next step in the journey. He does indeed weave the thread of change into the fabric of daily life in order to remind us of the pilgrim character of our lives in this world. We belong to the next world, and part of the process of sanctification is learning the lesson that He and He alone is changeless.

*"Thru life and all its changing scenes, and all the grief that intervenes;
Tis this supports my fainting heart, That Thou my Sanctuary art."*

What about mistreatment? How should a Christian think about the issue of injustice and mistreatment? The natural reaction is to fight back, to get even, to take up for ourselves. But the Christian is a person who does not have unrealistic expectations. He knows that in a sin-cursed world, he will inevitably be misunderstood, falsely accused, or victimized. Even our Savior suffered the pain of mistreatment. 1 Peter 4:19 says, "Let them that suffer according to the will of God commit the keeping of their souls to Him in well doing as unto a faithful Creator." Psalm 37 also helps us to think Biblically about mistreatment. The Christian remembers that just one glimpse of Him in glory will more than compensate for every perceived injustice down here.

Well, perhaps these examples will suffice to illustrate what I mean about the need to think Biblically. That's the challenge we all face. That's where the battle is fought -- in the theater of our thought patterns.

Understanding the Dynamics of Positive Change

Under this heading, I will develop the following sequence of thought:

1. People develop habits of reacting to life. God calls upon us to recognize sinful habits and to repent.

2. Change involves "putting off" old habits of thinking and living, (Scripture calls this "the mortification of sin"), and "putting on" new habits, or replacing the natural tendency to react with the Biblical and godly alternative. This is called "consecration".

3. The key to affecting this kind of positive change, or character transformation into Christ-likeness, is rooted in what one feeds into his/her mind. It doesn't happen by magic. Making progress in holiness is a matter of "abiding in Christ" through the spiritual

disciplines of prayer, Bible intake, Christian fellowship, meditation, public worship, etc.

Let's address each area separately.

1. People develop habits of reacting to life.

Horace Mann said, "Habit is a cable; we weave a thread of it every day until at last it is so strong, we cannot break it." I agree with the analogy, but disagree with the conclusion. Through the power of the Holy Spirit, life-dominating habits -- what old writers termed "besetting sins" -- can be broken. Philippians 4:13 should be the motto for every believer: "I can do all things through Christ who strengthens me." Learn to say to yourself, "Yes, I can be a nice person; I can control my temper; I can handle the pressures of the day; I can forgive my brother; etc. 'through Christ who strengthens me'."

But still, Mann is correct about the formation of a habit -- every day we weave a strand until it becomes a cable. There are four basic characteristics of a habit. A habit is something that a person does:

- automatically (like tying shoe laces)
- unconsciously (like which sock a person puts on first, the left or the right)
- skillfully (like driving an automobile)
- comfortably (like the way a person folds his arms, i.e. whether he puts left over right or right over left depends on which is most comfortable).

The point is that early in life, people learn what will maximize personal comfort and they begin to do things in the same way each day without consciously thinking about their actions. Can you imagine how long the simplest tasks in life would take if we didn't have this capacity for habit and had to consciously think about each little step to take?

This capacity for habit also touches the emotional dimension of life. People develop habits of thinking, behaving, and reacting to life based on many different influences, e. g. the way they observed their parents reacting to various situations, defense mechanisms arising from personal fears or unpleasant experiences in the past, etc. But at the root, these habits of thinking and living arise from the sin nature within us.

The most "comfortable" reaction to any given situation is the course of action to which a person is naturally inclined. Just as water naturally follows the path of least resistance and flows to the lowest point, so people naturally react to life situations in the way that is the most natural. But there's the rub; man's "natural" reaction is a sinful one. Man has been habituated as a sinner.

Let me illustrate. When someone criticizes me, it gives me personal pain and distress. I don't like pain and distress, so I've developed a natural habit of reacting to criticism in order to protect myself. I retaliate. That's a sinful habit.

Now here's how the dynamic works. The pain over past criticisms makes me fear future criticisms and guilt over those times that I've retaliated in kind causes me to fear the confrontation even more. So, in a very subtle way, I develop another habit of tailoring my action so as not to subject myself to criticism in the first place. This either takes the form of compromise or a total paralysis of action. For instance, criticism over things I've written makes me fear future criticism, tempting me either not to write at all or to write in an attempt to please my readers. Do you see how the dynamic works? That's just one of a myriad of different illustrations that could be cited to show how man's sinful nature habituates his approach to life.

In Ephesians 4:22-32, Paul identifies certain behaviors as instinctive habits to a person's "former conversation (or lifestyle)". That brings us to the second point.

2. Change involves dehabituation, or "putting off" old habits of thinking and living, and rehabituation, or "putting on" new godly habits in their place.

The theological terms employed to speak of these activities are "mortification" and "consecration". These are the two sides of the coin the Bible calls "sanctification". Ephesians 4:22-24 states the general principle, then verses 25-32 make specific application of this "put off/put on" dynamic. The "old man" is the fallen nature—the sinful person you were before God called you into new life. The "new man" is the new nature that God has created in the soul. The point of Paul's admonition is clear: "You are a new man in Christ; now live like it by deliberately rejecting the habits that characterized your old life and by replacing them with new habits."

Notice he does not say "taper off" or "cut down gradually." He says "Stop it!" *Let him that stole, steal no more.* This takes a conscious and deliberate decision to quit sinning. For the person who drinks, that means making the determination not to drink again. Now here's where many people go wrong. They make it easy to fall back into the sinful behavior by "making provision for the flesh to fulfill the lust thereof" (Rom. 13:14).

But the only way to make positive change is to take drastic steps with sin, whether it be a sinful behavior, like drunkenness, or a sinful attitude, like self-pity or pouting. Drastic maladies call for drastic remedies. One doesn't treat cancer with a bandaid.

This is precisely Jesus' point in Mt. 5:29-30: *"If thine eye offend thee, pluck it out; if thy hand offend thee, cut it off..."* Jesus is saying, "Take radical steps to deal with the steps that lead you to sin." If alcohol is a problem to you, he says, then cut the process short by getting rid of every drop of alcohol in your home and refusing to go into an establishment that offers it for sale. "*Mortify* (the word is the root of our noun "mortician", meaning "to put to death") *your members: fornication, uncleanness...covetousness*" (Col. 3:5; see also Rom. 8:13). Nail the flesh to the cross every day!

That's the meaning of Christ's call to discipleship: "*If any man will be my disciple, let him deny himself, take up his cross daily, and follow me.*" Putting off the old man, or mortification, involves saying "No" to the natural inclinations. Now this is admittedly painful. Jesus compares it, again, to the plucking out of an eye or the cutting off of a limb. The flesh will scream "bloody murder" and say, "No, I want that!" It will not die passively or quietly. But self-denial is basic to Christian living.

We don't need training to quit sinning. We just need to quit. But we do need training to be godly.

Notice Isaiah 1:16-17: "*Cease to do evil; Learn to do well.*" Every day, we must put off the attitudes and thought patterns that arise spontaneously from the sinful nature and learn new godly biblical habits of thinking and living in their place.

Consider Ephesians 4:22-32 again. Paul says, "Stop lying; then make a decisive effort to tell the truth. Don't allow anger to turn into ill-will and resentment, but close-out the anger account each day and refuse to carry the balance over from one day to the next. Stop stealing; start working and commit yourself to giving to others; Stop speaking biting sarcasms and acid comments and concentrate on speaking words that will be to the benefit of others...", etc.

Someone said that it takes approximately forty days of regular work to establish a new habit. I think that's probably accurate. But even then, because the old nature will never be completely eradicated this side of the grace of glorification, we must be aware that it is always on the lookout for an opportunity to reclaim its lost territory and to reestablish its former dominance.

3. The secret to change is "renewing the mind."

It is important to notice that between Ephesians 4:22 ('put off') and Ephesians 4:24 ('put on') is Ephesians 4:23 ("*And be renewed in the spirit of your mind*"). What does this mean? It means that a Christian must feed his mind with good thoughts if he will have the resources necessary to break old habits and replace them with new ones.

If a person will be self-forgetful instead of self-absorbed, great-hearted instead of narrow-spiritied, patient instead of quick-tempered, gentle instead of abrasive, courageous as opposed to timid, hopeful as opposed to cynical, pleasant instead of sour, etc., he must take in the kind of information necessary to feed the new man on a daily basis. He must "Think again!"

The common quip is true even in a spiritual sense: "Garbage in/Garbage out." But it is also true to say, "Nothing in/Garbage out," because by nature we are predisposed to sinful attitudes and behaviors. If I do not read God's word every day, I am operating in the energy of the flesh. It's comparable to trying to run my car on water instead of gasoline. It's just a matter of time before the engine locks and ceases to function at all.

Personally, I need constant input and stimulation. I am not a "self-starter" and in all candor, though I've met people who claimed they were, I do not believe that there is any such creature. No one is automatically or spontaneously spiritually-minded. I require daily Bible intake, sermons online, good literature, recordings of singing, fellowship with believers, and regular public worship just to keep my mind in the right frame. I wish I was more spiritual than that, but I'm not. I am growing in this area, though. I am developing new habits, if you please, in terms of the fact that it is generally easier to control my attitudes and moods now than it was several years ago. And growth, not a quantum leap or second blessing, is the Biblical metaphor for transformation in Christian character.

Interestingly, the word "renewed" in Ephesians 4:23 is the Greek word *ananehao*. It means "to think youthfully." Paul is saying, "Remind yourself of who your God is and what He has done for you and all of the cynicism and scar-tissue built up through years of disappointment, frustration, and battle fatigue will fade away, and the carefree and hopeful perspective of youth will return."

There is indeed a "fountain of youth" (Ps. 103:5). When people drink from this "living water," they can be forever young (Jno. 4:14; 7:37-39). Even in old age, they will still bear fruit (Ps. 92:13-14). In a day like ours when "even the youths" are cynical, still those who "wait upon the Lord shall renew their strength; they shall mount up with wings as eagles; they shall run and not be weary; they shall walk and not faint" (Is. 40:29-31).

How can a person drink from this fountain of living waters? By staying connected to the life supply -- the Lord Jesus Christ. He is the vine and we are the branches (Jno. 15:1). Severed from the vine, the branch cannot bear fruit. There will be no "love, joy or peace", no "longsuffering, goodness or faith", no "gentleness, meekness or temperance" -- no fruit of the Spirit manifested in the person's life who has been disconnected from Jesus Christ (Gal. 5:22).

Instead of producing fruit, the individual who allows himself to be distracted from the moment-by-moment habit of fellowship with Christ will only produce the "works of the flesh" (Gal. 5:19-21). Such will be the natural and inevitable outcome of a Christless life. He will not have to try to manifest these-the works of the flesh will spontaneously manifest themselves, for people are habituated as sinners. But by "abiding in Christ", the Christian can bear fruit.

Perhaps you wonder, "But how do I abide in Christ? How do I stay connected to the vine so that His life can flow through me and produce love, and faith, and joy, and kindness?" By practicing the spiritual disciplines of prayer, Bible intake, Christian fellowship, Biblical meditation, public worship, etc. God has given us resources like prayer, the Bible, other believers, the assembly of the saints, etc. not as a spiritual luxury but as a spiritual necessity. I must utilize these resources or I die. I cannot live without them.

The key, then, to successful discipleship is living proactively instead of reactively. Instead of waiting for a crisis to arise and then reacting "off the cuff", we should plan ahead for all eventualities -- preparing in advance for each day by drawing close to Christ in the morning. A person who does not spend time in the word of God and in prayer every day, feeding good thoughts into his mind and heart, simply cannot live a godly life. It is an impossibility. Apart from me, says Jesus, you can do nothing.

Summary

How do you help someone who is reeling beneath the burdens and difficulties of life? You say, "*There is lifting up*" (Job 22:29). You point that individual to the principles of the word of God and exhort them to trust in the God of the word. Will all be benefited by such an attempt to minister help to them? No. Only the individual who humbly submits to Scripture and commit himself to obeying it: "*When men are cast down, then thou shalt say, 'There is lifting up', and **He shall save the humble person***" [emphasis mine].

Tom Landry once entered the dressing room of the Dallas Cowboys after a humiliating defeat. He told his players, "Men, I told you how to win the game. You didn't do what I told you. That's why you lost." Then he made his exit. It is vital to a "helper's" sanity to remember that the person he/she is trying to help is ultimately responsible for implementing the counsel of Scripture.

In the final analysis, we cannot control whether or not another person submits to the help God gives in His word. People have a will of their own. None of us can be God in someone else's life. The individual who resists and rebels against the principles of Scripture, opting instead to follow his own impulses, will not be helped. But we are not responsible for the results. We are simply responsible to faithfully sow the seed. We are merely the "stretcher bearers" who, by faith, bring our paralyzed friends to the Master, even if we must tear a whole in the roof to get to Him. Jesus alone is *Jehovah-rapha*, the Lord our Healer. Perhaps when He sees your faith, He will be merciful to your friend, forgiving his sins and saying to him, "Rise, take up thy bed and walk."

Bibliography

Adams, Jay E. *How to Help People Change*, Zondervan, 1986.

_____. *Shepherding God's Flock*, Zondervan, 1974.

Baxter, Richard. *The Saint's Everlasting Rest* (1650), Christian Heritage, 2001.

Lewis, C. S. *The Last Battle (Chronicles of Narnia Series)*, Collier Books, 1970.

Menninger, Karl A. M.D. *Whatever Became of Sin?*, Hawthorn Books, Inc., 1975.

Murray, Iain H. *David Martyn Lloyd-Jones: The Fight of Faith 1939-1981*, Banner of Truth Trust, 1990.

Old School Hymnal Twelfth Edition, Old School Hymnal Company, Inc., 2001.

Osbeck, Kenneth W. *101 Hymn Stories*, Kregel Publications, 1979.

Oxford Universal Dictionary (The). Oxford Press, 1933.

Packer, J. I. *A Grief Sanctified: Passing Through Grief to Peace and Joy*, Servant Publications, 1997.

_____. *Never Beyond Hope*, InterVarsity Press, 2000.

_____. *Rediscovering Holiness*, Servant Publications, 1992.

Primitive Baptist Hymnal, Second Edition, Harmony Hill, A Primitive Baptist Foundation, 2004.

Sweeting, George. *Who Said That?*, Moody Press, 1994.

Warburton, John. *The Mercies of a Covenant God*, Reiner Publications, 1976.

Wiersbe, Warren. *Classic Sermons on Suffering*, Kregel Publications, 1984.

Yoakum, J. C. and Reba, "Hymn Time" (unpublished manuscript), Sovereign Grace Publications, owner.

www.gracegems.org/Watson.

www.ingramcontent.com/pod-product-compliance
Lightning Source LLC
Chambersburg PA
CBHW031243090426
42742CB00007B/292